# OCR Anthology for Latin AS and A Level Shorter Verse Authors

The following titles are available from Bloomsbury for the OCR specifications in Latin and Greek

**Cicero *pro Roscio Amerino*: A Selection**, with introduction, commentary notes and vocabulary by Neil Treble

**OCR Anthology for Latin AS and A Level Shorter Prose Authors**, covering the prescribed texts by Nepos, Tacitus and Apuleius, with introduction, commentary notes and vocabulary by Katharine Radice and Stuart R. Thomson

**OCR Anthology for Latin AS and A Level Shorter Verse Authors**, covering the prescribed texts by Lucretius, Tibullus and Ovid, with introduction, commentary notes and vocabulary by John Godwin

**OCR Anthology for Latin GCSE 2027–2028**, covering the prescribed texts by Pliny the Younger, Aulus Gellius, Apuleius, Ovid and Virgil, with introduction, commentary notes and vocabulary by Tim Chambers and Declan Lawell

**OCR Anthology for Classical Greek GCSE 2027–2028**, covering the prescribed texts by Herodotus, Lysias, Homer and Euripides, with introduction, commentary notes and vocabulary by Christopher Burnand and Andy Mylne

**OCR Anthology for Classical Greek AS and A Level: 2026–2028**, covering the prescribed texts by Aristophanes, Herodotus, Homer, Lucian, Plato and Sophocles, with introduction, commentary notes and vocabulary by Matthew Barr, John Claughton, Benedict Gravell, Rowena Hewes, Ellice Hetherington and Stuart R. Thomson

**Virgil *Aeneid* IV: A Selection**, with introduction, commentary notes and vocabulary by John Storey

Supplementary resources for these volumes can be found at https://bloomsbury.pub/OCR-editions-2026-2028

Please type the URL into your web browser and follow the instructions to access the Companion Website. If you experience any problems, please contact Bloomsbury at onlineresources@bloomsbury.com

# OCR Anthology for Latin AS and A Level Shorter Verse Authors

Selections from

Lucretius *De Rerum Natura* I.1–224
Tibullus *Elegies* I.2, I.5, II.4
Ovid *Metamorphoses* VII.1–227

With introduction, commentary notes and vocabulary by John Godwin

BLOOMSBURY ACADEMIC
LONDON • NEW YORK • OXFORD • NEW DELHI • SYDNEY

BLOOMSBURY ACADEMIC
Bloomsbury Publishing Plc
50 Bedford Square, London, WC1B 3DP, UK
1385 Broadway, New York, NY 10018, USA
29 Earlsfort Terrace, Dublin 2, Ireland

BLOOMSBURY, BLOOMSBURY ACADEMIC and the Diana logo are trademarks of Bloomsbury Publishing Plc

First published in Great Britain 2025

Copyright © John Godwin, 2025

John Godwin has expressed his right under the Copyright, Designs and Patents Act, 1988, to be identified as Author of this work.

Cover design: Terry Woodley
Cover image: Roman mosaic in Villa Adriana, Tivoli © Manakin/istockphoto.com

All rights reserved. No part of this publication may be reproduced or transmitted in any form or by any means, electronic or mechanical, including photocopying, recording, or any information storage or retrieval system, without prior permission in writing from the publishers.

Bloomsbury Publishing Plc does not have any control over, or responsibility for, any third-party websites referred to or in this book. All internet addresses given in this book were correct at the time of going to press. The author and publisher regret any inconvenience caused if addresses have changed or sites have ceased to exist, but can accept no responsibility for any such changes.

A catalogue record for this book is available from the British Library.

A catalog record for this book is available from the Library of Congress.

ISBN: PB: 978-1-3503-8441-5
ePDF: 978-1-3503-8442-2
eBook: 978-1-3503-8443-9

Typeset by RefineCatch Limited, Bungay, Suffolk
Printed and bound in Great Britain

To find out more about our authors and books visit www.bloomsbury.com and sign up for our newsletters.

# Contents

Preface — vii

**Lucretius: *De Rerum Natura* I.1–224**

    Introduction — 3
    Text — 33
    Commentary Notes — 41
    Vocabulary — 73

**Tibullus: *Elegies* I.2, I.5, II.4**

    Introduction — 95
    Text — 123
    Commentary Notes — 133
    Vocabulary — 165

**Ovid: *Metamorphoses* VII.1–227**

    Introduction — 189
    Text — 217
    Commentary Notes — 225
    Vocabulary — 257

**Endorsement statement**

The teaching content of this resource is endorsed by OCR for use with specification AS Level Latin (H043) and specification A Level Latin (H443).

All references to assessment, including assessment preparation and practice questions of any format/style, are the publisher's interpretation of the specification and are not endorsed by OCR.

This resource was designed for use with the version of the specification available at the time of publication. However, as specifications are updated over time, there may be contradictions between the resource and the specification, therefore please use the information on the latest specification and Sample Assessment Materials at all times when ensuring students are fully prepared for their assessments.

Endorsement indicates that a resource is suitable to support delivery of an OCR specification, but it does not mean that the endorsed resource is the only suitable resource to support delivery, or that it is required or necessary to achieve the qualification.

OCR recommends that teachers consider using a range of teaching and learning resources based on their own professional judgement for their students' needs. OCR has not paid for the production of this resource, nor does OCR receive any royalties from its sale. For more information about the endorsement process, please visit the OCR website.

# Preface

The text and notes found in this volume are designed to guide any student who has mastered Latin up to GCSE level and wishes to read any (or all) of the three poets in this book in the original.

The edition is, however, particularly designed to support students who are reading this poetry in preparation for OCR's AS/A level Latin examinations in June 2026–June 2028. (Please note this edition uses AS to refer both to AS and to the first year of A level, i.e. Group 3.)

The poets contained in this volume represent a wide range of Latin verse from the end of the republic and the early empire. There is some challenging philosophical poetry on the nature of the world in which we live, there is a wonderfully inventive account of the sorceress Medea and in the centre there are three love-poems of the poet Tibullus. Students can choose which of these poets to study for their examinations, but they will benefit from reading at least parts of all these authors in this volume and seeing how these three writers in their very different ways manage to use Latin verse to convey a picture of the world which is both strange and familiar. Lucretius anticipates much of classical Physics, Ovid is the ancient world's magic realist before the term was coined, and Tibullus is a case-study in heartbreak which rings as true today as it did then.

This edition contains detailed introductions to the context of the work of each of these three poets. The commentary notes aim to help students bridge the gap between GCSE and AS level Latin, and focus therefore on the harder points of grammar and word order as well as assisting students with difficulties in the philosophical and literary background. At the end of each section is a full vocabulary list, with words in OCR's Defined Vocabulary List for AS Level Latin flagged by means of an asterisk.

I am grateful to the anonymous reviewers of this book who saved me from error more times than I would like to admit. I also owe a debt of thanks once again to Alice Wright and her indefatigable team at Bloomsbury who made the writing and the publishing process a painless and happy experience for the author.

John Godwin<br>Shrewsbury, 2024

# Lucretius

De Rerum Natura *I.1–224*

# Introduction

## Lucretius and his times

We know almost nothing about Titus Lucretius Carus, the poet who wrote the *De Rerum Natura*. Cicero, in a letter written in 54 BC to his brother Quintus (*ad Quintum fratrem* I.10.3) comments that:

> *The poetry of Lucretius, as you say in your letter, contains many flashes of inspiration and also a good deal of poetic ability.*

Later writers also showed admiration for this poet. The poet Statius, writing over one hundred years after Lucretius, refers (*Silvae* II.7.76) to the *docti furor arduus Lucreti* ('the sublime frenzy of Lucretius the learned'). Virgil paid him the compliment of imitating him on many occasions in his own poems and may have explicitly referred to him (*Georgics* II.490) in his own didactic poem on the Italian countryside when he declared:

> *felix qui potuit rerum cognoscere causas* ('Happy the man who could get to know the reasons behind things').

All we have is the poem. We do not know the dates of his birth and death, but we do know a lot about the period in which he lived and worked, a time which he calls 'this troubled period for our fatherland' (I.41).

The late Roman republic was a place of political and military turmoil; army commanders with troops loyal to themselves rather than loyal to Rome were dominating the state – a process which ultimately turned the city from the Roman republic to something almost approaching a military dictatorship. Something of the military flavour of the times comes over in Lucretius' brilliantly sardonic account (I.62–79) of Epicurus the victorious general who conquered the dragon religion and traversed the whole universe with the power of his mind, bringing back the booty which outdid all other booty – namely the truth about the world itself, part of which is the truth that fighting battles is folly. Mock battles with all their pomp and weapons are described as taking place on the Campus Martius (II.40–3). Conservatives like Cicero could try to influence good men and maintain the republican system which he cherished – and he was quick to applaud when the dictator Caesar was assassinated on the Ides of March 44 BC – but his euphoria was short-lived as Caesar's heir Octavian and Caesar's consul Mark Antony between them carved up the Roman world and Cicero's body with it. If (as seems likely) Lucretius died in the late 50s BC, then he will have missed the Civil War of Julius Caesar and his former son-in-law Pompey the Great which began in 49 BC: but he will probably have had the misfortune to witness the brutal dictatorship of Sulla who imposed his rule on Rome in the late 80s BC and butchered many of his opponents, especially the wealthy.

63 BC was Cicero's finest hour when he thwarted the conspiracy of Catiline – a man who allegedly threatened to murder large numbers of Roman senators. Some of the conspirators were arrested and executed (without trial) and others were defeated in battle. If anyone needed a parable of the folly of political revolution, it was here: but the Saviour of the State, Cicero himself, did not find himself the hero for long and was quickly snubbed and later exiled, for all his unstinting service to the public good. He ended his days being butchered by the henchmen of Mark Antony in the proscriptions which followed the assassination of Julius Caesar in 44 BC, but before that he spent several years writing philosophy in Latin, and it is clear that he was not alone in devoting himself to the life of the mind in the age of military might. Why should the wise man get involved in politics on either side, when he will end up dead or disgraced whatever he does? What passed for political life could easily be seen as just dog-eat-dog and a waste of energy. Some of this emerges in passages like the following, where Lucretius is explaining the lust for money and power as forms of the fear of death:

Then greed and the blind longing for status, which force unhappy men to cross over the bounds of what is right, making them at times the allies and the servants of crime, striving night and day with overpowering might to get to the top – these sores of life are fed not least by the fear of death … and, driven by their false fear, men wish to run away, far far away, so they pile up property by civil bloodshed, they double their money greedily, heaping up death upon death, cruel men who are glad to see the sad funeral of a brother. They hate and fear the dinner table of their own kin.

III.59–73

The internecine strife and bloodshed of civil war is lurking behind this grim landscape of lust and violence, and the poet stresses the futility of it all. No wonder Lucretius uses the image of the serially unsuccessful politician when he later seeks to explain the mythological figure of Sisyphus, permanently condemned to push a heavy boulder up a hill only for it to fall down again at once. The term *amicitia* ('friendship') was used in Roman political life to mean 'alliance' and was often therefore a cynical and self-serving activity among competing aristocrats – a far cry indeed from the Epicurean ideal of friendship from which the wise will derive genuine support and affection. Finally, Roman politicians were not above abusing religious ritual for political ends: there were the faintly desperate tactics of a consul called Bibulus in 59 BC who constantly claimed to see 'bad omens' in the sky to halt public business of which he disapproved, and there were the terrible acts of brutality in which (for instance) Vestal virgins convicted of unchastity were buried alive. Fear of divine displeasure and the desire to secure the gods' approval made many Romans sacrifice animals as burnt offerings and give credence to the prophecies of soothsayers whose 'evidence' often consisted of nothing more reliable than the observed flight of a flock of birds or the state of a dead animal's entrails.

The message of Lucretius – that political ambition is a waste of time and that the gods are not listening to us – might well have seemed as blasphemous as it was dangerous to some, but must have struck others as attractive. The real danger here is not so much that the Gods might just prove that they were listening by destroying the state which allowed such free-thinking to go on: so long as the ritual was performed most Romans felt that the gods did not worry about this sort of 'free-thinking'. The danger was that if all the philosophers leave the political arena their places will easily be filled by the selfish and the greedy. As the statesman Edmund Burke famously observed in the eighteenth century, all it takes for evil to triumph is for good men to do nothing. Meanwhile, Epicureans pursued happiness in rural seclusion, living in their version of Epicurus' famous 'Garden', which was a kind of research centre for like-minded people. Here they could pursue the good life far away from the crowded city. It is difficult to blame them.

## Epicurus and his philosophy

So who was Epicurus and what did he teach? Long before Epicurus, Greek philosophers had been investigating the nature of the world. The philosophers before Socrates (the 'Presocratics') had speculated on whether the world consisted of one element (earth, air, fire, or water, say) or else a mixture of elements: the fifth-century atomists Democritus and Leucippus came up with the atomic theory which dominated scientific understanding of the nature of matter right up until the twentieth century, and Epicurus (341–270 BC) took over this theory and developed it into a full philosophy of life, summed up by the poet Philodemus as:

> God is not something to be feared. Death is not to be dreaded. What is good is easy to attain, what is terrible is easy to endure.

He was famous for living the simple life in his 'garden', accompanied by friends of both sexes, and his influence on later generations was immense.

### Atoms

In its simplest form the theory states that nothing exists except matter and empty space in the universe. This matter is made up of indivisible atoms (the Greek word *atomos* means 'uncuttable') which are too small for the eye to see but whose existence can be inferred in practice from (e.g.) the phenomenon of erosion (I.311–28). Their indivisibility and indestructibility was inferred from the continued existence of things: if matter could be subdivided to an infinite extent then (in an infinity of time) all things would have disintegrated to nothing by now (I.540–50). Everything in the world is the result of atoms coming together to form things and people: and death is the disintegration of the atomic compound which is a human being, allowing the indestructible atoms to form other compounds. There must be empty space for the atoms to move in – and also to explain the different weights and densities of different sorts of object, so that a lump of lead has more atoms and less space than a lump of wood and so is heavier. This empty space is infinite – for what limit can there be to nothingness? – and hence the universe is infinite in size. The number of different atomic shapes and sizes is finite – otherwise some would be big enough to be visible – but the number of individual atoms of each size and shape is infinite.

These atoms are always moving and colliding to form material compounds. Gravity makes things move downwards and so one would expect all the atoms to fall down in the same direction like raindrops. This cannot be happening, as it would leave no room for the atoms to collide sufficiently to form compounds. One might have thought that the heavier atoms would fall faster than the lighter ones and land on top of them but Epicurus pointed out that all atoms would fall at the same speed and invented the theory of the 'swerve' (*clinamen*) which states that atoms veer from the downward path on occasion and bang into each other, causing a ricochet of atoms which injects horizontal movement into the otherwise vertical stream. This is highly dubious as an argument and ignores other possibilities. It does have the virtue of adding an element of uncertainty into a mechanical universe and it also helps to account for free-will and volition.

Democritus had described the atomic nature of the world and saw no alternative to determinism in human nature as a result. If, after all, we are atomic compounds like the humblest brick, and if all such compounds obey the laws of atomic movement in an infinite universe where no gods tend to us, then our lives are determined by forces outside of ourselves. This is (of course) an argument which continues to rage today: to what extent are any of us 'free' to choose what to do? Our brains are physical objects, subject to all the forces of external causality (as Lucretius well describes in book III), and yet we have the impression that we are something more than simply a machine on legs. If taken to an extreme, this denial of free will might tend to deny any 'missionary' purpose to the poem – if I have no free will then I can no more change my way of life than my car can fix its own puncture. Lucretius, however, sees that we do have the power to move ourselves and sought to explain this in atomic terms as part of his account of perception and thought (IV.722–1036).

Perception is a major problem for the atomists: if all events are the atomic results of an atomic cause, then all perceptions must be (in some sense) 'true', but we see things in dreams which are not there, and optical illusions had long convinced the Sceptics to doubt the validity of *all* empirical experience. The oar which is straight when laid on the grass looks bent when submerged in water, so which is it? More tellingly, how can we see ghosts (as people do) unless dead people continue to live after death? This is a problem which mattered to Lucretius as the existence of ghosts would appear to disprove his theory that human life ends at death. He therefore broaches it early in the poem (I.127–35), arguing later on that ghosts are the confluences of images which left the living bodies and continue to exist simply as the remnants of what were once living bodies.

All perception, then, is the result of contact (II.434–5): atoms from the world hit our sense-organs, whereby (e.g.) sound atoms enter our ears, smell atoms enter the nose, and so on: Lucretius has a theory of the mind which has 'soul-atoms' (*anima*) spread all over the body, functioning very much as a nervous system and relaying messages to the mind when (for example) a spider crawls on our hand. Epicurus regarded sight as the passing of 'films' issuing from the surface of objects into the eyes, but had difficulties explaining how we see (for instance) an elephant if that means that the elephantine 'image' has to fit into our tiny eyes. Images come into the mind unsorted, leaving the mind to explain and interpret them, which effectively gets Epicurus off the Sceptics' hook as he can always say that the mind is mistaken in interpreting the bent oar as bent when it is in fact straight – the mind is being given images of oar and water which it is not able to interpret correctly and thus the perception is true but falsely read.

The challenge of the Sceptics was not easily defeated. The Sceptics refused to accept the validity of sense-experience – if some experience (e.g. a dream) is clearly not true, then how do we know that it is not *all* wrong? Diogenes Laertius in his life of the Sceptic Pyrrho reported how Pyrrho 'faced all risks – traffic, precipices, dogs' and was saved from harm only by his less sceptical friends who would pull him from out of the path of oncoming traffic. There was plenty of Scepticism in the philosophical tradition: even Democritus said that 'in reality we know nothing' (frag.117 KRS) and Socrates was famous for asserting that the only thing he knew was that he knew nothing. Lucretius is facing something of an uphill challenge to justify his belief in the possibility of knowledge even in the case of everyday experience, above all in his discussion of what cannot be seen.

## Gods

It is worth saying at the outset that neither Epicurus nor Lucretius were atheists in our modern sense of somebody who denies that gods exist. Gods (for Epicurus) are seen in visions and so there must be *something* there. Where he differed from most others of his time was in his conviction that these gods did not care about us and could not be swayed by our prayers or our misdeeds (I.49). Rather than seeing them as divine policemen or parent-figures, Lucretius made the gods reflect his notion of the good life. His gods were models of serenity, living in a cloudless windless paradise of detached contentment (I.44–9, III.18–24) in the gaps between the worlds. Their bodies are as deathless as the atoms of which all bodies are composed. They cannot be involved in the life of men, on the syllogistic reasoning that:

**A Level**

The gods enjoy a life free of all cares
If they cared about us they would not enjoy a life free of care
Therefore they do not care about us.

This means that the whole apparatus of personal and public religion is a waste of time if it seeks to acquire favours from unheeding gods. Lucretius attacks the practice of human sacrifice as an abomination (I.80–101) and mocks the folly of the impotent man praying for fertility (IV.1236–9). Epicurus' gods are not the bullying beings of myth who fling thunderbolts to punish us (and end up hitting their own temples, as Lucretius reminds us at VI.417–20). There is scope for 'prayer' but it is not communication with the gods but rather contemplation of their divine nature and meditation on their peaceful serenity. We ourselves can live a life worthy of the gods (III.322) if we follow their examples and banish fear and anxiety, using the gods as role-models rather than divine Godfathers to be placated and entreated. Epicurus managed this sort of felicity to such an extent that he deserves to be called a god (V.8), and the poet himself enjoys a state of 'divine pleasure' (III.28) when he uncovers the secrets of nature.

This is all very well, but it may be hard to see why people should surrender the colourful gods of myth for these faceless, idle *bon viveurs*, especially since the removal of the gods also removes one possible hope of manipulating the world. If we listen to Lucretius, we are left totally at the mercy of the random devastation of atomic collisions, as is brought out only too well in the section on the plague (VI.1138–1286). Why should this philosophy of atomic mechanisms appeal to the general public at all? To understand this we need to see Epicurus' moral and social philosophy and his concept of happiness.

## How should we live?

Morality for Epicurus is a matter of what is best for us both as individuals and as a society. The greatest good (he stated) is in fact pleasure, and Epicureans soon acquired a (false) reputation for being hedonistic 'epicures' addicted to gluttony, debauchery and luxury, people whose lives lurched from one orgy to the next. In fact Epicurus saw pleasure as a purely material atomic process involving the removal of want and pain. Our pleasure in (say) eating is proportionate to our hunger – the more hunger, the more pleasure from food – and once the pain of want has been removed, the pleasure cannot be increased but only varied. Excessive indulgence ends up becoming painful – as anyone who has overeaten will attest. He divided pleasures up into 'kinetic' and 'katastematic': kinetic pleasure involves movement of the sense-organs and is experienced in such things as the ingestion of food and drink or the ejaculation of sperm, while katastematic pleasure is the static equilibrium of not needing anything, the highest state of which is the Epicurean ideal of *ataraxia* ('not being disturbed') where the lucky individual is in a state of blissful contentment.

Kinetic pleasures fall into three categories:

a) natural and necessary (food and drink)
b) natural but not necessary (sex)
c) unnatural and unnecessary (luxuries)

The wise man will make use of the first sort as he needs, the second sort with the greatest caution and the third sort not at all. Expensive luxuries are no better than freely available goods and the Epicurean wise man will train himself to be content with a little (the famous 'little which is enough' (*parvum quod satis est*)) so that he will always be able to be content: all this produces an austere philosophy far removed from the 'epicure'. The man addicted to pleasure is a fool, and the poet satirises him in the burlesque of the daughters of Danaus in the Underworld (III.1003–10). If we develop our tastes so that bread will no longer please us but we must have caviar, then we have not increased our pleasures but merely increased the possibility of pain when the caviar runs out. Epicurus himself would live happily on bread and water – with a pot of cheese for a 'feast'. Similarly, the romantic attachment to one lover will produce frustration when that lover is unavailable or unwilling, and so Lucretius recommends multiple affections (IV.1065–6) as better calculated to free us from the pain of frustration. What goes for the body also goes for the mind: greed for power and money is unnecessary and insatiable and the wise man will eliminate this labour of Sisyphus (III.995–1002) altogether. If we pursue wealth, then no amount will ever be enough, whereas if we restrict our needs to what anyone can afford, we will always be well off. This leaves Epicurus with the paradox that 'poverty is the greatest wealth and unlimited wealth is great poverty' (*Vatican Sayings* 25): or as Lucretius puts it:

> 'if a man guides his life by true philosophy he will find ample riches in a modest livelihood enjoyed with a tranquil mind. There is never a shortage of a little.'
>
> V.1117–19

This might raise questions about the social duty of the wise man: traditional Epicureanism seems to espouse a selfish dedication to personal pleasure and freedom from attachment which would seem to make most social commitment undesirable. Cicero (*On Laws* 1.39) thought that we ought to act in the service of the state and he was quick to lambast the Epicurean garden-dwelling peaceniks as useless cowards. Cicero was not being fair to them, and some scholars argue that Epicurus did encourage some degree of civic virtue. Lucretius is perhaps seeking a more enlightened social life in what he claims is 'this troubled era for our country' (I.41) and Epicureanism urges us to improve our lives collectively as well as individually. As a response to atomism – in an uncaring universe we might as well practise enlightened self-interest – seeking pleasure is understandable, but does it leave any scope for morality?

One major factor here is Epicurus' insistence on the importance of friendship. This is not innate in man – early man was (he says) a lone wolf who only came together with others when it dawned on him that there was greater safety in numbers – but became the overriding ethical good for the wise man:

> Of all the things that wisdom acquires for the blessedness of life, the greatest by far is the possession of friendship.
>
> Epicurus *Key Doctrines* 27

Such friendship marked the advance of man from his earlier bestial state:

> Epicurus said that you should be more concerned at looking at the company with whom you are eating and drinking than at what you eat and drink. For feeding without a friend is the life of a lion and a wolf.
> 
> Seneca *Letters* 19.10

The friends in question are, of course, fellow-Epicureans and the Garden was open mainly to the sympathizers and not to the unenlightened rabble, although some Epicureans did promote their beliefs: Diogenes of Oenoanda had a summary of Epicurean teachings carved onto a giant wall in his home town to convert his fellow-citizens, and contact with the rest of humanity might generate more serenity in the world for all to enjoy.

If ever there was a society susceptible to the appeal of the apolitical tranquillity of the Epicurean garden, then, it was this Rome where the streets at times ran with blood, and where politics could become either a tragedy or a farce. The Epicurean apolitical stance did not come naturally to the people whose whole history was one of conquest and ambition, who learned from early on to pursue ideals of courage and glory even to death. Epicureanism offered hope of happiness even in the face of political and social upheaval.

## Forms of argument and use of evidence

How did Lucretius prove his statements? There are two sorts of proof – the evidence of the senses (what we call 'empirical' evidence) and logical deduction from that evidence. Clearly the evidence of the senses is primary, and Lucretius tells us this so many times with his repeated emphasis on 'seeing' the world as it really is and not how we would like it to be. We do not need to 'prove' statements such as that hemlock kills you, or that magnets attract iron filings; so long as the sceptics' case (that we cannot trust the senses at all) is refuted, then Lucretius is (so far) in the clear. Arguments based on empirical evidence are found especially useful in areas of science such as medicine, meteorology and biology: when we see iron rings suspended from a magnet, then that suggests that there is a force greater than gravity holding them in place. Where we see babies resemble both parents, we can assume that both parents must contribute something to the embryo, rather than seeing the child as entirely made by the father. We see that the body and mind are interlinked because things which affect the one also affect the other (such as drinking wine). This has its drawbacks of course – and we still often confuse cause with coincidence – but it certainly produces some tentative areas for study.

Empirical evidence of the senses is also surprisingly useful if (like Epicurus) you subscribe to a 'naturalist' style of ethical theory. If there are no divine commandments to obey, then why should we choose any one of the competing ethical systems on offer? If we can reduce ethics to a scientific basis in the empirical facts of human nature, then we can point to evidence for recommending a particular course of action. If happiness is the goal of all our endeavour, then Lucretius can easily point to examples of unhappy people as role-models of what not to do. We see in book V.1151–60 the force of guilt at our bad behaviour giving us bad conscience, poor sleep, risk of arrest: and all this wrecks our peace of mind. It must therefore be better to obey the laws since crime does not pay. The romantic lover moping after an unavailable girl (IV.1121–40) is visibly unhappy: he is unfulfilled, constantly beset by jealousy of possible rivals and wasting money on the pursuit of an illusion. All this ruins his happiness and peace of mind, and so better not to behave like this. Fear of the gods and political ambition can also cause appalling behaviour such as that of Agamemnon killing his daughter (I.80–101) out of a mixture of religious ignorance and political ambition to lead the great Greek fleet to Troy; *tantum religio potuit suadere malorum* ('so great is the evil that religion could urge men to perform'). Money does not make us healthy or happy, but rather the reverse: rich people become anxious about their wealth and always want more. Furthermore the rich still get sick, and do not recover any faster in expensive coverlets than they would if covered by a poor man's garment (II.33–6).

All of this reduces ethics to enlightened self-interest, but then that is what it is for Lucretius – or (in a different way) for Socrates who also (memorably on the final page of Plato's *Republic*) regarded doing good and doing well as the same enterprise. Ethics for Lucretius becomes a matter of common sense whereby we can see what sort of behaviour is conducive to happiness/pleasure and weigh up the pros and cons in a balance of profit and loss. We find it hard to rid ourselves of the pain surrounding death, but even here the poet makes a valiant attempt to free us from fear; given that we are all going to die whether we like it or not, it is up to us to do our best to rid ourselves of the terror. Brave men and cowards all die just the same. Philosophy like this faces the truth full in the face and should make sense to the reader.

More sophisticated arguments are needed for those tricky areas where the senses cannot go. Statements such as 'Julius Caesar was killed by his friends' or 'atoms have no colour' or 'there is an infinite number of worlds' cannot be established simply by looking out of the window. Even a generalisation (and this poet has to do a fair bit of generalising) such as 'all swans are white' (II.824) just needs one black swan to waddle along to be refuted – and who can inspect every swan that has ever been born or ever will be?

One way of doing this is to prove that things must be a certain way because of other known laws or facts. Lucretius uses logical inference to prove what cannot be seen from the evidence of what can be seen, most obviously in his atomic theory. Atoms last for ever as otherwise (in the infinity of past time) they would have crumbled to nothing by now and nothing would now exist. Things do exist, and so the atoms that make them up last forever. In an infinite universe, matter must also be infinite; or else by now matter would have been spread throughout space and not cohere in the things we see and are. The existence of 'things' proves this infinity. Atomic variety is finite; if there were an infinite variety of atomic shapes and combinations then there would be monsters and odd hybrids like centaurs, which palpably do not exist. A nice form of this argument is found in book V: early man must have been tougher than we are: we could not survive (let alone reproduce) without warm clothes and cooked food, but early man did (as otherwise we would not be here). Therefore he was tougher than we are.

The logical form of the argument in these cases is as follows::

if P, then Q
but not-Q
therefore not-P

and is an argument which we all still use without thinking about it. (How do you know it rained in the night? Because the grass is wet. If it had not rained it would not be wet, and so it probably rained.)

A second form of argument he uses is the *a fortiori* reasoning of the form:

if x>y, and if y>z, then x>z

such as one finds in everyday arguments such as: team A will win the cup as they have beaten team B who have themselves beaten team A's opponents last month. John is taller than Sam who is taller than Bernard, and so John must be taller than Bernard. In Lucretius we find examples such as these: sunlight is atomic and moves at a colossal speed; and yet the sunlight atoms have to travel past other atoms which impede them, and so the natural speed of atoms must be even faster than that.

It is even used for ethical purposes in book III in the diatribe against the fear of death: greater men than you (such as Epicurus himself) have died without complaining (and they represented a greater loss to the world), so you should not complain when you come to die.

The third sort of argument to demonstrate the invisible is that of analogy: x is like y, and y is φ, so x is also φ. This is clearly only as good as the comparison is sound and yet it is one of the most widespread arguments used in ancient philosophy; one thinks for example of Plato's analogy (*Republic* 488) of the ship of state and how in a well-ordered ship/state there is an expert hand on the rudder but how in democracy everyone thinks they can steer just as well as everybody else and the ship ends up going round in circles. Lucretius uses this to demonstrate (II.112–24) the movement of atoms in space, pointing to the way in which we can see dust motes dancing in a sunbeam: atoms are like dust-particles, so they dance too. Again, this argument is ethically useful and affords good scope for satire or advice, as in the analogy of life as a dinner-party: good guests know when to leave, and so you should be well-mannered about dying too. Sleep is like death; just as sleep is welcome and painless, so death also is welcome and painless. (The problem here is that we like sleep as we feel better afterwards, but there is no 'afterwards' after death in Lucretius' theory).

## The *de rerum natura*

The genre to which this poem belongs is that of the didactic epic: a branch of epic poetry whose purpose is to instruct the reader. The first ancient practitioner of the genre was the eighth-century Greek poet Hesiod, whose works *Theogony* (concerning the birth of the gods) and *Works and Days* (advice to the poet's brother Perses about farming and related matters) still survive. After Hesiod there are texts by philosophers such as Parmenides and Empedocles, who both wrote poems about the universe and who are thus important models for Lucretius. A great deal more didactic poetry was produced when the literary capital of the world moved from Greece to Egypt and the great cultural centre of Alexandria in the period after the death of Alexander the Great in 323 BC.

Here was a library of world-historical importance, staffed and used by men of wide-ranging scholarship and literary interest such as Callimachus, Apollonius Rhodius, Theocritus. Here, more than anywhere else in the world, a didactic poet could find all the information he wanted and transfer it to verse, and demonstrate both his mastery of arcane information and his dexterity in reproducing this knowledge in verse of dazzling ingenuity and lucidity. Here was born the 'metaphrast' – the poet who responds to the ultimate artistic challenge of producing poetry out of rather dull factual information and thus creates *tours de force* such as Nicander of Colophon's *Venomous Reptiles* and *Antidotes to Poisons*, works designed to be admired and enjoyed by a literary audience rather than being aimed at the wary hill-walker. The poet and textual critic A. E. Housman famously said of Manilius – a didactic poet from the first century AD who wrote about astronomy – that his peculiar genius was for 'doing sums in verse' and there used to be a fashion for deriding didactic poetry as arid poetic exhibitionism. The issue is not that the information contained in such poetry is not correct – the prose manuals which the poet consulted were generally the best available – but that there is a chasm between the audience *about* whom the poet was writing and the audience *for* whom he composed. The old notion of Nicander being consulted by the Alexandrian Ramblers' Association dies hard, but all that we know about this sort of poetry assures us that it was the entertainment of the salon rather than the handbook of the hills.

In Rome we have evidence of didactic poetry being written in Lucretius' own day. Cicero himself translated Aratus' *Phaenomena* into Latin, and we know of a (lost) poem called *De Rerum Natura* being written by an Egnatius, while a certain Sallustius wrote an *Empedoclea*. Was this a sign that poets were looking for something to write about but had nothing original to say?

Similar things might be said about Virgil's *Georgics*: a didactic poem in four books composed after Lucretius' death between 37 and 30 BC and concerned to expound the techniques of farming. The poem shows enormous poetic and literary skill and a good deal of enthusiasm for the subject and for the land of Italy, but less evidence of first-hand knowledge of farming on the part of the poet. It may be disillusioning to realise that all the information contained in the *Georgics* could have been picked up from (say) the prose *De Re Rustica* of Virgil's contemporary Varro. To feel that this line of argument undermines the poem would be a mistake, however. Long gone are the days when poetry was seen as a document of real life whose ostensible 'meaning' was obviously its 'purpose'. Virgil composed a poem about farming which possesses a beauty and a wonder which continue to astonish the reader: such beauty and wonder is not compromised by the question of whether or not the poet actually had a farm.

## Lucretius: Missionary and/or poet?

These questions are still central to much discussion of Lucretius and the debate about this poem still ranges around the polar opposition between those who regard him as a missionary, preaching the good news of Epicurus with a view to converting the reader, and those who regard him as a poet first, picking up the challenge to compose Latin verses on the subject of atomic physics and producing a literary masterpiece out of the most unpromising material. On the one hand, the poet *claims* to be aiming at the conversion of the addressee to the way of life espoused by Epicurus, and yet on the other hand there are many ways in which this does not seem to be the case. The vast majority of the text is concerned with the scientific details of atomic physics, branching out into such arcane matters as the magnet, the waterspout, the question of the infinity of the universe and the finite number of atomic shapes. Little of this (it might be argued) is much use in telling us how to live, and much of it reads like the poet rather than the preacher, creating coherence, beauty and meaning out of the apparently random and mechanical movements of insensate atomic particles. A poetic triumph, but not (at first glance) calculated to inspire a change in how you live your life. The poet claims to be against religion and to despise those who pray to the gods for help – and yet he does so himself when he prays for help to the goddess Venus in the prelude of the poem (I.24). He ends his poem with a ghastly picture of the plague at Athens in 430 BC – an ending hardly likely to inspire positive joy and pleasure in the readers and one which might more easily fill them with despair in the face of such degradation and death.

There are 'ethical' passages in the poem which advise us on matters such as the limits of pleasure, the fear of death, and the correct attitude to love and sex, and these are the passages which are often anthologised and praised. These ethical passages only add up to a tiny proportion of a long poem, however, and Lucretius leaves the reader adrift in a scientific sea for huge stretches of verse with little to anchor this knowledge to the 'moral' purpose of the poem. When we get to the ethical material it is often more satirical than logical: the poet caricatures society types such as the bored rich man (III.1060–7), the insane lover (IV.1058–1191), the ambitious politician (III.995–1002), the impotent man (IV.1233–8), the canny sex-workers (IV.1180–7), villains who murder their kinfolk for power (III.59–73) or to make the wind blow (I.80–101). We might even feel that the ethical material in the poem is drawn from the comic stage rather than experienced Roman life: and the caricatured extremes of bad behaviour do not address the more delicate issues of ethical practice which the real convert would certainly need to discuss – such as the issue of whether to engage in politics or not. Lucretius claims that the poetry is merely the 'honey' on the 'medicine' of his philosophy (I.936–50) and that therefore his 'missionary' purpose is paramount, but (if so) there has to be a sense in which all the poetry is of ethical as well as aesthetic importance.

One way to account for the preponderance of science here is to remember that for Lucretius the pursuit of pleasure is the highest good, and that the study of nature was for him a source of deep pleasure. When he describes his writing of this poetry he does so in terms of 'nights of serenity' (I.142–5). If we were to ask Lucretius how he thought we should live our lives, he might well say 'as I do' and urge us to devote ourselves to the study of the world. Just as pleasure is the removal of pain, so correct knowledge of the world will remove the pain of fear (of the gods and of death) and so is a form of pleasure in itself. Knowledge is the force which will remove the fear born of ignorance and the human misery which results from delusion in all areas of life: it is also a positive source of pleasure in giving us aesthetic joy in seeing the world as it is.

## Pleasure-poetry

*'Only as an aesthetic experience are existence and the world justified'*
Nietzsche *The Birth of Tragedy* 38

The choice of Epicureanism was in fact ideal for a poet of this greatness. In the first place, Epicureanism stresses the primacy of the senses and our capacity to see the truth if we will but open our eyes and look, and this approach suits well the poet with an eye for detail who will paint the world around us with clarity and sharpness. We see through the poet's eyes such things as rainstorms (VI.256–61), leaps of historical imagination such as the description of early man (V.925–1447) and social behaviour such as that of people mourning their loved ones (III.894–911) or the foolish lover (IV.1121–91) satirized and dramatized with pitiless accuracy. In the second place, Epicureanism is primarily an ethical creed based on a scientific reading of the world; but the physics is also invested with an emotional power of its own. For the poet who found ideas interesting in their own right, who could invest cerebral concepts with both colour and emotional significance, this philosophy was perfect. Time after time he applies scientific facts to the values we will infer from them, the physics to the ethics: not content with proving our mortality, he goes on to show how we do (in fact) behave and then how we ought to behave in the face of the grim reaper: not content with explaining the facts of reproduction he tells us how to conduct our sex lives: he explains the spread of disease and then (astonishingly) ends his poem with a stark picture of the plague at Athens. Nowhere does the poet hide behind the stark objectivity of his teaching and fail to draw the human consequences of his beliefs. The artist's eye for detail convinces the reader of the truth of what he describes and the mixture of logical argument and rhetorical diatribe hammers home the points and puts down the opposition, while the indefinable emotional effects of the poetry make it the ideal medium for this instructor of minds and convertor of souls.

The poet claims at two points in the poem that the poetry is the honey smeared onto the bitter medicine of the philosophy, but this dichotomy does not do full justice to this poet. In his love and admiration for the natural world there is no bitterness but a great deal of poetry; ultimately the question of how we ought to live is answered in the manner in which Lucretius shows us as much as in the theories he explains. We ought to live without fear of death or the gods, and in a constant state of curious joy and interest in the world around us. This *rerum natura* is freely available to all of us all of the time, and the study of it will give us understanding. This understanding will give us freedom from pain and fear, and what is more will grant us the 'divine' life of pleasure which this poem both celebrates and creates in verbal form.

## The poet at work

To conclude this brief introduction to Lucretius' poetry, let us look at two short sections of the set text and see all the above in action while also addressing the issues raised.

### (a) The Prelude

The poem begins with a prelude invoking the goddess Venus. This is one of the most surprising features of a surprising poem, since the poet frequently tells us that the gods do not listen to our prayers. The imagery of the gods as serenely untroubled which we find in lines 44-9 and again at 3.18-24 is a mile away from the exquisite portrayal of gods here enjoying a sexual embrace and being asked to bring peace to a troubled world. Many attempts have been made to explain this 'inconsistency' between the poet's theory and his practice.

One suggestion is that Venus here is symbolic for the 'force of nature' or vital energy which makes all things reproduce and which brings into being the myriad life-forms we see. Venus is at once glossed as *hominum divumque voluptas* ('pleasure of men and gods') which reminds us that the Epicurean saw pleasure as the highest good: and the lavish colourful description of the world inspired by Venus shows us furthermore that the Epicurean view of the world is no cold grey place full of dull atoms but is the greatest show on earth. We will soon learn that all these wondrous things are formed by atomic movements, but at this point in the poem it is important for the poet to show us how the pleasure of gazing at the world in all its variety mirrors the pleasure which it shows at work in reproducing life-forms and enjoying the world around us. This is to read the prelude as an allegory – but then that had been done of Aphrodite many time before both in poetry (see e.g. *Homeric Hymn to Aphrodite* 1–5, Euripides *Hippolytus* 447–50) and also in philosophy (by Empedocles (frs. B17, 22, 35,71) and Parmenides (B12.3–6)). This use of a divine name as a stand-in for something else (which critics term 'metonymy') is allowed later on by the poet (II.655–60) provided that the reader refrains from 'polluting his mind with foul superstition'.

A simpler reading is produced if we see these poetic images of the gods as being the sort of 'prayer' which the poet later on (VI.58–79) espouses as being likely to influence our behaviour and encourage us to emulate the 'serenity' (*ataraxia*) of the gods, so that here exchanging the 'image' of war for that of 'peace and creativity' is good for all of us, including the poet.

Finally, the passage begins with the 'patronymic' term 'descendants of Aeneas' (*Aeneadum*) – a form familiar from epic – and the poem is in the tradition of didactic epic in which gods play an active part in the lives of men. It is conceivable that Lucretius writes in this 'epic' manner to hook his readers into a poem which will undermine the epic view of the world: a neat form of irony which uses poetry (which Epicurus famously disapproved of) to correct the 'poetic' view of the world but which makes it clear throughout the text that removing false ideas about the world will not remove the colour and the pleasure from life. There is a feeling that the devil should not have all the best tunes and that poetry such as this will give pleasure even though it speaks of a world which is going to be rediscovered through Atomic philosophy very soon.

### (b)  199–204: giants on the sea

After three separate proofs of the statement that 'nothing will come of nothing', Lucretius brings out his most daring yet.

*denique cur homines tantos natura parare*
*non potuit, pedibus qui pontum per vada possent*
*transire et magnos manibus divellere montes*
*multaque vivendo vitalia vincere saecla,*
*si non, materies quia rebus reddita certa est*
*gignundis, e qua constat quid possit oriri?*

The argument is familiar from elsewhere in the poem:

> if things could appear and grow without atoms, then by now we would have massive people able to stride across the ocean and to live for centuries.
> There are no such people.
> Therefore atoms are needed for creation and growth.

This is the latest in a line of counterfactual absurdities amounting to a *reductio ad absurdum*: if atoms were not essential to growth, we would see people appearing out of nowhere from the sea, apple trees bearing pears and cows giving birth to sheep, roses growing in winter and grapes in spring, little children turning into grown men overnight and crops growing without rain. The argument in 199-205 is different, however, and rests on the principle that every atom is a separate thing and there are limits to the speed and quantity of growth – a limit which we also see in the imperceptible reduction of things being eroded (311-21). Growth is a matter of the snowballing of atomic layers over a period of time. The argument is inductive in that it rests on our perception of the world and could (in theory) be disproved if such giants turned up one day. What matters for us is the way the poet uses this argument to create poetry.

To begin with he gives us the picture of giants bestriding the seas – an epic picture which reminds the educated reader of the god of the sea Poseidon striding from Samothrace to Aigae in four steps (Homer *Iliad* 13.20-1), the one-eyed Cyclops Polyphemus who 'tore off the head of a great mountain' in Homer's *Odyssey* (9.481) and of course the Giants Otus and Ephialtes who ripped off the top of one mountain (Pelion) to put on top of another (Ossa) when they tried to scale

Olympus and unseat the gods. Here he has his cake and eats it: he can enjoy the language of epic mythology while also debunking its content. He certainly gives it the full epic flavour: note the 'p' alliteration as this giant paces over the seas, and the 'm' alliteration as he rips off the heads of mountains. Note how the poet lets us see through the eyes of the giant, who regards what is to us a deep ocean (*pontum*) as 'shallow waters' (*vada*). The vast epic scenery of lines 199–200 is undercut by the quiet but determined verb *non potuit*, stressed in enjambement. In line 202 the lifespan is stretched out verbally by the heavy vowels and the repetition of ideas in *vīvēndō vītālia* (literally 'by living living'), as well as the framing of the line with the 'many ages' (*multa saecula*) which this man lives through, whose long life recalls the epic longevity of Nestor in Homer's *Iliad* (1.250–2). The poet tells us that the reason why these things cannot happen is that 'fixed matter' has been assigned to things as they are created – matter which determines 'what can and cannot arise'. Again, the poet makes the argument come to life with his mode of presentation: the enjambed long syllables of *gignundis* expressing the achingly slow process of generation, the repetition of *re-* sounds in *rebus reddita* showing the accretion of atoms, the emphasis on *certa est* at the end of the line picked up by the central placing of *constat* to assert that there is no argument about this and you get what is put in and no more. Line 204 has a preponderance of heavy syllables:

> *gīgnūndīs ē quā cōnstāt quīd pōssĭt ŏrīrī*

and this cannot be an accident in a line which is putting the brakes so heavily on growth.

Lucretius is a poet of surprises. Even when we may think he is at his most prosaic in content he is working on the poetic form to enact and to enliven his point, and when it comes to inventive ways of illustrating his atomic theories there is simply no limit to his creative powers.

## Summary of book I

### Introduction

| | |
|---|---|
| 1–49 | prayer to Venus |
| 50–61 | appeal to Memmius |
| 62–79 | praise of Epicurus |
| 80–101 | the impiety of religion |
| 102–35 | there is no punishment after death |
| 136–45 | the difficulty of the task |

### Existence of atoms

| | |
|---|---|
| 146–214 | nothing can be made out of nothing |
| 215–64 | nothing can be destroyed, only broken down to its constituent atoms |
| 265–328 | matter is made of invisible particles |

### Existence of space

| | |
|---|---|
| 329–417 | the universe contains space as well as matter |

### Everything is made of matter and space

| | |
|---|---|
| 418–48 | there is no third form of existence after matter and space |
| 449–82 | all qualities and properties are accidents of matter and space |
| 483–634 | atoms cannot be destroyed |

### False theories of matter refuted

| | |
|---|---|
| 635–704 | Monists who think the universe is all one thing |
| 705–829 | Pluralists who think the universe is made of two or more substances |
| 830–920 | Anaxagoras and his theory of 'homoeomeria' |

A Level

## The nature of the universe

921–1007   the universe is infinite in space
1008–1051  and infinite in matter
1052–1113  there is no gravitational centre in the universe

## Conclusion

1114–1117  encouragement to the reader

## The metre of the poem

Latin poetry was written in a fairly rigid system of metres, all of which in turn relied on the 'weight' of each syllable as either 'heavy' or 'light'. A syllable is light if the vowel is short and not followed by two (or more) consonants, whereas syllables containing long vowels, or diphthongs, or in which a vowel is followed by a succession of consonants, are heavy. A syllable is reckoned to be a single vowel sound, followed either by nothing (an 'open' syllable) or by a consonant (a 'closed' syllable): usually a single consonant following a vowel is reckoned to be the first consonant of the following syllable (e.g. *ca-li-gi-ne*) and does not affect the weight of the syllable.

Where two or more consonants follow a vowel, the first one is included in the first syllable (*men-sa*) which is thus 'closed' and becomes heavy – the exceptions being combinations of mute and liquid consonants (b, c, g, p, t followed by r: and c, p, t, followed by l) where both letters are considered as belonging to the following syllable (*ma-tris*) and need not affect the rhythm of the line. Diphthongs (double vowels pronounced as a single sound such as ae, eu, au) are always long by nature: single vowels can in many cases change their quantity in different forms of a word: the final -a of *mensa* is long in the ablative case, short in the nominative, and the perfect tense of the verb *vĕnio* is *vēni*, for instance. This needs to be considered before any judgement is made about assonance – if the vowels have different quantities then there cannot be assonance and the only way to be sure is to scan the line.

In cases where a word ending with a vowel (or a vowel + m such as *naturam*) is followed by a word beginning with a vowel or h, the two syllables usually merge ('elide') into a single syllable, as at 126 where *coepisse et rerum naturam expandere dictis* (fifteen syllables) is scanned *coepiss' et rerum natur' expandere dictis* (thirteen syllables).

– means a heavy syllable
U means a light syllable
× means a syllable which may be either heavy or light
// means the caesura (word-end in the middle of a foot of a hexameter).

The hexameter is the 'epic' metre used by Homer and all later epic and didactic poets. The line is divided into six 'feet', each of which is either a dactyl (a heavy syllable followed by two light syllables (–UU in conventional notation)) or a spondee (two heavy syllables (– –)). The last foot is always dissyllabic, and the last syllable of all may be either heavy or light. The metrical analysis of a line is called 'scansion' and a typical hexameter line (1.1) may be scanned thus:

U U /–   U U/ –//  U  U/–   –/–    U U/– ×
*Aéneadúm genetríx,// hominúm divúmque volúptas*

where the // sign shows the 'caesura' – the word-break in the middle of a foot – which occurs in the third foot (as here) or else in the fourth.

Latin also had a stress accent, whereby most words of more than one syllable were stressed on the penultimate syllable, or on the antepenultimate if the penultimate contained a short vowel. Thus, line 2 would be spoken:

<u>al</u>ma <u>Ven</u>us <u>cae</u>li <u>sub</u>ter la<u>ben</u>tia <u>sig</u>na

but 'scanned' metrically as:

<u>al</u>ma Ven<u>us</u> cae<u>li</u> sub<u>ter</u> la<u>ben</u>tia <u>sig</u>na

Here we can see that the metrical beat or 'ictus' clashes with the speech 'accent' in the first four feet and only coincides with it in the final two feet. This is common in all hexameter verse: occasionally poets avoid coincidence of ictus and accent in the final two feet as at 116, where the metrical ictus falls thus:

<u>an</u> pecu/d<u>es</u> ali/<u>as</u> div/<u>in</u>itus/ <u>in</u>sinu/<u>et</u> se

but the line is spoken thus:

<u>an</u> <u>pe</u>cudes <u>al</u>ias div<u>in</u>itus ins<u>in</u>uet <u>se</u>

## Key literary terms

**Alliteration**: repetition of consonants in successive words as at 68–9 (*minitanti murmure*) or 94 (*patrio princeps*).

**Anaphora**: repetition of a key word, often for rhetorical effect, as in the repetition of *privata* at 47.

**Assonance**: repetition of vowel sounds such as the 'i' sounds at 72 (*vivida vis animi pervicit*)

**Chiasmus**: a pair of matching phrases where the second reverses the order of the first, forming an abba pattern as at 174 (*vere rosam frumenta calore*)

**Enacting**: where the words used conjure up the thing described, as in the rumbling thunder of *minitanti murmure* (68–9) or the tiny word *res* at 216 showing the tiny amount of matter left behind.

**Enjambement**: where the sentence runs over the end of the line and continues into the next line: see e.g. *sensit* at the start of line 90.

**Epanalepsis**: repetition of a word after several other words, such as at 61 (*prima…primis*)

**Framing**: where a key word or phrase is expressed with two words which begin and end a line, such as *maestum… parentem* at 89.

**Juxtaposition**: placing two words next to each other for emphasis or for ironic contrast, as at 30 (*sopita quiescant* – emphasis) or 19 (*incutiens blandum* – contrast).

**A Level**

**Metaphor:** a comparison which uses terms appropriate for one thing in describing another: in line 8 the seas are said to 'laugh' (*rident*). See also (e.g.) 21, 50, 62, 76–7.

**Metonymy:** the substitution of a name for a thing: the goddess Venus is arguably used metonymically for a combination of sexual love and the life force in the opening prelude (1–43).

**Oxymoron:** putting words side by side with opposite meanings, as *casta inceste* (98).

**Pathetic Fallacy:** in which inanimate and insentient objects are described as if they had feelings: see e.g. the personification of the seasons at lines 174–5.

**Polyptoton:** repetition of the same word in a different grammatical form: e.g. *omni/ omnibus* (26–7).

**Spondee:** two long syllables forming a single measure of the line (see metre).

**Tricolon (crescendo):** a group of three phrases of increasing emphasis, often beginning with the same initial word as at line 6 (*te dea, te fugiunt venti, te nubila caeli/ adventumque tuum*)

# Further reading

### English Translations of the *de rerum natura* include:
*On the Nature of the Universe* (translated in prose by R. Latham, edited with notes by John Godwin (Penguin Classics, 1994))

*On the Nature of Things* (translated in verse by A. E. Stallings, with introduction by Richard Jenkyns (Penguin Classics))

*On the Nature of the Universe* (translated in verse by R. Melville with notes by Don and Peta Fowler (Oxford World's Classics))

The whole poem is available with a facing English translation by M. F. Smith in the Loeb Classical Library series (Harvard, 2nd edition, 1982)

The standard edition of the poem with full text, translation and commentary is the magisterial work of Cyril Bailey (3 vols, Oxford, 1947)

### Editions of Book I include:
J. D. Duff (Cambridge, 1950)

J. H. Warburton-Lee (Macmillan, 1964)

P. M. Brown (Bristol Classical Press, 1984)

**General books on Lucretius include:**

| | |
|---|---|
| Clay, D. | *Lucretius and Epicurus* (Cornell, 1983) |
| Gale, M. R. | *Myth and Poetry in Lucretius* (Cambridge, 1994) |
| Gale, M. R. | *Lucretius and Didactic Epic* (Bloomsbury, 2001) |
| Godwin, J. | *Lucretius* (Bloomsbury, 2004) |
| Johnson, W. R. | *Lucretius and the Modern World* (Duckworth, 2000) |
| Kenney, E. J. | *Lucretius* (*Greece and Rome* New Surveys in the Classics 11, 2nd edition, 1995) |
| Pope, M. | *Lucretius and the End of Masculinity* (Cambridge, 2023) |
| Sedley, D. | *Lucretius and the Transformation of Greek Wisdom* (Cambridge, 1998) |
| Taylor, B. | *Lucretius and the Language of Nature* (Oxford, 2020) |
| West, D. | *The Imagery and Poetry of Lucretius* (Edinburgh, 1969) |

**On the role of Ennius in Lucretius' work see:**
Nethercut, J. *Ennius Noster: Lucretius and the Annales* (Oxford, 2020)

**Collections of essays on Lucretius can be found in:**
Dudley, D. R. (ed.) *Lucretius* (London, 1965)
Gale, M. R. (ed) *Lucretius* (Oxford Readings in Classical Studies, Oxford, 2007)
Gillespie, S. and Hardie, P. (edd.) *The Cambridge Companion to Lucretius* (Cambridge, 2007)
O'Rourke, D. *Approaches to Lucretius: Traditions and Innovations in Reading the de rerum natura* (Cambridge, 2021)

**General accounts of Epicureanism include:**
Long, A. A. *Hellenistic Philosophy: Stoics, Epicureans and Sceptics* (Duckworth, 1986)
Rist, J. M. *Epicurus: An Introduction* (Cambridge, 1972)
Sharples, R. W. *Stoics, Epicureans and Sceptics: An Introduction to Hellenistic Philosophy* (Routledge, 1996)

**For the Presocratic background, see:**
Barnes, J. *The Presocratic Philosophers* (London, 1982)
Waterfield, R. A. *The First Philosophers: the Presocratics and Sophists* (translation of the key texts with notes: Oxford World's Classics, 2009)

**For the texts of the Hellenistic philosophers translated into English see:**
Long, A. A. and Sedley, D. N. *The Hellenistic Philosophers* (Cambridge, 1987)

**For the growth and spread of Epicureanism in Rome see:**
Jones, H. *The Epicurean Tradition* (London, 1989)
Yona, S. and Davis, G. *Epicurus in Rome: Philosophical Perspectives in the Ciceronian Age* (Cambridge, 2022)

**For the political world of Lucretius' own day see (e.g.):**
Syme, R. *The Roman Revolution* (Oxford, 1939)
Crawford, M. *The Roman Republic* (London, 4th edition, 1988)
Jones, P. and Sidwell, K. *The World of Rome* (Cambridge, 1997)

**A good general introduction to Roman Literature is:**
Braund, S. Morton *Understanding Latin Literature* (2nd edition, Routledge, 2017)

**For a highly readable account of the rediscovery of Lucretius in the Renaissance see:**
Greenblatt, S. *The Swerve: How the Renaissance Began* (Vintage, 2012)

The **text** printed here is largely that of Bailey's Oxford Classical Text (reprinted 1974): I have however printed lines 44–9 (which Bailey omits) in this text. In two places (14–15 and 155) the order of the lines was clearly wrong in some early manuscripts and I have printed the generally accepted rearrangement of these lines.

I have printed 3rd declension accusative plurals as *-es* rather than *-is* and assimilated prefixes as in the *Oxford Latin Dictionary* (and so printed (e.g.) *affectis* where Bailey prints *adfectis* at 1.133).

A Level

# Text

Aeneadum genetrix, hominum divumque voluptas,
alma Venus, caeli subter labentia signa
quae mare navigerum, quae terras frugiferentes
concelebras, per te quoniam genus omne animantum
concipitur visitque exortum lumina solis:  5
te, dea, te fugiunt venti, te nubila caeli
adventumque tuum, tibi suaves daedala tellus
summittit flores, tibi rident aequora ponti
placatumque nitet diffuso lumine caelum.
nam simul ac species patefacta est verna diei  10
et reserata viget genitabilis aura Favoni,
aëriae primum volucres te, diva, tuumque
significant initum perculsae corda tua vi.
inde ferae pecudes persultant pabula laeta
et rapidos tranant amnes: ita capta lepore  15
te sequitur cupide quo quamque inducere pergis.
denique per maria ac montes fluviosque rapaces
frondiferasque domos avium camposque virentes
omnibus incutiens blandum per pectora amorem
efficis ut cupide generatim saecla propagent.  20
quae quoniam rerum naturam sola gubernas
nec sine te quicquam dias in luminis oras
exoritur neque fit laetum neque amabile quicquam,
te sociam studeo scribendis versibus esse,
quos ego de rerum natura pangere conor  25
Memmiadae nostro, quem tu, dea, tempore in omni
omnibus ornatum voluisti excellere rebus.
quo magis aeternum da dictis, diva, leporem.
effice ut interea fera moenera militiai
per maria ac terras omnes sopita quiescant;  30

nam tu sola potes tranquilla pace iuvare
mortales, quoniam belli fera moenera Mavors
armipotens regit, in gremium qui saepe tuum se
reicit aeterno devictus vulnere amoris,
atque ita suspiciens tereti cervice reposta                 35
pascit amore avidos inhians in te, dea, visus
eque tuo pendet resupini spiritus ore.
hunc tu, diva, tuo recubantem corpore sancto
circumfusa super, suaves ex ore loquelas
funde petens placidam Romanis, incluta, pacem;             40
nam neque nos agere hoc patriai tempore iniquo
possumus aequo animo nec Memmi clara propago
talibus in rebus communi desse saluti.
omnis enim per se divum natura necesse est
immortali aevo summa cum pace fruatur                      45
semota ab nostris rebus seiunctaque longe;
nam privata dolore omni, privata periclis,
ipsa suis pollens opibus, nil indiga nostri,
nec bene promeritis capitur nec tangitur ira.
quod superest, vacuas aures animumque sagacem              50
semotum a curis adhibe veram ad rationem,
ne mea dona tibi studio disposta fideli,
intellecta prius quam sint, contempta relinquas.
nam tibi de summa caeli ratione deumque
disserere incipiam et rerum primordia pandam,              55
unde omnes natura creet res, auctet alatque,
quove eadem rursum natura perempta resolvat,
quae nos materiem et genitalia corpora rebus
reddunda in ratione vocare et semina rerum
appellare suemus et haec eadem usurpare                    60
corpora prima, quod ex illis sunt omnia primis.

humana ante oculos foede cum vita iaceret
in terris oppressa gravi sub religione,

quae caput a caeli regionibus ostendebat
horribili super aspectu mortalibus instans, 65
primum Graius homo mortales tollere contra
est oculos ausus primusque obsistere contra;
quem neque fama deum nec fulmina nec minitanti
murmure compressit caelum, sed eo magis acrem
irritat animi virtutem, effringere ut arta 70
naturae primus portarum claustra cupiret.
ergo vivida vis animi pervicit et extra
processit longe flammantia moenia mundi
atque omne immensum peragravit mente animoque,
unde refert nobis victor quid possit oriri, 75
quid nequeat, finita potestas denique cuique
quanam sit ratione atque alte terminus haerens.
quare religio pedibus subiecta vicissim
obteritur, nos exaequat victoria caelo.
illud in his rebus vereor, ne forte rearis 80
impia te rationis inire elementa viamque
indugredi sceleris. quod contra saepius illa
religio peperit scelerosa atque impia facta.
Aulide quo pacto Triviai virginis aram
Iphianassai turparunt sanguine foede 85
ductores Danaum delecti, prima virorum.
cui simul infula virgineos circumdata comptus
ex utraque pari malarum parte profusa est,
et maestum simul ante aras adstare parentem
sensit et hunc propter ferrum celare ministros 90
aspectuque suo lacrimas effundere cives,
muta metu terram genibus summissa petebat.
nec miserae prodesse in tali tempore quibat,
quod patrio princeps donarat nomine regem;
nam sublata virum manibus tremibundaque ad aras 95
deducta est, non ut sollemni more sacrorum
perfecto posset claro comitari Hymenaeo,

sed casta inceste nubendi tempore in ipso
hostia concideret mactatu maesta parentis,
exitus ut classi felix faustusque daretur.                               100
tantum religio potuit suadere malorum.
tutemet a nobis iam quovis tempore vatum
terriloquis victus dictis desciscere quaeres.
quippe etenim quam multa tibi iam fingere possunt
somnia, quae vitae rationes vertere possint                              105
fortunasque tuas omnes turbare timore!
et merito; nam si certam finem esse viderent
aerumnarum homines, aliqua ratione valerent
religionibus atque minis obsistere vatum.
nunc ratio nulla est restandi, nulla facultas,                           110
aeternas quoniam poenas in morte timendum.
ignoratur enim quae sit natura animai,
nata sit an contra nascentibus insinuetur
et simul intereat nobiscum morte dirempta
an tenebras Orci visat vastasque lacunas                                 115
an pecudes alias divinitus insinuet se,
Ennius ut noster cecinit, qui primus amoeno
detulit ex Helicone perenni fronde coronam,
per gentes Italas hominum quae clara clueret;
etsi praeterea tamen esse Acherusia templa                               120
Ennius aeternis exponit versibus edens,
quo neque permaneant animae neque corpora nostra,
sed quaedam simulacra modis pallentia miris;
unde sibi exortam semper florentis Homeri
commemorat speciem lacrimas effundere salsas                             125
coepisse et rerum naturam expandere dictis.
quapropter bene cum superis de rebus habenda
nobis est ratio, solis lunaeque meatus
qua fiant ratione, et qua vi quaeque gerantur
in terris, tunc cum primis ratione sagaci                                130
unde anima atque animi constet natura videndum,

et quae res nobis vigilantibus obvia mentes
terrificet morbo affectis somnoque sepultis,
cernere uti videamur eos audireque coram,
morte obita quorum tellus amplectitur ossa.   135
    nec me animi fallit Graiorum obscura reperta
difficile illustrare Latinis versibus esse,
multa novis verbis praesertim cum sit agendum
propter egestatem linguae et rerum novitatem;
sed tua me virtus tamen et sperata voluptas   140
suavis amicitiae quemvis efferre laborem
suadet et inducit noctes vigilare serenas
quaerentem dictis quibus et quo carmine demum
clara tuae possim praepandere lumina menti,
res quibus occultas penitus convisere possis.   145
hunc igitur terrorem animi tenebrasque necesse est
non radii solis neque lucida tela diei
discutiant, sed naturae species ratioque.
    principium cuius hinc nobis exordia sumet,
nullam rem e nilo gigni divinitus umquam.   150
quippe ita formido mortales continet omnes,
quod multa in terris fieri caeloque tuentur,
quorum operum causas nulla ratione videre
possunt ac fieri divino numine rentur.
quas ob res ubi viderimus nil posse creari   155
de nilo, tum quod sequimur iam rectius inde
perspiciemus, et unde queat res quaeque creari
et quo quaeque modo fiant opera sine divum.
    nam si de nilo fierent, ex omnibus rebus
omne genus nasci posset, nil semine egeret.   160
e mare primum homines, e terra posset oriri
squamigerum genus et volucres erumpere caelo;
armenta atque aliae pecudes, genus omne ferarum,
incerto partu culta ac deserta tenerent.
nec fructus idem arboribus constare solerent,   165

A Level

sed mutarentur, ferre omnes omnia possent.
quippe ubi non essent genitalia corpora cuique,
qui posset mater rebus consistere certa?
at nunc seminibus quia certis quaeque creantur,
inde enascitur atque oras in luminis exit, 170
materies ubi inest cuiusque et corpora prima;
atque hac re nequeunt ex omnibus omnia gigni,
quod certis in rebus inest secreta facultas.
   praeterea cur vere rosam, frumenta calore,
vites autumno fundi suadente videmus, 175
si non, certa suo quia tempore semina rerum
cum confluxerunt, patefit quodcumque creatur,
dum tempestates adsunt et vivida tellus
tuto res teneras effert in luminis oras?
quod si de nilo fierent, subito exorerentur 180
incerto spatio atque alienis partibus anni,
quippe ubi nulla forent primordia, quae genitali
concilio possent arceri tempore iniquo.
nec porro augendis rebus spatio foret usus
seminis ad coitum, si e nilo crescere possent; 185
nam fierent iuvenes subito ex infantibus parvis
e terraque exorta repente arbusta salirent.
quorum nil fieri manifestum est, omnia quando
paulatim crescunt, ut par est semine certo,
crescentesque genus servant; ut noscere possis 190
quidque sua de materia grandescere alique.
   huc accedit uti sine certis imbribus anni
laetificos nequeat fetus summittere tellus
nec porro secreta cibo natura animantum
propagare genus possit vitamque tueri; 195
ut potius multis communia corpora rebus
multa putes esse, ut verbis elementa videmus,
quam sine principiis ullam rem exsistere posse.
   denique cur homines tantos natura parare

non potuit, pedibus qui pontum per vada possent 200
transire et magnos manibus divellere montes
multaque vivendo vitalia vincere saecla,
si non, materies quia rebus reddita certa est
gignundis, e qua constat quid possit oriri?
nil igitur fieri de nilo posse fatendum est, 205
semine quando opus est rebus, quo quaeque creatae
aëris in teneras possint proferrier auras.
  postremo quoniam incultis praestare videmus
culta loca et manibus meliores reddere fetus,
esse videlicet in terris primordia rerum 210
quae nos fecundas vertentes vomere glebas
terraique solum subigentes cimus ad ortus;
quod si nulla forent, nostro sine quaeque labore
sponte sua multo fieri meliora videres.
huc accedit uti quidque in sua corpora rursum 215
dissolvat natura neque ad nilum interimat res.
nam si quid mortale e cunctis partibus esset,
ex oculis res quaeque repente erepta periret;
nulla vi foret usus enim, quae partibus eius
discidium parere et nexus exsolvere posset. 220
quod nunc, aeterno quia constant semine quaeque,
donec vis obiit, quae res diverberet ictu
aut intus penetret per inania dissolvatque,
nullius exitium patitur natura videri.

# Commentary Notes

## 1–43

Address to the goddess Venus. This is surprising, as the poet frequently tells us that the gods do not listen to our prayers as they could not enjoy divine contentment if they were constantly being bothered by us. For further discussion see the introduction.

**1 Aeneadum genetrix** – Lucretius addresses Venus as 'mother of the sons of Aeneas'. *Aeneadum* is the genitive plural of *Aeneades*, a 'patronymic' word indicating the parentage of the person described, often used in epic poetry. Aeneas was a Trojan prince, son of the goddess Venus and a mortal Anchises, and legendary founder of the Roman race.

**hominum divumque voluptas** – Venus is described as 'pleasure of men and gods', thus linking her with the Epicurean school which declared that pleasure was the highest good. The phrase is also reminiscent of epic language.

**2 alma** – 'nourishing' derives from *alo* ('I feed'). The 'gliding signs of the heavens' are the stars: the poet ranges from sky to sea (**mare**) and earth (**terras**) in a sequence, with repeated **quae** and parallel pattern of noun and adjective.

**3 navigerum... frugiferentes** – note the epic compound adjectives and the balanced repetition of *quae* + noun + adjective.

**4 concelebras:** the verb is emphasised in enjambement. The poet now begins a sequence of second person pronouns (*te...te...te...te... tibi...tibi*) which accentuate the direct address ('apostrophe') to the goddess.

**4–5** In crude mechanical terms, if Venus is the power of sexual love, then she is responsible for all mammalian reproduction. The poet expresses this elegantly: the 'type of living things' is 'conceived' and at once 'sees' the light of the sun.

**6** Note the tricolon crescendo of three phrases all beginning with *te*.

**6–7 tuum tibi** is effective juxtaposition. **suaves** agrees with **flores** in the next line. **daedala** here means 'skilled' and is usually applied to the works of human craftsmen – here the earth is personified as a skilled producer of flowers. The original Daedalus was the brilliant craftsman who devised wings for himself and his son Icarus to allow them to escape from King Minos on Crete, as narrated in Ovid *Metamorphoses* VIII.183–235.

**8 rident** – the metaphor of the sea 'laughing' is effective.

**9 diffuso lumine** – the ablative absolute construction is also explanatory: 'the calmed sky shines with light outpoured'.

**10 species...verna diei** – 'the face of springtime': the adjective **verna** is transferred from **diei** (here meaning 'season') to **species**. Many animals and birds mate or produce their young in the spring, and so (as Venus is the goddess of sexual love) it is Venus herself who is welcomed in the spring.

**11 reserata** – (literally) 'unlocked', suggesting the cave where King Aeolus keeps the winds locked up in Homer *Odyssey* 10. The rest of the line emphasises the creative power of the wind: **viget** suggests health, **genitabilis** (recalling *genetrix* in line 1) suggests 'capable of giving life'. **genitabilis** could be either nominative or genitive singular but is perhaps best taken with **aura**.

**12 aëriae** is scanned as four syllables (*āĕrĭae*). The poet addresses Venus again as 'goddess' (**diva**: cf. *dea* in line 6).

**13 corda** – accusative of respect: 'struck as to their hearts'. The monosyllabic ending to the line creates a bumpy rhythm which stresses the energy being described.

**14–15 ferae pecudes** – not to be taken together, as *fera* means a 'wild beast' while *pecudes* are herds of tame animals. The omission of 'and' is a device known as asyndeton and here suggests the rapid listing of types of animals all inspired by Venus. In this line and the next the poet again employs a varied sentence structure of verb-noun-adjective (**persultant pabula laeta**) followed by adjective-verb-noun (**rapidos tranant amnes**). *rapidus* has the obvious sense of 'rapid' but also has the sense of 'snatching' from its root *rapio* and thus here depicts the river in full flood carrying all with it, as in *rapaces* in line 17. The vigour of the river is matched by the richness of the fields: **laeta** when applied to fields usually means 'rich, fruitful' but its common meaning of 'happy' is not out of place in the context of 'laughing' seas and leaping flocks. The poet also notably uses effective alliteration in **pecudes persultant pabula** and then strong assonance of *a* in **rapidos tranant amnes**. These two lines appeared in some manuscripts in reverse order but scholars all agree that they should be transposed as in the text printed.

**15-16   lepore**: this is a quality of elegance and charm: this is a surprising use of the word here in the military metaphor of **capta…sequitur** suggesting that the hardness of war is captivated by the soft charms of Venus – a theme which the love of Mars and Venus at lines 29–40 will continue to develop. In this sentence the subject of **sequitur** is *quaeque* ('each beast') supplied from **quamque** which also agrees with *capta*: 'thus captivated by your charm (each beast) follows you eagerly wherever you go on to lead each [beast].' Any actions induced by Venus will have quality of 'desire' in them and so **cupide** is appropriate.

**17-18   maria… montes fluviosque… domos…campos** – the topography of animal life is listed: seas and mountains are simply mentioned, but the poet uses descriptive adjectives so that the rivers are **rapaces**, the trees are the 'leaf-bearing homes of birds' and the plains are 'lush green'. The impression created by this rapid tour is one of energy (**rapaces**) health (**virentes**) and also that beneath the surface of something as ordinary as a tree there is a whole world of hidden life.

**19-20   amorem…propagent** – if Venus strikes love into their hearts, then they will breed: this truism is made more impressive by the language used – **incutiens** is a violent word whereas **blandum** means 'coaxing, affectionate', the juxtaposition producing an oxymoron which brings out both the power and the charm of Venus: then line 20 is framed by the verbs, with **cupide** appropriate to the acts of the mother of Cupid, and **generatim saecla** going well together. **generatim** ('each according to its kind', so that sheep do not breed cows) will be explained further at 159–73. **saecla** (a shortened form of *saecula*) here means the same as *genera* ('species' or 'kinds' of animal).

**21–7** The poet prays to Venus to assist him and names his addressee; since Venus alone 'steers' the *rerum naturam* then it is appropriate that she should also steer the poem *de rerum natura*. Later on the poet utters the more conventional address to the Muse Calliope (VI.92–5).

**21    gubernas** – this is a metaphor from steering a ship.

**22    nec . . . quicquam** – 'nor does anything'. The periphrasis 'arises into the bright shores of light' for 'is born' is a lively epic formula: the adjective **dias** is from *divus* and has the primary sense 'bright' but a clear undertone of 'divine' – it is appropriate that a *diva* should produce living things into the **dias** 'shores of light'.

**23    laetum . . . amabile** – Venus does not merely produce life – but also joy and lovability, both of which will engender more life in their turn and (in the case of the poem) communicate to the reader this joy and love. Note how the two lines are framed by the parallel phrases **nec. . . quicquam. . .neque. . . quicquam**.

**24    scribendis versibus** – a dative of purpose (cf. 184) after **sociam** (a 'partner for the purpose of writing verses'). Note the heavy alliteration of 's' and the sense of **studeo** as 'I am keen for'.

**25    de rerum natura** – the poet signposts the title of the poem. **pangere** properly means 'to construct' and suggests the building of a house – there is a touch of modesty in **conor** ('I am attempting') which fits well with the prayer to the goddess.

**26    Memmiadae** – Gaius Memmius was an important man in the politics of the late Roman Republic. He had literary interests (Ovid *Tristia* II.433) and was as well known for his political ambition as for his sexual activities – he even tried to seduce the wife of Pompey the Great. He was thus a perfect candidate for Epicurean conversion. Here the poet uses the elegant patronymic (as at line 1) 'to the scion of Memmius' as *Mēmmiō* would not scan in a hexameter.

**26–7 omni/omnibus** – the remark that Venus 'wanted Memmius to excel in all things at all times' is interesting: on the one hand, the coinage of the Memmii have the goddess Venus on them and so she may be the family patroness, and on the other hand his sexual appetites were so legendary that the poet may here be alluding to his devotion to Venus – the goddess of sexual love – 'at all times'. Notice here the polyptoton of **omni omnibus** over the line-break in fulsome praise of Memmius.

**28 quo magis** – the prayer sums up: Venus should be 'all the more' willing to assist the poet as Memmius is her favourite. Most surprising is the poet's wish for 'eternal' (*aeternum*) grace to be given to the poem as he frequently tells us how we ourselves will die and all the world with us. Note here the sequence of alliterative words **da dictis diva** and the final juxtaposition of **diva leporem** indicative of the way in which she is the source of *lepos* (15) and lovability (23).

## 29–49

The mythology becomes more involved as the poet now invokes the goddess to bring peace, drawing on the traditional imagery of her love-affair with the god of war (Mars) and the topical allusion to Memmius' political involvement in the turbulent days of the late Roman republic.

**29–30 moenera militiai** – earlier on Venus was credited with awakening all living things everywhere to life, but now she is credited with the reverse power to send to sleep the 'wild works of warfare' 'through seas and all the lands'. *moenus* is an archaic form of the noun *munus* meaning 'task, drill' and also 'duty' and even 'gladiatorial show'. *militiai* is the archaic genitive form of *militia*. **sopita quiescant** is an emphatic juxtaposition.

A Level

**31 tu... potes** – Venus is divine, and has the power to send us good things anyway, but she has a special power over the god of war whom she can distract with her charms.

**32 belli fera moenera** – the phrase recalls line 29 and sets up the alliteration of *moenera Mavors*, the name (for Mars) being both archaic and suggestive of the word *mors* ('death'). It also neatly frames the line which began with *mortales*.

**32–3** Mars rules war – but Venus rules over Mars, and so Venus can rule over war. *armipotens* is a grand compound adjective for a grand warrior-god who 'rules' (*regit*) even what is 'savage' (*fera*). The grandeur is however soon dissipated as the wargod throws himself into the lap of Venus, the verbal juxtaposition of *tuum se* bringing their embrace to life. This happens 'often' and his love is an 'eternal' wound.

**34 devictus** – there is nice irony here in the conqueror being conquered, the wounds inflicted on this warrior being those of love and not war. Unlike ourselves, the gods are immortal and so his wound is also 'eternal' (*aeterno*). For the tale of how Mars (Ares) was seduced by Venus (Aphrodite) and then caught and humiliated by her husband Mulciber (Vulcan) see Homer *Odyssey* 8.266–369.

**35–40** The poet describes the scene in lavish and highly visual detail, concentrating on how Venus is above Mars and dominant over him in their embrace. The description of the scene suggests the composition of a work of art.

**35 tereti cervice reposta** – an ablative absolute construction, with *reposta* a contracted form of *reposita*. Mars' neck is *teres* – 'rounded' and even 'beautiful'.

**36** The imagery here is striking: Mars 'gasping, feeds his greedy eyes on you with love', with *avidos* and *inhians* juxtaposed for effect and the broken rhythm of *te dea visus* may perhaps suggest the panting of the amorous god. *visūs* (accusative plural: literally 'the act of seeing') here means 'eyes'.

A Level

**37** The close contact of the gods is beautifully brought out by the 'breathing' of the war-god 'hanging' from the mouth of the goddess (*spiritus ore* juxtaposed verbally as in life) as he lies back (*resupini*). *pendet* adds to the feeling of the passivity of the war-god, as does *super* in line 39.

**38 corpore sancto** – the ablative term can be taken with both participles *circumfusa* and *recubantem*. *sancto* is an interesting choice of word: as applied to a goddess it means primarily 'divine, holy' but also has the sense 'pure, chaste' and also 'untouchable, inviolate'.

**39 super** – continues the idea of domination from *suspiciens...pendet resupini... recubantem. suaves* agrees with *loquelas. ex ore* may sound redundant – what else is she going to speak from? – but here continues the emphasis of *eque... ore* in 36 with focus on the lovely mouth of the goddess.

**40 funde** – Venus is *circumfusa* and is now told to *funde*, the imperative followed by *petens* which functions as another command. She is coaxingly addressed as *incluta*, (an archaic word meaning 'renowned'). *placidam..pacem* might seem something of a tautology but (apart from the 'p' alliteration) it affords a greater emphasis on the quiet and peace being sought which sounds very close to the *ataraxia* (serenity) which for Epicurus was the highest good.

**41 agere hoc** here means something like 'do my job'. The phrase ('in this troubled era for our country') suggests that the lines were being written in the darkest days of civil war (49–45 BC).

**42** The adjective **aequo** picks up *iniquo* from the previous line and seals the logic of *possumus*: if things are not *aequus*, then we cannot work with an *aequus* mind. The phrasing *Memmi clara propago* ('the noble offspring of Memmius') suggests an attitude of *noblesse oblige* whereby so noble a citizen has to get involved in his country's turmoil.

**43 communi ... saluti** almost suggests Cicero's dictum *salus populi suprema lex* ('the safety of the people is the highest law'). Epicureanism was notoriously apolitical, but the wise man might act to preserve social safety. The sentence as a whole is both praise of Memmius as indispensable to his country and also a neat conclusion to the prayer for peace.

## 44–9

These lines recur in 2.646–51 and fit badly into the context here, and were possibly added here by a later scribe to be shaped into a passage 'correcting' the false theology of the prelude which seems to contradict the Epicurean view of divine serenity. If they were placed here by the poet, the connection of thought must be: 'give the Romans peace, for the gods enjoy unbroken peace'. Later on (III.322) the poet tells us that we too can 'live a life worthy of the gods' (*dignam dis degere vitam*) and perhaps this passage acts as a contrast to the troubled times of Rome and a paradigm of the sort of peace which is being sought.

**44–5 divum** – a contraction of the genitive plural *divorum*. The subjunctive *fruatur* is to be taken after *necesse est* – 'it is necessary that divine nature enjoys'.

**46 semota ab nostris rebus** – 'removed from our affairs'. This is the major area of conflict with what has preceded: if the gods have no connection with us, why should Venus assist Rome and the poet now? Note here the duplication of *semota... seiunctaque*.

**47 privata** – notice the anaphora of *privata* and alliteration of 'p'.

**48 indiga** takes the genitive case and **nostri** here simply means 'us'.

**49 nec...nec** – gods are often expected to reward good deeds and to punish the wicked: Lucretius assures us that neither is the case.

## 50–3

The poet sets out his intention to explain the atomic theory, and the first four lines express (understandable) concern that the reader will find this difficult and dismiss it before it is understood.

**50 quod superest** – this phrase simply means 'next'. The poet calls for 'attentive (literally 'empty') ears' and the following line suggests that we will need to give this matter our full attention. **sagacem** is a metaphor from the keen noses of hunting dogs: cf. 130.

**51 semotum a curis** is both good sense – it is no use trying to read philosophy when your mind is on other things – and very good Epicureanism, as Epicurus prized *ataraxia* ('freedom from worry, serenity') as the height of happiness. *ratio* is a difficult word with a range of meanings: here it connotes 'philosophy'.

**52-3 ne... relinquas** – a negative purpose clause ('to prevent you from abandoning') addressed to Memmius. The poet presents his philosophy as 'gifts' (*dona*) which have been paid out with care and fidelity to Epicurus (*studio... fideli*): such gifts do not deserve to be 'despised' (*contempta*) 'before they have been grasped'.

## 54-61

The poet promises the truth about the telescopic and the microscopic: the sky, the gods and the atoms. The paragraph concludes with some enticing technical language to convince the reader that he will learn something here from a poet who is an authority on the subject. It is interesting that he hooks the reader with astronomy and meteorology – which the poem will not discuss until the last two books – and only then mentions the atomic theory which will occupy much of the first two books. the syllabus for books 3 and 4 will not appear until lines 131–5.

**54 summa** ('lofty') is applied to the explanation (*ratione*) of both the heavens and the gods. *deum* is the contracted form of *deorum*.

**55** The line is framed by the two important verbs **disserere** and **pandam**. The *rerum primordia* are the 'first-beginnings of things' or the atoms.

**56 natura** is personified here as active creator and 'dissolver'. Later on (III. 931–77) she even speaks to the man reluctant to die, but none of

**A Level**

this implies that Lucretius believed that there was a personal deity at work creating the world as we see it. The exuberant energy of nature is brought out by the sequence of three verbs *creet. . .auctet alatque* for the threefold activity of creating, making to grow and then feeding.

**57** Nature causes things to break up and return to their atomic state again (*rursum*) when they are destroyed (*perempta*): the atoms of which things (**res**) are constructed are eternal. **eadem** and **perempta** are neuter plural to go with the *omnia* implied in **omnes res**.

58–61 The poet lists some of the various synonyms for 'atoms' in Latin: **materiem** (literally 'matter'), **genitalia corpora** ('bodies which give life'), **semina rerum** ('the seeds of things') and **corpora prima** ('first bodies'), while at the same time finding synonyms for the verb 'to call' (*vocare, appellare, usurpare*).

**58** **materiem** sounds as if it has *mater* ('mother': cf. 170–1) in it and leads well onto *genitalia* ('life-giving') and then *semina* ('seeds'). **rebus** is a possessive dative going with *genitalia corpora* ('the life-giving bodies of things').

**59** **reddunda in ratione**: *reddere rationem* is properly to 'render an account' and is a financial term: here it refers to the poet giving us his explanation of the world.

**60** **appellare ... usurpare** – the two synonymous words for 'call' frame the line: *sŭēmus* is scanned as three syllables and is the contracted form of *suevimus* (perfect tense of *suesco*).

**61** The line makes better sound than sense: the epanalepsis of **prima ... primis** is rhetorically effective but the meaning is (at this point in the poem) elusive and will await further explanation later when the poet will show how 'things' (*rerum*) are made up of atoms.

## 62–79

Praise of Epicurus, especially for his subjugation of religion. Books III, V and VI similarly open with praise of Epicurus. The language here borrows in places the epic register of the conquering general as Epicurus defeats the monster which has kept humanity grovelling in fear and superstition: there is also a sense here that the mortal Epicurus vanquished the gods themselves, as we see (rarely) in epic poetry.

**62  ante oculos** means here 'for everyone to see'. The metaphor of 'lying prostrate' in **iaceret** (with 'human life' as its subject) is continued in the following lines to create a spatial image of religion towering above mortal men.

**63**  The plural **terris** indicates that it was not merely Greece which suffered but all nations. *religio* here means 'religious fear', rather than 'true religion' which Lucretius discusses at VI.68–79 and which can inspire men to a life of 'divine' serenity. The final five-syllable word **religione** suggests the weight already implied in the juxtaposition of **oppressa gravi: gravi** agrees with **religione**, and **oppressa** agrees with **vita** in 62.

**64–5**  **quae** picks up **religione**. The poet plays with words here: *religio* came down from the **caeli regionibus**, while *superstitio* was the force which was **super instans**. Religion here glares down from the clouds – an apt image as many people derived their fear of gods from their incomprehension of meteorological phenomena (as Lucretius explores in book VI). Note the heavy, threatening slowness of the fifth-foot spondee **ostendebat**.

**66  mortales** – accusative agreeing with *oculos* in the next line but effectively juxtaposed here with *homo* to stress Epicurus' humanity. Epicurus' fame is such that the poet does not need to name him, but there is also something special about this man who was just a 'Greek man' defeating the might of the gods. The struggle of Epicurus against the gods is well emphasised by the repetition of **contra** at the end of two consecutive lines, and his status as 'first' man to do this is stressed by the repetition **primum . . . primusque** (and **primus** in 71).

**68–9  deum** stands for *deorum* as in 54. **fama** refers to the legends of divine retribution, **fulmina** are thunderbolts while the thunder itself is enacted with the alliterative **minitanti murmure**. The poet mocks the unenlightened with the pathetic fallacy of **minitanti** ('threatening') – the fearful think that the heavens are threatening them but the wise man knows otherwise. **neque … nec … nec** – note the tricolon crescendo and a good deal of alliteration of 'f' 'm' and 'c' to convey the menace of the religion he faced. It is surprising that three subjects govern a singular verb **compressit**. The active verb **compressit** continues the imagery of the passive form **oppressa** from line 63 and contrasts the behaviour of Epicurus with that of everybody else: religious feelings which terrify others have the opposite effect on him (**eo magis acrem** ('all the more keen')).

**70-9** The imagery of military conquest now becomes prominent as Epicurus shatters the bolts of the gates of nature, marches forth and brings back victory over religion.

**70  irritat** – the third syllable is scanned long as the word is a contraction of *irritavit*. The locks on the gates of nature are 'tight' (**arta**) and his quest to shatter them is brought out by the alliteration of 'p' and 'c'. Nature is not Epicurus' enemy, but the power of *religio* would be defeated when the secrets of nature were unlocked. Epicurus has raided the locked cabinet of Nature like a victorious general sacking a city.

**71  primus** – the poet again says that Epicurus was 'first' even though he was in fact but one in a long line of Greek philosophers who sought and helped to find the truth about Nature (see Introduction).

**72  vivida vis animi pervicit** – the rhetoric continues with repetition of consonantal 'v' and assonance of 'i'. The enjambement onto line 73 suggests the onward march of Epicurus.

**73  flammantia moenia mundi** – the 'flaming walls of the world' refers to the ether which surrounds our world and which is literally a wall of fire. At this point in the poem the reader is not expected to understand the cosmology but will be impressed by the imagery of the daring of this general who faced cosmic fire in his quest for the truth.

**74  mente animoque** – Epicurus did all this without leaving the earth and simply by using his mind: far from underplaying the victory, this makes his achievement even more impressive. **omne** here means 'the universe' while **immensum** ('boundless') looks forward to the discussion of the infinity of the universe later (I.921–1007).

**75  refert** – like any victor, Epicurus brought back the spoils of his campaign: but *his* spoils are factual truths about the limitations of matter and the universe. 'What can arise and what cannot' is very much to the point in the victory over superstition which frightens us with things which cannot possibly exist such as monsters and the torments of the dead.

**76–7  quanam ratione** – this introduces the indirect question: Epicurus showed us 'on what (scientific) principle' the power of each thing (**cuique**) is limited (**finita … sit**). The 'deepset boundary stone' (which marked the edge of a person's property) gives the passage a legalistic and Roman tone: the Romans even worshipped *terminus* as a divinity, which gives added point here. The victorious general might be expected to set up a 'trophy' to mark his victory but this 'general' set up a (metaphorical) 'stone' showing the limits of nature.

**78–9  religio** used to have mortal men under her feet (62–5): the tables are now turned (**vicissim**) and *religio* is the one being 'trampled' (**obteritur**), with **victoria** picking up *victor* from line 75. The heavens glared down at us (64–5) before, but Epicurus' triumph has raised us up the sky and we are the equals and not the subjects of the heavenly realms.

## 80–101

The rejection of religion has often been seen as offering a licence to be immoral; Lucretius counters this by showing that it is more often religion which produces wicked behaviour and cites the famous example of human sacrifice from the start of the Trojan War.

**80  illud** refers to the fearing clause **ne … rearis** + indirect statement.

**81–2  impia** – the word is stressed at the beginning of the line: the word **elementa** often denotes the 'rudiments' or 'first principles'. The word shows that Memmius is regarded as a total novice in philosophy. Note the metaphor of movement here (**inire ... indugredi**) and the mock-moralising tone of 'walking upon the path of crime'. **indugredi** is an archaic form of the present infinitive of *ingredior*.

**82–3   peperit** – the metaphor is of giving birth (from *pario*). The poet neatly rounds off the sentence with a repetition of **impia**.

## 84–101

The Greek fleet – going to attack Troy to reclaim Helen of Sparta from her Trojan abductor Paris – was becalmed at Aulis in Boeotia. The priests said this was because the goddess Artemis was angry with them, and the Greek leader Agamemnon summoned his daughter Iphigenia (on the false pretext that she was to marry Achilles) so that he could sacrifice her to placate the goddess. The use here of this legendary tale is perhaps odd: the slaughter of a mythical virgin before a legendary war does not (it might be urged) have the same contemporary power to persuade Roman readers to change their (Roman) behaviour. The advantage of the tale of Iphigenia here is that it is well-known to the Roman reader from the accounts in Greek and Roman tragedies (Aeschylus' *Agamemnon* and especially Ennius' *Iphigeneia* which was still being performed in Lucretius' day) and so carries emotional resonance that the poet can exploit – a sort of persuasive short-cut. There is a further possibility that this passage is a description of a famous painting of the sacrifice of Iphigenia which Cicero (*Orator* 74) tells us of.

**84   quo pacto** – 'just as' introduces the evidence for Lucretius' assertion in 83. The goddess *Trivia* (literally the 'deity of three roads') is 'Diana of the crossroads' who was the Roman equivalent of the Greek goddess Artemis to whom Iphigenia was sacrificed. **virginis** is pointed – a virgin was offered to a virgin, and the word might be taken either with **Triviai** or with **Iphianassai**.

**85   turparunt** (=*turpaverunt*) is pejorative: the leaders of the Greeks were doing what they thought was the right thing but they 'fouled' the altar. Altars were made for blood-sacrifice – but not the blood of one's own child. *Iphianassa* is an alternative form of the girl's more common name 'Iphigenia'.

**86 ductores** – the men killing the girl are sardonically entitled with full pomposity with strong alliteration of 'd'. After the panegyric of the 'generalship' of Epicurus in the previous section, these Greek generals sound very-much second-rate as their victim is a helpless girl.

**87 simul** – here means 'as soon as' (=*simulac*). The *infula* was the ribbon of twisted wool worn by sacrificial victims and Vestal virgins: Iphigenia was expecting the hairband (*vitta*) of a bride. The accusative **comptus** is governed by the *circum* in **circumdata** ('put around her hair').

**88 ex utraque pari** – the poet stresses that the ribbon fell down her cheeks evenly on both sides: every care was taken to make this 'offering' acceptable to the god. **ex** here has the meaning 'down from', while **malarum** is a partitive genitive with **ex utraque** ('down from each of her cheeks'): **pari** goes with **parte** in an adverbial phrase (in equal proportions').

**89–90 maestum … parentem** – the 'sad parent' frames line 89 and his sadness is brought out by the assonance of 'a' throughout.

**90** The subject of the main verb **sensit** (stressed in enjambement) is the girl herself: the verb introduces the indirect statement clauses with accusative and infinitive. **hunc propter** means 'next to this man'. The servants are hiding the weapon (**ferrum**) but she has already seen this (**sensit**) and so their efforts to spare her fears are in vain.

**91 cives** – 'citizens' may connote the Greek soldiers or else the citizens of Aulis itself. **aspectu suo** means 'at the sight of her' but also carries the sense of 'at the look on her face': just as Iphigenia was seen to see (*sensit*) earlier on, we now see others seeing her seeing.

**92 muta metu** ('dumb with fear') is a fine phrase both for sound and also sense as her fear makes her speechless: her limbs then react ('let down by her knees she sank to the ground').

**A Level**

**93–4 quibat** is from *queo* ('to be able') and its subject is the whole clause of line 94 (*quod… regem*): her status as her father's first child did her no good at all. **in tali tempore** recalls lines 41 and 43: the construction is 'she had been the first to endow the king with the name of father', with **donarat** as the contracted form of the pluperfect *donaverat*. The scorn in the words is brought out by the spitting 'p' alliteration of *patrio princeps* and also by the faint undertone of 'chief' in *princeps* which applies to Agamemnon more than to the helpless victim. The clash of roles was well remembered by Ovid (*Metamorphoses* XII.30) who put the situation concisely: *rexque patrem vicit*.

**95 sublata** is the perfect participle passive of *tollo*. Her helplessness is brought out by the way in which she is carried by the hands of (nameless) men to the altars and her emotion is conveyed in the word 'trembling' (**tremibunda**).

**96 deducta** – *deductio* was the technical term for the escort of the bride to her new husband's home. Iphigenia was expecting to be married, so here the term *deducta* brings out the travesty of this incident. The contrast between the marriage and her execution is now explicitly emphasised by the poet in sneering terms. *solemni more sacrorum* is vague ('the solemn manner of sacred rites') and could as well describe either a sacrifice or a wedding.

**97 perfecto** – take with the **solemni more sacrorum** in the previous line as an ablative absolute. **Hymenaeo** – *Hymenaeus* was the formal wedding song, which had the customary refrain 'Hymenaeus' addressing the god Hymen who was the god of weddings. Note the alliteration of 'p' and 'c'. **claro** here means 'loud'.

**98 casta inceste** – a pointed oxymoron: the mention of *nubendi* is unnecessary but stresses both the girl's youth and the deception required to arrange her presence.

**99 maesta** is an understatement but recalls *maestum* used of Agamemnon at line 89. Lucretius has Agamemnon perform the killing himself to bring out the barbarism of the deed. The terms **hostia concideret** are correct for an animal sacrifice but icily cold here for a parent to do to his child, as brought out by the postponement of **parentis** to the end of the line.

**100** **exitus** – the inadequate reason for the sacrifice is stated bluntly with strong emphasis on the juxtaposed near-synonyms **felix faustusque** (it was hardly *felix* for Iphigenia) which in turn contrast with the word **maesta** in the previous line. **classi** is dative as the indirect object of **daretur**.

**101** **tantum ... malorum** – the poet sums up the message of the preceding twenty lines in a devastating single line which refers us back to the point with which this passage began (80): if you think *ratio* is immoral, just look at what *religio* has done. The word *suadere* is well chosen as religious ideas do not 'force' us to kill our daughters but they 'persuade' us to do so if we listen to them. **malorum** is a partitive genitive going with **tantum** ('so much [of] evil').

## 102–35

The poet continues the anti-religious theme and explains why it is so important to understand the nature of the world if we are rid ourselves of superstitious fears.

**102** **tutemet** is a strongly emphasised form of the pronoun *tu*, placed to contrast with **nobis**. **quovis** (from *quivis*: 'at some time or other') adds a touch of uncertainty to the strong future indicative *quaeres*. **vatum**: *vates* is an old word for 'priest' and 'poet' used here critically of the bardic seers who invent tales of divine agency.

**103** **terriloquis** is another compound adjective (literally 'terror-talking'). **desciscere** is a strong metaphor whose primary meaning is to 'defect' from an army or a cause.

**104** **quippe etenim** – 'yes, because ...' The subject of **possunt** is the priests.

**105** **somnia** ('dreams') is stressed in enjambement. The phrase **vitae rationes vertere** literally means 'to overthrow the principles of your life' but may also be a financial metaphor for 'wreck your accounts'. **possint** may be a consecutive subjunctive ('[enough] dreams to be able to...') or a potential subjunctive (which 'could' wreck your life [if you let them]).

**106** **fortunas . . . turbare** – literally means 'to upset all your fortune' but is also perhaps a financial metaphor (to render you bankrupt). The key word in all this is postponed to the end of the line and the sentence: **timore** is the means of your mental destruction.

**107** **merito** – 'with good reason'. The subject of **viderent** is **homines** in 108. The sentence is an unreal conditional in present time with two imperfect subjunctives ('if men saw … they would be able …'). The 'fixed endpoint' (**certam finem**) envisaged here is death which (the poet argues) is the end of our existence, making torments after death impossible.

**108** **aerumnarum** is a suitably long and heavy word to suggest seemingly endless suffering.

**109** **religionibus** here means 'superstitious beliefs'. **vatum** is a subjective genitive (fears coming from the priests).

**110** **nunc** has the sense 'but as things are'. **restandi** goes with both **ratio** and **facultas**: there is no means, mental or physical, to stand up to these terrors. Notice the thundering repetition of **nulla**.

**111** **timendum** (*est*) is an impersonal use of the gerundive of obligation ('one must fear') taking the accusative **aeternas... poenas** as its object.

**112** **ignoratur** is another impersonal verb, followed by the indirect question **quae sit**. **animai** is an archaic genitive form for *animae* – see *militiai* (29) – and is scanned as four syllables (*an-im-a-i*). The *anima* is the 'soul': that part of the person which animates the body and is thought by some (such as Socrates) to survive death.

A Level

**113** Is the soul born with (and as part of) the body? Or does it enter the body from a pre-birth existence – which would mean that it can live without the body and so survive death? **nata** ('born') picks up *natura* from 112 and steers us towards the assumption that the soul is indeed born with the body. **nascentibus insinuetur** is a clever debunking of the idea of pre-existence, suggesting that the soul somehow 'worms it way into' us while we are in the act of being born.

**114–16** The poet continues the binary questions: does the soul die with the body or else somehow go to the underworld or even worm its way into beasts? The subject of **intereat** is the *anima*. Orcus was the Italian god of the underworld: here the name may mean either the god or his realm. The phrase **vastasque lacunas** ('gaping chasms') is again contemptuous.

**116** **pecudes alias** – 'beasts instead of ourselves' (not 'other beasts'). The theory of transmigration of souls – whereby souls pass at death from person to person and from person to animal – is attributed to the Greek mathematician and philosopher Pythagoras.

**117–18** Ennius (239–169 BC) was the first great poet in Roman literature and his epic poem *Annales* told the story of Rome from its foundation to his own time. In it he narrated how he had a dream of the first Greek epic poet Homer who told him that Ennius' soul had previously resided in the bodies of Homer, Pythagoras, and a peacock. Lucretius aptly calls him 'our' (**noster**) and uses the verb **cecinit** (from *cano*) which is commonly used of the epic poet 'singing' his tales as in the first line of Virgil's *Aeneid*. Lucretius awards Ennius the distinction of being the first (cf. 66, 71) to produce poetry worthy of the Muses, expressing this in suitably poetic language of his own. Ennius brought down the 'garland' (**coronam**) from 'lovely' (**amoeno**) Mount Helicon (the home of the Muses in Boeotia) with its evergreen leafage (**perenni fronde**: with a pun on the name Ennius). **perenni fronde** is an ablative of quality.

**119** **quae** refers to the **coronam**, and the subjunctive clueret is consecutive ('so as to win renown'). The heavy alliteration of **clara clueret** is itself suggestive of Ennius' style of rugged epic.

**120    etsi** – 'even though'. **Acherusia** refers to Acheron, one of the fabled rivers of the underworld. **templa** here means 'realms' rather than 'temples'.

**121    aeternis** ('everlasting') may sound odd (cf. 28n.) from a poet who tells us that death is the end of all our works but is here a term of praise for the poetry (**versibus**).

**122    quo** picks up the *templa* of 120: 'to which place'. **permaneant** means 'abide' or 'stay' and we have to supply something like 'to where the souls cannot [go and] stay' to make sense of **quo**. The subjunctive is in indirect statement, reporting what Ennius said.

**123    simulacra** here means 'visions' or 'ghosts': the word is used in book IV for the 'films' which objects emit to allow us to see them. **modis. . . miris** are to be taken together ('in amazing ways') and **pallentia** suggests the pallor of the dead – even though these dead beings have neither body nor soul.

**124–6**    The construction is: 'he narrates (**commemorat**) that the image of Homer arose from this place (**unde** – i.e. the underworld) and began to pour out salt tears and to expound. . .'

**124    sibi** refers to the subject of the main verb and so here indicates Ennius himself. Just as Ennius utters 'deathless' (*aeternis*) verses, so Homer's ghost is 'ever fresh' (**semper florentis**).

**125**    Homer's initial response is one of tears, couched in suitably epic language.

**126    rerum naturam** is the subject of the present poem and it is ironic that Ennius should have seen Homer offer his own mythological version of the matter.

**127–30    cum. . . tunc** – 'not only. . . but also'. **habenda nobis est ratio** is a gerundive of obligation ('we must give an account'). **superis de rebus** (literally: 'about matters on high') includes all aspects of meteorology, which the poet will address fully in book VI. Here he promises to deal with the movements of the sun and moon and explain 'on what principle they come about' (**qua fiant ratione**).

**129–30   quaeque** (from *quisque*) – 'each single thing'. **in terris** shows that here Lucretius is thinking of the atomic theory itself as well as of terrestrial phenomena, such as he will discuss in book V.

**130-1   cum primis** – 'especially' makes it clear that the topic of the soul is more important for the removal of superstitious fear than the science of the previous lines. **videndum** is another impersonal gerundive of obligation (cf. 111). For the metaphor of **sagaci** see line 50. For Lucretius the human person has a body (*corpus*), a mind (*animus*, also called *mens*) and a soul (*anima*). The *animus* is the governing part of the mind and its emotional 'heart', while the *anima* is the part of the soul which ensures sensation throughout the body, keeps us alive, and leaves us at death. Lucretius analyses the nature of the soul later (III.94–416).

**132–5**   A major source of the belief in life after death is the common human experience of seeing ghosts, and Lucretius intends to explain these away, while acknowledging that they are a terrifying (**terrificet**) and a vivid (**coram**) experience.

**132–3   quae res** – 'what [is] the thing which…': **res** is singular as **obvia** makes clear. People see visions both when awake (**vigilantibus**) during a bout of illness (**morbo affectis**) and also when 'buried in sleep' (**somnoque sepultis**). Lucretius will explain that all perception is caused by thin 'films' (*simulacra*) which emanate from objects and hit the eyes, giving us the sensation of sight.

**134   cernere … videamur** – 'we seem to be seeing' implies that we are not actually seeing anything of the kind. The fact that we can hear (**audire**) ghosts is a problem for the *simulacra* theory: if the films just crop up randomly it is strange that appropriate sound-films also happen to occur just at the right time.

**135**   The phrase is a lengthy way to refer to the dead: (literally: 'those people whose bones the earth embraces after death has been met'). **morte obita** is an ablative absolute.

## 136–45

Lucretius admits that conveying the 'obscure discoveries of the Greeks in Latin verses' is not easy owing to the 'poverty of the language' and the novelty of the subject-matter: but he expresses hope for the pleasure of Memmius' friendship as his reward.

**136** **nec me animi fallit** – 'I am under no illusions' (literally 'nor does it deceive me in my mind', with *animi* a locative use). The phrase then introduces the indirect statement (**difficile . . . esse** + infinitive).

**136–7** Notice the contrast of **obscura** (dark) and **illustrare** ('to shine a light on'). The theme of light vs darkness will be continued in 144–8.

**138** 'especially since (**cum**) we have to deal with (**agendum**) many things with new words'. **multa. . . agendum** is an impersonal gerundive as at 131 and stands for *multa sint agenda*.

**139** Greek had developed a very full philosophical vocabulary over the centuries, and many Roman philosophers found themselves unable to match Greek terms with Roman equivalents: Lucretius himself ends up discussing the *homoeomeria* theory of Anaxagoras (1.830–920) using the Greek term and not trying to translate it.

**140** **virtus** literally means 'manly quality' and often 'courage': here it must simply mean 'excellence' in a general sense. **voluptas** ('pleasure') is the utmost good for the Epicurean (cf. line 1 above).

**141–2** **suavis amicitiae**: 'friendship' is one of the highest moral benefits of the wise man and **suavis** shows that its value is also one of pleasure. The pleasure of the friendship is expressed also by the repetition of **suavis. . .suadet**. The effort involved is considerable – the poet is ready to undertake 'any effort' to secure the rewards – and this involves burning the midnight oil (**noctes vigilare**). **serenas** alludes to the 'contentment' which is the greatest pleasure for an Epicurean.

**143** The writing process is twofold: find the right words (**dictis**) and then transform them into poetic form (**carmine**).

**144–5** **possim** and **possis** are potential subjunctives. **res... penitus convisere** means 'to see deep into the heart of things'. **quibus** picks up *lumina* from the previous line.

**146–8** This short passage occurs several times in the poem. It is ideally placed here after the strong light vs dark imagery of the previous lines to undercut the metaphorical light and explain that this 'light' is not physical but intellectual illumination. The construction is *necesse est* + subjunctive: 'as for this terror … it is necessary not for rays of the sun to dispel it, but …'.

**147** **radii solis** – the rays of the sun are in fact the same as the **lucida tela diei**.

**148** **naturae species ratioque** – the process of illumination involves looking at the appearance (**species**) of nature and then understanding how it works (**ratio**).

## 149–214

The first principle of Epicureanism for Lucretius is that nothing can arise out of nothing or be reduced to nothing – what we might call the law of conservation of matter.

**149–50** The 'first-principle' (**principium**) will take its initial beginnings (**exordia**) from this statement (**hinc**), that no thing arises (**gigni**) out of nothing'. The accusative and infinitive express the principle as an indirect statement.

**150** **divinitus** – 'by divine means'. Lucretius in fact states that creation is impossible by any means, but he nails his anti-theological colours to the mast again here and goes on to explain his reasons in the following lines.

**151–4** *People see things coming about without understanding how this happens, and they assume that it must be the work of the gods.*

**151** **quippe** introduces an explanation, and **ita** means 'as we see'. **formido** (fear) is personified as holding 'all of mankind' (**mortales** …

**omnes**) prisoner: Lucretius is overstating his case here, as presumably Epicureans were not prisoners of such fear.

**152   tuentur** ('they see that') introduces the accusative and infinitive **multa . . . fieri**.

**153–4** 'By no rational thought can they see the causes of these things, and think that they come about by divine power'. Notice the contrast of **ratione** and **numine**, and the way line 154 is framed by the verbs **possunt . . . rentur**.

**156   quas ob res** – 'for this reason'. Take **posse** before **creari**: 'that nothing can be created . . .'

**157   quod sequimur** is figurative – 'that which we are seeking' (i.e. 'the object of our enquiry'). **rectius** is the comparative adverb of *rectus* ('more correctly').

**157–8   queat** is from *queo* (to be able). The subjunctives are in indirect question ('we shall see from where each thing can be made . . .'). **quo** goes with **modo** to mean 'how'. **sine** is postponed: translate as *sine opera divum* ('without the work of gods'). **divum** is the short form of the genitive plural of *divus* (for *divorum*). **et . . . et . . .** means 'both . . . and . . .'. Line 158 appeared as line 155 in the early manuscripts: it was correctly placed here by the humanist scholar Michael Marullus (1458–1500), and his revision has been accepted by all modern editors.

**159–214**   *Logical proofs of this statement.*

The form of argument used is counterfactual, as discussed in the introduction:

*If P then Q*
*But not-Q*
*Therefore not-P.*

If things could arise out of nothing, then anything could arise out of nothing, things would suddenly appear out of nowhere, things would not need feeding and would grow out of season and things/people would grow to massive size.

Since none of these things is true, we can deduce that things do not in fact arise out of nothing.

The argument is inductive, relying on our sense-experience (188) and so is always subject to correction if any such things started to happen.

**159–60** **si . . . egeret** – the sentence is an unreal conditional in present time with imperfect subjunctives. 'If [things] were made out of nothing, then every kind of thing would be able to be born from every thing, with no need for a seed'. The subject of **egeret** is either **nil** or **omne genus** – in which case **nil** is adverbial ('not at all'). The final 's' of **omnibus** has to be elided for the line to scan: elision of final 's' is more common in early Latin but dropped out during Lucretius' lifetime.

**161–2** The poet illustrates his point with amazing counterfactual events of men coming out of the sky, fish out of the earth, and birds suddenly appearing in the sky, all elegantly placed over the two lines. The poet covers earth, sea and sky as he did in lines 2–3. **mare** is here the ablative case (normally *mari*). Fish are alluded to with the epic periphrasis **squamigerum genus** (the 'breed of scale-bearing things'), where **squamigerum** is a contracted genitive plural (=*squamigerorum*). **posset** is a potential subjunctive.

**163–4** **armenta . . . pecudes** – 'cattle and other farm animals' are contrasted with 'every breed of wild beast' to argue that (if animals could appear randomly) farm animals would live in the wild and wild beasts on farms: **incerto partu** ('with unpredictable birthing') suggests that the cattle could even give birth to the wild beasts and vice versa.

**165–6** From animals to plants: trees would produce random different fruits. **constare** has the sense of 'remain consistent'.

**167–8** If living things were born randomly, how could we predict what would be born and from what? **quippe** introduces an explanation ('since'). **genitalia corpora** are literally 'the particles which give life' which would be seeds of every kind, and **cuique** means here 'in the case of each species'. **qui** – 'how?' Note the rhetorical juxtaposition of **consistere certa**. **mater** (literally 'mother') is more appropriate for animals than plants, but Lucretius uses the term here loosely for the thing which produces each living thing.

**169** **nunc** means 'as things are' and not 'now'. **quaeque** indicates 'each and every living thing'. *semina* for Lucretius can be atoms themselves (see 58–9) but here have the more common meaning of 'seeds'.

**170-1** **inde...ubi** – 'from that source...where its constituent matter and primary particles are'. **cuiusque** is essential: each thing has its own source material. **materies** echoes *mater* in 168 and makes the animal-centred focus of the previous lines more generally atomic, as is shown by the poet redefining **materies** as **corpora prima**. **oras in luminis exit** (literally 'comes into the shores of light', repeated at 179) is a lovely epic phrase for 'to come into existence'.

**172** **hac re** – 'for this reason'. Lucretius now reasserts the principle slightly more gently: 'nothing comes of nothing' becomes 'it is impossible for anything to come of anything'.

**173** **certis** here must mean 'specific'. **secreta facultas** is a 'capacity peculiar to itself'.

**174-83** *Lucretius' second argument is that if anything could come from anything, then things would not be produced only in certain seasons of the year.*

**174-5** Spring, summer and autumn have their own typical plants, conveyed in a tricolon crescendo and with chiasmus of **vere rosam frumenta calore**. **calore** ('heat') here means 'summer'. The ablatives **vere**, **calore** and **autumno** are all taken with **suadente** in an ablative absolute construction. Note the pathetic fallacy of the seasons 'urging' their crops: and the pregnant use of **fundi** (which has to be taken with roses and corn as well as grapes) hinting in 175 at the 'pouring forth' of the wine which these grapes produce.

**176–7** Translate 'if it were not owing to the fact that when specific seeds of things have gathered together at their due season, then whatever is being created appears ...'.

**178–9** **tempestates** here are 'seasons' of the year. **tuto** is adverbial: 'in safety' as being protected from inhospitable weather conditions, which is how the earth can cause tender plants to grow.

**180–1** As at 159–60, the argument is counterfactual: crops would grow in each other's (**alienis**) seasons if they could grow out of nothing. **subito** adds a surreal note – one minute nothing, the next moment a plant is there. **incerto spatio** – *spatium* here (as in 184 below) indicates a measure of time rather than space and the phrase means 'at unpredictable intervals'.

**182–3** 'seeing that there would be no constituent elements (**primordia**) which could be prevented (**arceri**) from life-generating union by the hostile season'.

**184–91** Third proof: if living things came from nothing, then they would do so instantaneously without needing time to grow.

**184** **spatio foret usus** means 'there would be need of time'. **augendis rebus** is a dative of purpose (cf. 24): 'for the purpose of growing things'.

**185** **ad** here indicates purpose: 'for the coming together of constituent seeds'. Birth and growth are (for Lucretius) parallel processes, both of which involve the accumulation of constituent particles.

**186–7** A wonderfully bizarre image of little infants all at once (**subito**) becoming grown young men and trees jumping (**salirent**) out of the earth.

**188–91** Lucretius summarises the argument and its conclusion in reverse order: first the slowness of growth, and then the consistency of species proving that each thing comes out of its own constituent matter.

**188** 'It is obvious that none of these things happens'.

**189** **semine certo** explains **par est**: this is only to be expected since the seeds have to be the right ones.

**190–1** **possis** is a potential subjunctive. **grandescere** ('to grow larger') is itself a suitably large verb, while the tiny verb **alique** ('and to be fed' from *alo*) shows the imperceptible accumulation of size as a result of feeding.

**192–8** *Fourth proof: if living things could arise spontaneously they would not need rain and nourishment.*

**192** **huc accedit uti** – a common formula in Lucretius to introduce a new point: translate 'an additional point is that'. **certis** again means 'specific', here applied to the rainy seasons (**imbribus anni**).

**193** Mother earth is described as if she were having babies – she brings forth **fetus** (here meaning 'produce' but commonly meaning human births) which give joy (**laetificos**), although the joy is here given to the animal life which feeds off her crops. **nequeat** is a potential subjunctive ('would be unable').

**194** **secreta cibo** – 'deprived of food'. **natura animantum** means essentially 'animal life' but the periphrasis with **natura** adds to the sense that this is built into animal physiology.

**195** The poet points out that without food animals would be unable to reproduce or maintain their lives both as individuals and as species.

**196–8** The fact that plants need rain and animals need food shows that neither life-form is independent of nourishment. Lucretius astutely adds that as the animals eat the plants which the earth produces, then there must be elements common to both the rain and the plants. The construction is this: the result is that (**ut**) you should think (**putes**) that many elements are shared by many things rather than (**potius**) [to think] that anything can exist without constituent particles. **putes** is subjunctive after **ut** but it also has jussive force ('you should think').

**197** Lucretius enjoys the analogy with letters of the alphabet which are shared between different words: he expands this at I.911–14 where words like *ignes* and *lignum* have common elements but very different meanings because these elements are set in a different order. The verbal analogy here is underscored by the repetition of words (**multis... multa**).

**199–207** *Fifth proof: if things could grow out of nothing they would grow to immense size.* The first six lines constitute one enormous question, thus verbally enacting the massive size of the beings (not) produced. For literary analysis of lines 199–204 see the Introduction.

**199 denique** – 'then again'.

**200–1 qui** is a consecutive relative after **tantos** in the previous line ('so big that they could'). These giants would be able to walk through the ocean (**pontum**) as if through shallows (**vada**) and their massive size would give them the massive strength to tear down mountains. The examples of supersized men are taken from the giants and gods of mythology: Poseidon could walk from Samothrace to Aigae in four steps (Homer *Iliad* 13.20–1), while the Cyclops Polyphemus 'tore off the head of a great mountain' in Homer's *Odyssey* (9.481) and of course the Giants Otus and Ephialtes ripped off the top of one mountain (Pelion) to put on top of another (Ossa) when they tried to scale Olympus and unseat the gods. The epic stories are well conveyed with epic language and abundant alliteration.

**202** If living things did not need food and atomic nourishment to be born and to live, then they could survive indefinitely on atomic hunger-strike. **vivendo ... vincere** – 'to outlive' (literally: 'to defeat by living'). **vitalia ... saecla** – 'generations of living things'.

**203–4** 'If it were not for the fact that specific matter has been assigned to the birth of things – matter which determines what could arise'. **rebus** is the indirect object of **reddita** but the phrase **rebus gignundis** is a gerundive dative of purpose as at 24.

**A Level**

**205 fatendum est** – 'we must admit'.

**206 opus est** ('there is need') takes a dative of the person needing and an ablative of the thing needed: so here 'things need a seed'): **quo** picks up **semine**.

**207 proferrier** is the archaic present passive infinitive of *profero* (equivalent to *proferri*). The line is highly poetic with the detail of the 'soft breezes' suggesting the warm airs of spring.

**208–14** *Sixth proof: we would not need to bother cultivating the soil.*

**208 postremo** – 'finally'. **incultis** is an ablative of comparison after **praestare** ('to be better than').

**209 manibus** is dative with **reddere**: cultivated lands give superior crops 'to hands [which work them]'.

**210 videlicet** is here literal and takes the accusative and infinitive of indirect statement: 'it is possible to see that there exist in the earth …' **primordia** are 'basic particles' which (the poet tells us) are buried in the earth and only brought to the surface by agriculture.

**211 vomere** – the ploughshare, used to 'turn' the 'fertile clumps of earth'.

**212 terrai** is the archaic genitive singular form of *terra* (cf. *animai* 112). **solum subigentes** is a powerful phrase for 'subduing the soil' by (literally) 'working it from below (*sub*))'. **ortus** indicates that the plough raises these *primordia* to the surface of the land.

**213–14** The construction is an unreal conditional in present time: 'if there were no (*primordia*) then you would see (**videres**) …' **quaeque** ('each of these things') is the object of **videres**. **sine** goes with **nostro labore**. Lucretius adds a surprise touch with **sponte sua multo fieri meliora**: if our work is not necessary then it is potentially damaging and the crops would be 'much better' if they grew without it. There is perhaps here a wry hint at the 'golden age' mythology whereby in the early days of humanity crops grew without the need to cultivate them.

A Level

## 215–24

Lucretius now inverts the previous argument. If nothing comes from nothing, then (by the same reasoning) nothing can be reduced to nothing.

**215** **huc accedit uti** – cf. 192n. **natura** is the subject of **dissolvat** and **quidque** the object.

**216** The final monosyllable **res** forces a clash of ictus and accent and enacts the diminution of things with the tiny monosyllable.

**217** **mortale** – 'perishable'. **e cunctis partibus** – 'in all its parts' i.e. 'totally'.

**218** Spontaneous destruction is as impossible as spontaneous birth (argued at lines 159–83). Here the unpredictable destruction is well described with the adverb **repente** ('without warning') and the reinforcing of **periret** with **erepta**.

**219–20** For the construction of **usus** + ablative (**nulla vi**) see 184. **discidium** is the technical term for the 'splitting up' of things into their constituent atoms and the action is well shown in the imagery of untying (**exsolvere**) the web of connections (**nexus**) which hold the parts (**partibus**) together as a whole.

**221** **nunc** – 'as things are' (cf. 110). **aeterno** – these 'seeds' are everlasting: one of the key elements of the atomic theory is that atoms are indestructible (see 483–684).

**222–3** Things do not spontaneously vanish but only break up when external force is applied to them from without or from within, which takes perceptible time to work. **donec** takes the indicative. **obiit** is interesting: *obeo* often means 'die' (as in 'obituary') but here has its basic meaning of 'encounter'. The three potential subjunctive verbs are expressive: **diverberet** is to 'smash apart', **penetret** indicates 'breaking into' (reinforced by **intus**) and **dissolvat** the 'breaking up' of the whole into its parts. The atomic theory stated that matter is made up of atoms and empty space (*inane*) (argued for at 329–97) and that relative density of different objects shows the amount of *inane* in each thing.

**224  natura** – nature is once again personified as 'permitting' the witnessing of destruction. **videri**: 'to be seen' (not 'to seem').

*The poet continues his proofs that nothing can be destroyed totally as follows:*

225–37   there would by now be nothing to make new things and people

238–49   everything could be destroyed

250–64   in fact death leads to birth in the cycle of life.

*The remainder of the book discusses:*

265–328   the invisible nature of atoms

329–97   the existence and nature of 'void' (*inane*) in the universe

398–417   readers may think of other proofs for themselves

418–82   matter can only be explained in terms of atoms and void

483–634   matter is made of atoms

635–920   Lucretius attacks competing theories of matter

921–1117   the universe is infinite.

# Vocabulary

While there is no Defined Vocabulary List for A-level, words in the OCR Defined Vocabulary List for AS-level are marked with * so that students can quickly see the vocabulary with which they should be particularly familiar, although the meanings given in this book are not necessarily the same as the ones in the DVL as this vocabulary is tailored to this text.

This vocabulary lists every word in the text. Nouns are listed with their genitive singular, and verbs are listed with all their four principal parts. Adjectives are listed with the endings of the different genders (e.g.: **aequus -a -um**) except where the three genders are the same in the nominative where the genitive is listed (e.g.: **teres, teretis**). Long vowels are marked as such with macra (e.g. **cūra**). Where a word has different meanings in different lines this is indicated.

| | |
|---|---|
| *a, ab (*preposition + ablative*) | by, from |
| *ac | and |
| accēdō, accēdere, accessī, accessum | to approach |
|     hūc accēdit uti | in addition to this, there is the fact that … |
| *acer, acris, acre | keen, fierce |
| Acherūsius -a -um | belonging to the Underworld |
| *ad (*preposition + accusative*) | to, towards |
| adhibeō, adhibēre, adhibuī, adhibitum | to apply, direct |
| adstō, adstāre, adstitī | to stand by |
| *adsum, adesse, adfuī | to be present |
| adventus -ūs *m.* | coming, arrival |
| Aeneadēs -ae *m.* | descendant of Aeneas |
| aequor, aequŏris *n.* | plain, flat surface |
| *aequus -a -um | untroubled |
| āēr, āĕris *m.* | air |
| āĕrius -a -um | of the air |
| aerumna -ae *f.* | trouble, distress |

A Level

| | |
|---|---|
| aeternus -a -um | everlasting |
| aevum -ī *n.* | lifespan |
| afficiō, afficere, affēcī, affectum | affect |
| *agō, agere, ēgī, actum | to do (41), to handle (138) |
| alō, alere, aluī, altum | to feed, nourish |
| aliēnus -a -um | not their own |
| aliquī, aliqua, aliquod | some |
| *alius -a -um | other |
| almus -a -um | nourishing, nurturing |
| *altē (*adverb*) | deeply |
| amābilis -e | lovely |
| amīcitia -ae *f.* | friendship |
| amnis -is *m.* | river |
| amoenus -a -um | pleasant, lovely |
| *amor, amōris *m.* | love |
| amplectōr, amplectī, amplexus sum | to embrace |
| *an | or |
| anima -ae/āī *f.* | soul |
| animans, animantis *m./f.* | living thing |
| *animus -ī *m.* | mind |
| *annus -ī *m.* | year |
| *ante (*preposition + accusative*) | before, in front of |
| appellō, -āre, -āvī, -ātum | to call, name |
| *ara -ae *f.* | altar |
| *arbor, arboris *f.* | tree |
| arbusta -ōrum *n.pl.* | trees |
| arceō, arcēre, arcuī | to prevent, restrain |
| armenta -ōrum *n.pl.* | cattle |
| armipotens, armipotentis | mighty in arms |
| artus -a -um | tight |
| aspectus -ūs *m.* | gaze (65) appearance (91) |
| *at | but |
| atque | and |
| auctō, auctāre | to cause to grow |
| *audeō, audēre, ausus sum | to dare |
| *audiō, audīre, audīvī, audītum | to hear |
| *augeō, augēre, auxī, auctum | to increase, enlarge |
| Aulis, Aulidis *f.* | Aulis |
| aura -ae *f.* | breeze |

# Vocabulary 75

| | |
|---|---|
| auris -is *f.* | ear |
| *aut | or |
| autumnus -ī *m.* | autumn |
| avidus -a -um | greedy |
| avis -is f | bird |
| | |
| *bellum -ī *n.* | war |
| *bene (*adverb*) | well |
| blandus -a -um | alluring |
| | |
| *caelum -ī *n.* | sky, heavens |
| calor -ōris *m.* | heat |
| *campus -ī *m.* | plain |
| *canō, canere, cecinī, cantum | to sing |
| *capiō, capere, cēpī, captum | to seize (14) to overcome (49) |
| *caput, capitis *n.* | head |
| carmen, carminis *n.* | poetry |
| castus -a -um | chaste, undefiled |
| *causa -ae *f.* | cause |
| *cēlō, cēlāre, cēlāvī, cēlātum | to hide |
| *cernō, cernere, crēvī, crētum | to see |
| *certus -a -um | fixed (107, 189, 192, 203) specific (168-9, 173, 176) |
| cervix, cervīcis *f.* | neck |
| *cibus -ī *m.* | food |
| ciō, cīre, cīvī, citum | to summon, stir |
| circumdō, circumdāre, circumdedī, circumdatum | to bind, go round |
| circumfundō, circumfundere, circumfūdī, circumfūsum | to bend around, envelop |
| *cīvis -is *m.* | citizen |
| clārus -a -um | distinguished (42) loud (97) renowned (119) clear (144) |
| classis -is *f.* | fleet |
| claustra -ōrum *n.pl.* | locks, bolts |
| clueō, cluēre | to be known, to be spoken of |
| *coepī, coepisse, coeptum | to begin |
| coitus -ūs *m.* | gathering, coming together |
| comitō, comitāre, comitāvī, comitātum | to escort |
| commemorō, -āre, -āvī, -ātum | to narrate |

A Level

# 76 Lucretius: De Rerum Natura I.1–224

| | |
|---|---|
| commūnis -e | public (43), shared (196) |
| comprimō, comprimere, compressī, compressum | to stop, restrain |
| comptus -ūs *m.* | lock of hair |
| concelebrō, -āre, -āvī, -ātum | to fill with living things |
| concidō, concidere, concidī | to fall, collapse |
| concilium -ī *n.* | atomic union, fusion |
| concipiō, concipere, concēpī, conceptum | to conceive |
| confluō, confluere, confluxī | to stream together |
| *cōnōr, cōnārī, cōnātus sum | to attempt |
| *consistō, consistere, constitī | to stand fixed |
| constō, constāre, constitī | to consist of (131, 204), remain constant (165), be by nature (221) |
| contemnō, contemnere, contempsī, contemptum | to despise |
| contineō, continēre, continuī, contentum | to hold prisoner |
| *contrā (*adverb*) | in opposition (66–7), to the contrary (82, 113) |
| convisō, convisere | to see into |
| cor, cordis *n.* | heart |
| cōram (*adverb*) | in person |
| corōna -ae *f.* | garland |
| *corpus, corporis *n.* | body (38, 122) particles (58, 61, 167, 171) elements (196, 215) |
| creō, creāre, creāvī, creātum | create |
| cresco, crescere, crēvī, crētum | grow |
| culta -ōrum *n.pl.* | cultivated land (164) |
| cultus -a -um | cultivated |
| *cum (*preposition + ablative*) | with (45) |
| *cum (*conjunction*) | when (62, 177) since (138) |
| cum...tunc... | not only...but also (127-30) |
| cum prīmīs | especially (130) |
| *cunctus -a -um | all |
| *cupidē (*adverb*) | greedily |
| *cupiō, cupīre, cupī(v)ī, cupītum | to desire, seek |
| *cūr | why |
| *cūra -ae *f.* | concern, care |
| daedalus -a -um | creative, inventive |
| Danaī, Danaum *m.pl.* | the Greeks |

A Level

# Vocabulary

| | |
|---|---|
| *dē (*preposition + ablative*) | about (54, 127), out of (157, 159, 180, 191, 205) |
| *dea -ae *f.* | goddess |
| dēdūcō, dēdūcere, dēduxī, dēductum | escort, lead off |
| dēligō, dēligere, dēlexī, dēlectum | to select |
| dēmum (*adverb*) | in the end |
| *dēnique | lastly (199), to put it briefly (17, 76) |
| dēsciscō, dēsciscere, dēscīvī, dēscītum | to defect, desert |
| dēserta -ōrum *n.pl.* | uncultivated lands, deserts |
| dēsum, dē(e)sse, dēfuī (+ *dative*) | to fail, let down |
| dēferō, dēferre, dētulī, dēlātum | bring down from |
| *deus -ī *m.* | god |
| dēvincō, dēvincere, dēvīcī, dēvictum | conquer |
| dicta -ōrum *n.pl* | words |
| *dies, diēī *m.* | day (147), season (10) |
| *difficilis -e | difficult |
| diffundō, diffundere, diffūdī, diffūsum | pour out |
| dirimō, dirimere, dirēmī, diremptum | break up |
| discidium -ī *n.* | shattering, breaking up |
| discutiō, discutere, discussī, discussum | dispel, scatter |
| dispōnō, dispōnere, disposuī, dispositum | set out |
| disserō, disserere, disseruī, dissertum | discuss, explain |
| dissolvō, dissolvere, dissolvī, dissolūtum | dissolve |
| dīus -a -um | bright, divine |
| dīva -ae *f.* | goddess |
| dīvellō, dīvellere, dīvellī, divulsum | tear down |
| dīverberō, dīverberāre, dīverberāvī, dīverberātum | shatter |
| dīvīnitus (*adverb*) | by divine power |
| dīvīnus -a -um | divine |
| dīvum *contracted genitive plural of* dīvus | of the gods |
| *dō, dare, dedī, datum | give |
| *dolor, dolōris *m.* | pain |
| *domus -ī/ūs *f.* | home |
| *dōnum -ī *n.* | gift |
| donec | until |
| dōnō, dōnāre, dōnāvī, dōnātum | endow |
| ductor -ōris *m.* | leader |
| *dum | while |

A Level

# 78 Lucretius: De Rerum Natura *I*.1–224

| | |
|---|---|
| *****e** (*preposition + ablative*) | out of, from |
| ēdō, ēdere, ēdidī, ēditum | proclaim, utter |
| efferō, efferre, extulī, ēlātum | carry out (141) bring forth (179) |
| *****efficiō, efficere, effēcī, effectum** (+ ut+ *subj.*) | bring about that |
| effringō, effringere, effrēgī, effractum | shatter, break open |
| effundō, effundere, effūdī, effūsum | pour out |
| *****egeō, egēre, eguī** (+ *ablative*) | need |
| egestās, egestātis *f.* | poverty |
| *****ego, meī** | I, me |
| elementa -ōrum *n.pl.* | rudiments (81) letters (197) |
| ēnāscor, ēnāscī, ēnātus sum | be born |
| *****enim** | for |
| Ennius -ī *m.* | Ennius |
| ēripiō, ēripere, ēripuī, ēreptum | snatch away |
| *****ergō** | therefore |
| ērumpō, ērumpere, ērupī, ēruptum | burst out, hatch |
| *****et** | and |
| et…et… | both…and… |
| etenim | for I tell you |
| *****etsī** | even though |
| *****ex** (*preposition + ablative*) | from out of, down from (88) |
| exaequō, exaequāre, exaequāvī, exaequātum | make equal to, level with |
| excellō, excellere | to be pre-eminent |
| exeō, exīre, exī(v)ī, exitum | to come out |
| *****exitium** -ī *n.* | destruction |
| exitus -ūs *m.* | way out, outcome |
| exordium -ī *n.* | initial starting point |
| exorior, exorīrī, exortus sum | spring into existence, come forth (124) |
| expandō, expandere, expandī, expansum | set out, unfold |
| expōnō, expōnere, exposuī, expositum | set out, claim |
| exsistō, exsistere, exstitī | exist |
| exsolvō, exsolvere, exsolvī, exsolūtum | untie, undo |
| extrā (*preposition + accusative*) | beyond |
| | |
| facta -ōrum *n.pl* | deeds |
| facultās -ātis *f.* | ability (110) capacity (174) |
| *****fallō, fallere, fefellī, falsum** | to fool, escape one's notice |

A Level

# Vocabulary 79

| | |
|---|---|
| *fāma -ae f. | legend |
| fateor, fatērī, fassus sum | admit, acknowledge |
| faustus -a -um | favoured by the gods, propitious |
| Favōnius -ī m. | the west wind |
| fēcundus -a -um | fertile |
| *fēlix -īcis | lucky, fortunate |
| fera -ae f. | wild animal |
| *ferō, ferre, tulī, lātum | bear, bring forth (166) |
| *ferrum -ī n. | blade, weapon |
| ferus -a -um | savage, fierce |
| fētus -ūs m. | offspring, produce |
| *fidēlis -e | faithful |
| fingō, fingere, finxī, fictum | make up, invent |
| fīniō, fīnīre, fīni(v)ī, fīnītum | limit |
| *fīnis -is f. | end |
| *fīō, fierī, factus sum | become (23, 186) come into existence (129, 152, 155, 159, 180, 205, 214) be caused (154) occur (188) |
| flammō, flammāre, flammāvī, flammātum | blaze |
| flōreō, flōrēre, flōruī | flourish |
| flōs, flōris m. | flower |
| fluvius -ī m. | river |
| *foedē (*adverb*) | foully, disgustingly |
| forem | imperfect *subjunctive* of **sum** (=essem) |
| formīdo, formīdinis f. | fear, dread |
| *forte | perhaps |
| *fortūna -ae f. | fortune |
| frondiferus -a -um | leaf-bearing |
| frons, frondis f. | foliage, leaf |
| fructus -ūs m. | produce, fruit |
| frūgiferens, frūgiferentis | fruit-bearing |
| *frūmenta -ōrum n.pl. | corn |
| fruor, fruī, fructus sum (*deponent* + *abl*.) | enjoy |
| *fugiō, fugere, fūgī, fugitum | flee from |
| fulmen, fulminis n. | thunderbolt |
| fundō, fundere, fūdī, fūsum | pour out |
| | |
| generātim (*adverb*) | each according to their kind |
| genetrix, genetrīcis f. | mother |

A Level

| | |
|---|---|
| genitābilis -e | life-giving |
| genitālis -e | life-giving |
| *gens, gentis f. | race, people |
| genū -ūs n. | knee |
| *genus, generis n. | kind, species |
| *gerō, gerere, gessī, gestum | do, make happen |
| gignō, gignere, genuī, genitum | give birth to |
| glēba -ae f. | clod of earth |
| Graius -a -um | Greek |
| grandescō, grandescere | grow large |
| *gravis -e | weighty |
| gremium -ī n. | lap, bosom |
| gubernō, gubernāre, gubernāvī, gubernātum | direct, steer |
| | |
| *habeō, habēre, habuī, habitum | see ratio |
| haereō, haerēre, haesī, haesum | be fixed, stick |
| Helicōn -ōnis m. | Mt Helicon |
| *hic, haec, hoc | this |
| hinc | from this |
| Homērus -ī m. | Homer |
| *homō, hominis m. | man (*plural:* people) |
| horribilis -e | dreadful |
| hostia -ae f. | sacrificial victim |
| *hūc | see accedō |
| hūmānus -a -um | human |
| Hymenaeus -ī m. | wedding-song |
| *iaceō, iacēre, iacuī | to lie flat |
| | |
| *iam | now, as things are (104) |
| ictus -ūs m. | blow |
| *īdem, eadem, idem | the same |
| *igitur | therefore |
| ignōrō, ignōrāre, ignōrāvī, ignōrātum | not to know |
| *ille, illa, illud | that (person/thing) |
| illustrō, illustrāre, illustrāvī, illustrātum | shed light on |
| imber, imbris m. | rain-shower |
| immensus -a -um | immeasurable, immense |
| immortālis -e | undying |

# Vocabulary

| | |
|---|---|
| impius -a -um | wicked |
| *in (*preposition* + *accusative*) | into |
| *in (*preposition* + *ablative*) | in, on, at |
| inānis -e | empty, void |
| incertus -a -um | unpredictable |
| incestus -a -um | impure, unchaste |
| *incipiō, incipere, incēpī, inceptum | begin |
| inclutus -a -um | glorious, illustrious |
| incultus -a -um | uncultivated |
| incutiō, incutere, incussī, incussum | strike into |
| *inde | next (15), then (157), from that source (170) |
| indigus -a -um (+ *genitive*) | having need of |
| indūcō, indūcere, induxī, inductum | lead |
| indugredior, indugredī | set foot on |
| *ineō, inīre, ini(v)ī | enter into |
| infans, infantis *m./f.* | infant |
| infula -ae *f.* | woollen ribbon |
| inhiō, inhiāre, inhiāvī, inhiātum | gaze upon |
| inīquus -a -um | troubled (41), unfavourable (183) |
| initus -ūs *m.* | arrival |
| insinuō, insinuāre, insinuāvī, insinuātum | worm its way into |
| instō, instāre, institī | stand over |
| insum, inesse, infuī | be in |
| intellegō, intellegere, intellexī, intellectum | understand |
| *interea | meanwhile |
| intereō, interīre, interi(v)ī, interitum | perish |
| interimō, interimere, interēmī, interemptum | destroy |
| intus (*adverb*) | inside |
| Īphianassa -ae/āī *f.* | Iphianassa |
| *ipse, ipsa, ipsum | himself, herself, itself |
| *īra -ae *f.* | anger |
| irritō, irritāre, irritāvī, irritātum | stir up, provoke |
| *is, ea, id | he, she, it |
| *ita | in this way |
| Italus -a -um | of Italy |
| *iuvenis -is *m.* | young man |

A Level

| | |
|---|---|
| *iuvō, iuvāre, iuvī, iūtum | help |
| *labor, labī, lapsus sum | move smoothly |
| *labor -ōris *m*. | toil, effort |
| lacrima -ae *f*. | tear |
| lacūna -ae *f*. | chasm |
| laetificus -a -um | joy-bringing |
| *laetus -a -um | fruitful, joyful |
| Latīnus -a -um | Latin |
| lepor, lepōris *m*. | charm |
| lingua -ae *f*. | language |
| loca -ōrum *n.pl*. | areas |
| *longē (*adverb*) | far |
| loquēla -ae *f*. | utterance |
| lūcidus -a -um | bright |
| lūmen, lūminis *n*. | light |
| lūna -ae *f*. | moon |
| | |
| mactātus -ūs *m*. | sacrificial slaughter |
| maestus -a -um | sad, mournful |
| *magis (*adverb*) | more |
| *magnus -a -um | great |
| mālae, mālārum *f.pl*. | cheeks |
| *malum -ī *n*. | wickedness |
| manifestus -a -um | evident |
| *manus -ūs *f*. | hand |
| *mare, maris *n*. | sea |
| *māter, mātris *f*. | mother |
| māteria -ae *f*. | matter |
| māteriēs -ēī *f*. | matter |
| Māvors, Māvortis *m*. | Mars |
| *mē | see **ego** |
| meātus -ūs *m*. | path, course |
| *melior, melius | better |
| Memmius -ī *m*. | Memmius |
| Memmiadēs -ae *m*. | descendant of the Memmii family |
| *mens, mentis *f*. | mind |
| meritō (*adverb*) | rightly, with good reason |
| *metus -ūs *m*. | fear |
| *meus -a -um | my |

A Level

## Vocabulary

| | |
|---|---|
| mīlitia -ae/āī f. | warfare |
| minae -ārum f.pl. | threats |
| minister, ministrī m. | attendant |
| minitor, minitārī, minitātus sum | threaten |
| mīrus -a -um | amazing |
| *miser, misera, miserum | wretched |
| *modus -ī m. | way, manner |
| *moenia -ium n.pl. | walls |
| moenus, moeneris n. | work |
| *mons, montis m. | mountain |
| *morbus -ī m. | disease, sickness |
| *mors, mortis f. | death |
| *mōs, mōris m. | custom |
| mortālis -e | mortal, perishable |
| mortālēs -ium m.pl. | human beings |
| *multus -a -um | much, many |
| mundus -ī m. | world |
| murmur, murmuris n. | rumble |
| mūtō, mūtāre, mūtāvī, mūtātum | change |
| mūtus -a -um | dumb, unspeaking |
| | |
| *nam | for |
| *nascor, nascī, nātus sum | be born |
| *nātūra -ae f. | nature |
| nāviger, nāvigera, nāvigerum | ship-bearing |
| *nē (+ subjunctive) | so that…not (50) that (80) |
| *nec/neque | nor |
| *nec…nec… | neither…nor… |
| *necesse est | it is necessary |
| nequeō, nequīre, nequī(v)ī | be unable |
| nexus -ūs m. | web of connections |
| *nīl | not at all, in no way |
| *nīlum -ī n. | nothing |
| niteō, nitēre, nituī | shine |
| *nōmen, nōminis n. | name |
| *nōn | not |
| *nōs, nostrī | we, us |
| nōbiscum | with us |
| noscō, noscere, nōvī, nōtum | realise, get to know |

# 84 Lucretius: De Rerum Natura I.1-224

| | |
|---|---|
| *noster, nostra, nostrum | our |
| *novus -a -um | new |
| novitās, novitātis f. | unfamiliarity |
| *nox, noctis f. | night |
| nūbila -ōrum n.pl. | clouds |
| nūbō, nūbere, nupsī, nuptum | marry |
| *nullus -a -um | not any |
| nūmen, nūminis n. | divine power |
| *nunc | as things are |
| | |
| *ob (preposition + accusative) | because of |
| *obeō, obīre, obi(v)ī, obitum | encounter |
| obscūrus -a -um | dark, unclear |
| obsistō, obsistere, obstitī (+ dative) | defy, stand up to |
| obterō, obterere, obtrīvī, obtrītum | crush underfoot |
| obvius -a -um | presenting itself |
| occultus -a -um | hidden, obscure |
| *oculus -ī m. | eye |
| *omnis, omne | all, every |
| opera -ae f. | work, effort |
| opēs, opum f.pl. | power |
| *opprimō, opprimere, oppressī, oppressum | crush |
| *opus, operis n. | thing (153) |
| *opus est + ablative | there is need of |
| *ōra -ae f. | shore |
| Orcus -ī m. | Orcus (god of the Underworld) |
| orior, orīrī, ortus sum (deponent) | arise, come into existence |
| *ornō, ornāre, ornāvī, ornātum | make distinguished |
| ortus -ūs m. | coming into being |
| *ōs, ōris n. | mouth |
| os, ossis n. | bone |
| *ostendō, ostendere, ostendī, ostensum | reveal, show |
| | |
| pābula -ōrum n.pl. | pastures |
| pactō | see under quo |
| palleō, pallēre, palluī | be pale |
| pandō, pandere, pandī, pansum | expound |
| pangō, pangere, pepigī, pactum | construct, create |

# Vocabulary

| | |
|---|---|
| *pār, paris | equal (88) reasonable (189) |
| *parens, parentis *m.* | parent |
| *pariō, parere, peperī, partum | bring about |
| *parō, parāre, parāvī, parātum | create |
| *pars, partis *f.* | part, season (181) |
|   e cunctis partibus | totally (217) |
| partus -ūs *m.* | birth |
| *parvus -a -um | small |
| pascō, pascere, pāvī, pastum | feed |
| patefaciō, patefacere, patefēcī, patefactum | reveal |
| patefīō, patefierī | be revealed (passive of patefacio) |
| *patior, patī, passus sum | allow, permit |
| *patria -ae/āī *f.* | fatherland |
| patrius -a -um | belonging to a father, paternal |
| *paulatim | gradually |
| *pax, pācis *f.* | peace |
| pectus, pectoris *n.* | heart, breast |
| pecus, pecudis *f.* | tame animal |
| pendō, pendere, pependī, pensum | hang |
| penetrō, penetrāre, penetrāvī, penetrātum | pierce, penetrate |
| penitus (*adverb*) | deeply |
| peperit | see **pario** |
| *per (*preposition + accusative*) | through |
|   per se | by itself |
| peragrō, peragrāre, peragrāvī, peragrātum | roam through |
| percellō, percellere, perculī, perculsum | strike, hit |
| perennis -e | evergreen |
| *pereō, perīre, periī, peritum | perish |
| *perficiō, perficere, perfēcī, perfectum | perform, complete |
| pergō, pergere, perrexī, perrectum | go on, proceed |
| *perīc(u)lum -ī *n.* | danger |
| perimō, perimere, perēmī, peremptum | destroy |
| permaneō, permanēre, permansī, permansum | stay |
| perspiciō, perspicere, perspexī, perspectum | see clearly |

A Level

# 86 Lucretius: De Rerum Natura I.1–224

| | |
|---|---|
| persultō, persultāre, persultāvī, persultātum | leap throughout |
| pervincō, pervincere, pervīcī, pervictum | be victorious |
| *pēs, pedis *m*. | foot |
| *petō, petere, petī(v)ī, petītum | ask for (40), fall towards (92) |
| placidus -a -um | quiet |
| plācō, plācāre, plācāvī, plācātum | calm, pacify |
| *poena -ae *f*. | punishment |
| pollens, pollentis | powerful |
| pontus -ī *m*. | sea |
| porrō | furthermore |
| *porta -ae *f*. | gate |
| *possum, posse, potuī | be able |
| *postrēmō | finally |
| potestas -ātis *f*. | power |
| *potius... quam... | rather...than... (196–8) |
| praepandō, praepandere | spread out |
| praesertim | especially |
| praestō, praestāre, praestitī (+ *dative*) | be better than |
| *praeterea | besides |
| prīmordia -ōrum *n.pl*. | beginnings, basic elements |
| *prīmus -a -um | first |
| cum prīmīs | especially |
| prīmum (*adverb*) | first of all |
| *princeps, principis | first |
| principium -ī *n*. | beginning (149), basic element (198) |
| *prius quam | before |
| prīvō, prīvāre, prīvāvī, prīvātum (+ *ablative*) | deprived of |
| *prōcēdō, prōcēdere, prōcessī, prōcessum | march onwards |
| prōferō, prōferre, prōtulī, prōlatum | bring out |
| profundō, profundere, profūdī, profūsum | let flow, pour |
| prōmeritum -ī *n*. | meritorious act |
| propāgō, propāgāre, propāgāvī, propāgātum | reproduce |
| propāgo, propāginis *f*. | offspring |
| *propter (*preposition* + *accusative*) | by the side of (90), because of (139) |

A Level

# Vocabulary 87

| | |
|---|---|
| prōsum, prōdesse, prōfuī (+ *dative*) | be of benefit to |
| *putō, putāre, putāvī, putātum | think |
| | |
| *quaerō, quaerere, quaesīvī, quaesītum | seek, search for |
| *quam | how (104) than (198) |
| *quandō | since |
| quāpropter | therefore |
| quārē | therefore, and so |
| queō, quīre, quī(v)ī, quītum | be able |
| *quī, quae, quod | who, which, what |
| quī | how? (168) |
| *quia | because |
| quīcumque, quaecumque, quodcumque | whoever, whatever, whichever |
| *quīdam, quaedam, quiddam | a certain |
| quiescō, quiescere, quiēvī, quiētum | rest, fall still |
| quīnam, quaenam, quodnam | which, what (77) |
| quippe | since, seeing that |
| *quis, quid | who, what? |
| *quisquam, quicquam | anyone, anything |
| *quisque, quaeque, quidque | each |
| quīvis, quaevis, quidvis | any… at all |
| *quō | to where (16,122) into which (57) |
| quō… magis | by which… all the more (28) |
| *quoniam | since |
| quō pactō | just as how |

| | |
|---|---|
| radius -ī *m.* | ray |
| rapax, rapācis | violent |
| rapidus -a -um | swift, rushing |
| *ratio, ratiōnis *f.* | reasoning (51, 130) explanation (54, 148) principle (77, 105, 129) philosophy (81) method, way (108, 110, 153) |
|     rationem habeō/reddō | give an account |
| *rectius (*comparative adverb*) | more correctly |
| recubō, recubāre, recubuī, recubitum | lie back |
| *reddō, reddere, reddidī, redditum | assign (203) produce (209) |
| referō, referre, retulī, relātum | bring back |
| regiō, regiōnis *f.* | area, region |
| *regō, regere, rexī, rectum | rule over |

A Level

| | |
|---|---|
| rēiciō, rēicere, rēiēcī, rēiectum | throw back |
| rēligiō, rēligiōnis *f.* | religion, superstitious fear (109) |
| *relinquō, relinquere, relīquī, relictum | leave, abandon |
| reor, rērī, ratus sum | think |
| *repente | suddenly |
| reperta -ōrum *n.pl.* | discoveries |
| repōnō, repōnere, reposuī, repostum | lay back |
| *rēs, rēī *f.* | thing, matter (80), situation (43), affair (46) |
| reserō, reserāre, reserāvī, reserātum | unlock |
| resolvō, resolvere, resolvī, resolutum | break up |
| restō, restāre, restitī | stand up to, resist |
| resupīnus -a -um | lying on one's back |
| *rex, rēgis *m.* | king |
| rīdeō, rīdēre, rīdī, rīsum | laugh |
| Rōmānus -a -um | Roman |
| rosa -ae *f.* | rose |
| *rursum | back again |
| | |
| sacra -ōrum *n.pl.* | religious rituals |
| saec(u)la -ōrum *n.pl.* | races, generations |
| *saepe | often |
| *saepius | more often |
| sagax, sagācis | shrewd (50) keen (130) |
| saliō, salīre, saluī, saltum | leap |
| salsus -a -um | salty |
| *salūs, salūtis *f.* | safety |
| sanctus -a -um | sacred |
| *sanguis, sanguinis *m.* | blood |
| scelerōsus -a -um | criminal |
| *scelus, sceleris *n.* | crime |
| *scrībō, scrībere, scripsī, scriptum | write |
| *sē, suī | himself, herself, itself |
| sēcernō, sēcernere, sēcrevī, sēcrētum | keep apart from (194) |
| sēcrētus -a -um | peculiar to itself (173) |
| *sed | but |
| sēiungō, sēiungere, sēiunxī, sēiunctum | keep at a distance |
| sēmen, sēminis *n.* | seed |
| sēmoveō, sēmovēre, sēmōvī, sēmotum | remove, detach |

# Vocabulary

| | |
|---|---|
| *semper | always |
| *sentiō, sentīre, sensī, sensum | sense, be aware of |
| sepeliō, sepelīre, sepelī(v)ī, sepultum | bury |
| *sequor, sequī, secūtus sum | follow |
| serēnus -a -um | untroubled, calm |
| *servō, servāre, servāvī, servātum | preserve, maintain |
| *sī | if |
| significō, significāre, significāvī, significātum | make known |
| *signum -ī n. | sign |
| *simul (ac) | as soon as |
| *simul (adverbial) | at the same time (114) |
| simulacrum -ī n. | image |
| *sine (+ ablative) | without |
| si quis, si quid | if anyone, anything (217) |
| socia -ae f. | ally |
| *soleō, solēre, solitus sum | be in the habit of |
| *sōl, sōlis m. | sun |
| sollemnis -e | solemn, traditional |
| solum -ī n. | soil (212) |
| sōlus -a -um | alone |
| somnium -ī n. | fantasy |
| *somnus -ī m. | sleep |
| sōpiō, sōpīre, sōpī(v)ī, sōpītum | make to sleep |
| *spatium -ī n. | interval (181), period of time (184) |
| speciēs -ēī f. | appearance, apparition (125) |
| *spērō, spērāre, spērāvī, spērātum | hope |
| spīritus -ūs m. | breath |
| sponte suā | of their own accord, spontaneously |
| squāmigerī -ōrum/um m.pl. | scaly creatures (162) |
| studeō, studēre, studuī | wish ardently |
| *studium -ī n. | zeal, ardour |
| suādeō, suādēre, suāsī, suāsum | urge, induce |
| suāvis -e | pleasant, delightful |
| *sub (preposition + ablative) | underneath |
| subiciō, subicere, subiēcī, subiectum (+ dative) | cast down |
| subigō, subigere, subēgī, subactum | subdue |
| *subitō | suddenly |

A Level

| | |
|---|---|
| sublāta | see **tollo** |
| subter (*preposition + accusative*) | below |
| suescō, suescere, suēvī, suētum | be accustomed to (60) |
| *sum, esse, fuī | be, exist |
| summittō, summittere, summīsī, summissum | send up (8, 193), lower down (92) |
| *summus -a -um | utmost (45) highest (54) |
| *sūmō, sūmere, sumpsī, sumptum | take, adopt |
| super (*adverb*) | from above (39, 65) |
| *superus -a -um | on high |
| suspiciō, suspicere, suspexī, suspectum | look up at |
| *suus -a -um | his own, her own, its own, their own |
| *tālis -e | of such a kind |
| *tamen | however |
| *tangō, tangere, tetigī, tactum | touch, affect |
| *tantum (+ *partitive genitive*) | so much (101) |
| *tantus -a -um | so large |
| tellus, tellūris *f.* | earth |
| *tēlum -ī *n.* | shaft |
| *tempestas, tempestātis *f.* | season |
| *templum -ī *n.* | realm |
| *tempus, temporis *n.* | time (26, 41, 98, 102) situation (93) season (176, 183) |
| tenebrae -ārum *f.pl.* | darkness |
| *teneō, tenēre, tenuī, tentum | occupy (164) |
| tener, tenera, tenerum | delicate, soft |
| teres, teretis | shapely |
| terminus -ī *m.* | boundary stone |
| *terra -ae *f.* | earth, land |
| terrificō, terrificāre | terrify |
| terriloquus -a -um | frightening |
| *terror, terrōris *m.* | terror |
| *timeō, timēre, timuī | fear |
| *timor, timōris *m.* | fear |
| *tollō, tollere, sustulī, sublātum | lift up |
| trānō, trānāre, trānāvī, trānātum | swim across |
| tranquillus -a -um | tranquil |
| transeō, transīre, transi(v)ī, transitum | cross, move through |

## Vocabulary

| | |
|---|---|
| tremibundus -a -um | trembling |
| Trivia -ae/āī *f.* | goddess of crossroads, Diana |
| *tū, tuī | you (*singular*) |
| tueor, tuērī, tūtus sum | observe (152), preserve (195) |
| *tum | then |
| tunc | then |
| turbō, turbāre, turbāvī, turbātum | upset, confound |
| turpō, turpāre, turpāvī, turpātum | pollute |
| tūtemet | = *strengthened form of* tū (102) |
| *tūtō (*adverb*) | safely |
| *tuus, tua, tuum | your (*singular*) |
| | |
| *ubi | when (156) since (167, 182) where (171) |
| *ullus -a -um | any |
| *umquam | ever |
| *unde | from which source (56, 131, 158), from where (75, 124) |
| ūsurpō, ūsurpāre, ūsurpāvī, ūsurpātum | name |
| *ūsus est (+ *ablative*) | there is need of (184, 219) |
| *ut (+ *subjunctive*) | so that |
| *ut (+ *indicative*) | as (117, 189, 197) |
| *uterque, utraque, utrumque | each (of two) |
| | |
| vacuus -a -um | unoccupied |
| vadum -ī *n.* | shallow water |
| *valeō, valēre, valuī | be strong enough to |
| vastus -a -um | gaping, vast |
| vātēs, -is *m.* | priest, seer |
| *ventus -ī *m.* | wind |
| Venus, Veneris *f.* | Venus |
| vēr, vēris *n.* | spring |
| verbum -ī *n.* | word |
| *vereor, verērī, veritus sum | fear |
| vernus -a -um | vernal, belonging to spring |
| versus -ūs *m.* | line of poetry |
| *vertō, vertere, vertī, versum | overturn (105), turn (211) |
| *vĕrus -a -um | true |
| *via -ae *f.* | road, path |
| vicissim | in its turn |

A Level

| | |
|---|---|
| *victor -ōris *m.* | victor |
| *victōria -ae *f.* | victory |
| vidēlicet | we may see that (210) |
| *videō, vidēre, vīdī, vīsum | see |
| *videor, vidērī, vīsus sum | seem (134), be seen (224) |
| vigeō, vigēre, viguī | be strong |
| vigilō, vigilāre, vigilāvī, vigilātum | stay awake |
| *vincō, vincere, vīcī, victum | defeat, overcome |
| virens, virentis | lush green |
| virgineus -a -um | of a girl |
| virgō, virginis *f.* | unmarried girl |
| *vir, virī *m.* | man |
| *virtus, virtūtis *f.* | excellence, strength of character |
| *vīs, vim *f.* | force |
| vīsō, vīsere, vīsī | go to see |
| vīsus -ūs *m.* | eye |
| vīta -ae *f.* | life |
| vītālis -e | living |
| vītis -is *f.* | vine |
| vīvidus -a -um | lively, energetic |
| *vīvō, vīvere, vixī, victum | live |
| *vocō, vocāre, vocāvī, vocātum | call |
| *volō, velle, voluī | want |
| volucer, volucris *f.* | bird |
| voluptas, voluptātis *f.* | pleasure |
| vōmer, vōmeris *m.* | ploughshare |
| *vulnus, vulneris *n.* | wound |

# Tibullus

Elegies *I.2, I.5, II.4*

# Introduction

## Why read Tibullus?

The ancient world was a very strange place, and much of Latin literature concerns aspects of life which are very different to that lived today. Few of us will fight in hand-to-hand combat on the battlefield like the men depicted in Virgil, Livy and Caesar, or declaim in the forum and the lawcourts as did Cicero, or worship Jupiter by sacrificing animals. This is part of the fascination which the Romans continue to have for us, of course, and it could well be said that the differences between us and them are less than the shared humanity which shines through the most alien pages of their literature. It can still be a struggle, however, to see the beating heart beneath the armour and the toga, and this is where poetry such as that of Tibullus is more immediately accessible to modern readers.

The great charm of the poetry of Tibullus is that he deals in that most universal of human arenas – romantic love. Most of us will fall in love and most of us will at times find the course of true love less than smooth, and so when the speaker in these poems exposes his own romantic illusions and disappointment, he could be writing today. Tibullus is not the only Augustan poet to do this, of course: Propertius, Ovid and Horace also produced love poetry of exquisite beauty and insight. Where Tibullus scores – and where he has oddly been criticised by some scholars – is in the fact that his verses are composed in relatively straightforward Latin, lacking in the mythological baggage which can make reading other poets a difficult task for the reader new to Latin poetry. Propertius will describe his girlfriend Cynthia and then spend many lines comparing her to a mythological heroine: Horace wrote in a lapidary and highly polished poetic form which can make the sense hard to decipher in the mosaic of interlocking words. Ovid created an amazing range of poems in a variety of genres: but here again the artistry is so intense that we often feel that we are reading poetry written for experienced readers rather than for beginners. Only Catullus has the same degree of forthright and (apparently) heartfelt power as Tibullus, but the range of moods in Catullus is wider and the register of his language more varied than will be found in this poetry.

Tibullus depicts himself much of the time as a man in mental and emotional anguish. Happiness (they say) writes white: there is not much literary mileage in describing a happy love-affair, and so most love-poetry is the poetry of longing more than fulfilment. Love-poetry is also more about the poet than it is about the beloved, and so while this poet lets us see very little of the two women whom he loves in these three poems, he shows us the workings of his own heart in acute and painful detail. There are some elements which are less common today – most lovers do not camp outside the locked door of their beloved as this man does in I.2. and I.5, and witchcraft is less commonly used as a means of securing or removing affection, as discussed in I.2.42–58 – but the emotions of a man who is unable to sort out his love life ring all too true and should provoke lively discussion. Tibullus' position of being the 'slave' of his 'mistress' (in II.4) may make readers squirm but it is not so far from the alarmingly common phenomenon of emotionally abusive relationships in which one partner exerts coercive control over the other. In Tibullus the relationship is also transgressive in gender terms. We are always told that in ancient Rome men ruled the household and women were usually treated as inferior beings who stayed at home and made wool while their men enjoyed themselves, but here we see a reasonably well-off Roman male putting himself into situations of ludicrous expense and humiliation in the service of a woman who evidently does not love him. Who were these women and what was their status in society? How can we fit the power-dynamics expressed here into what we know of Roman law and society? Three of his elegies express the poet's desire for a younger man (Marathus): does this mean that same-sex desire in Roman society of this period was acceptable? Would it be fair to say that this poet falls in love with a person and is clearly not embarrassed by the gender of the beloved?

The language Tibullus uses is generally easy to understand, but the ideas discussed are adult and will also provoke thought and discussion. When, for instance, Delia had left him for another man, the poet tried to use promiscuous sex to divert his obsessive love for her. He openly tells us (I.5.39–40) of the embarrassing result:

*saepe aliam tenui: sed iam cum gaudia adirem*
*admonuit dominae deseruitque Venus.*

('I often embraced another woman: but just when I was reaching orgasm/ Venus reminded me of my mistress and abandoned me.')

Guilt-induced impotence is here depicted in elegant but stark terms, and it is not surprising that the great German poet Goethe used this couplet to introduce his own wonderful poem on the same theme (*Das Tagebuch* (1810)). As with much of this poetry, the style here is harmonious and fluent but the content is anything but. From the turmoil of a wrecked relationship this poet seems able to create lines of astonishing beauty.

Tibullus is often described as a pastoral poet, and he does depict rural life in idyllic terms on many occasions. Unimaginative scholars have taken him to task for the imprecise nature of his knowledge of farming as if his words are to be taken at face value, not seeing that the context of these vignettes of country life is ironic. He lives in the city but dreams of living in the countryside (e.g. I.1, I.2.71–4) with a woman whose own way of life is thoroughly urban. In the first elegy (I.1) he tells us that he owns a rural property ('once prosperous but now poor' I.1.19) but much of his description of his agriculture is couched in wishful subjunctives (I.1.1–10) and he obviously lived the life of a soldier ('if only I could be … not always subject to the long march' (I.1.25–6)) as he details later in I.3 and I.7. At I.5.21–34 he itemises the elements of farming life – crops, grapes, flocks, religious ritual – with Delia in charge of the food and the entertainment when his patron Messalla comes for dinner – only to snarl that this was all so much fantasy (*haec mihi fingebam* ('I dreamed all this up') frames this section) and that any hopes he may have had have been blown to the four winds.

The rural idyll is seen as a poetic fantasy, part of his longing to have his girl to himself in a 'safe' setting and perhaps no more to be taken literally than that of the banker Alfius in Horace's second *Epode* (who is 'any day now going to live in the countryside' but still works in the bank).

The 'reality' behind this text is elusive, and the rustic charms are yet another tissue of poetic material which this master-poet uses to show his own disillusion with his life in Rome. It could be suggested that Tibullus loves farming because in his mind it represents a potential escape from the rat-race of his romantic jockeying for power between himself, his mistress and his rivals for her affection in the city where money talks and love is up for sale. We know little about Tibullus the man, and we know better than to take his verses as simple confessions of his own lived experience, but reading them we get a glimpse into a world which is both familiar and unfamiliar at the same time, a window into the past but also a mirror into our own lives and our own emotions.

## Tibullus and his times

The ancient biographical sketch of the poet describes him thus:

> *Albius Tibullus, Roman knight, handsome in appearance and conspicuous in his attention to his bodily appearance. Above all others he loved the orator Corvinus Messalla, and shared his quarters in the war in Aquitania where he was awarded military decorations. Many people think that Tibullus was the best of the elegists. His 'love-letters' though brief are thoroughly useful. He died young, as his epitaph indicates.*

Young indeed – he may have been no more than thirty on his deathbed – but he certainly lived through very interesting times. He was born somewhere between 55 BC and 48 BC and the date of his death is secured by his epitaph (written by Domitius Marsus) which has this poet die not long after Virgil (who died in 19 BC). Latin love elegy itself also died not so long after him, and the short but intense flowering of this genre overlapped with what has been dubbed 'the Roman revolution'.

Tibullus was born into a republic in which political power overlapped with military authority, where competing aristocrats were eclipsed by competing generals such as Pompey and Caesar, and where the so-called free republic was struggling to maintain a large and unwieldy empire abroad. Caesar famously crossed the Rubicon – the river bordering his province in Gaul – in 49 BC and thus started a civil war against the Roman government. The senate appointed the great general Pompey to lead their defence and this man ended up a headless corpse, murdered by the Egyptians after he lost the battle of Pharsalus in 48 BC. Julius Caesar returned to Rome and ruled as dictator for the few years before his own assassination on the Ides of March 44 BC. There followed a bloodbath in which those who supported the assassins – including Tibullus' patron Messalla and the poet Horace – fought with Brutus and Cassius against the dead dictator's supporters led by his former consul Mark Antony and his heir Octavian. The assassins were defeated at Philippi in 42 BC, and the conflict then polarised between Octavian and Antony who met in the crucial battle at Actium on 2 September 31 BC. This battle left Octavian in sole control and it was he who returned to Rome to be renamed Augustus and to be the first of the Roman emperors, ruling from 27 BC until his death in AD 14. The final eight years of Tibullus' life will have been lived under this new autocracy and it was in the first year of this regime (27–26 BC) that Tibullus published his first book of *Elegies*. This was autocracy under the light disguise of a 'restored republic': there were still meetings of the senate and the old offices of state (consuls, praetors, aediles and tribunes) continued to be elected and to serve. Nobody was fooled, of course. Tacitus (*Annals* I.2) comments drily that:

> *By seducing the soldiers with gifts, the masses with grain and everybody with the pleasures of peace, he (Augustus) increased his powers little by little, taking to himself the roles of the senate, the magistrates and the laws, with no resistance. The most energetic men had died ... and the other nobles acquired wealth and distinction in proportion to their hunger for servitude.*

It may be more than a coincidence that this new world of enforced pacification after many years of bloodshed should produce a poet whose own aspirations are rural rather than urban, romantic rather than military, who begins a key poem with the rhetorical question:

> Who was it who first invented dreadful swords? How savage (ferus), how iron-hearted (ferreus), he was. Then it was that slaughter and fighting began for the human race, then it was that there opened up a short-cut to horrific death.
>
> I.10.1–4

We can never really disentangle the 'life' from the 'art' of any poet, and we will find that these three elegies in this book elude even straightforward mapping onto 'real life'. It is clear, however, that the genre of love elegy, with its subjection of war to peace, of masculine self-assertion to romantic emasculation, and with its elevation of the life of love over that of the life of duty, coincided with a period in which thoughtful and sensitive Roman males may well have felt increasingly alienated from the status quo and drawn to the counter-culture expressed in these quiet but devastating poems.

## Messalla

It is very hard to make a living as a poet, then or now, and patronage was vital to some poets. Horace and Virgil both enjoyed the direct financial and social support of Augustus' associate Maecenas. Juvenal, over a century later, complained of the dearth of patrons (*Satires* 7.59–62) and commented that 'miserable poverty cannot sing . . . as it lacks the money which the human body needs'. Patronage was entrenched in Roman political and social life during the republic: the powerful senator would have his 'clients' who would greet him in the morning and escort him down to the forum in return for his support in their own lives (and the promise of food on a regular basis). These friends (*amici*) of slender means depended on their patron for protection in the sometimes chaotic world of Roman society.

Tibullus, however, seems to have been different. For one thing he was of equestrian status when he served in the army and so must have had access to a large amount of money to qualify, although he seems to have lost at least some of his estate in the land confiscations brought about by Octavian in 41–40 BC and then in 36 and 31 BC. He does describe (I.1.19) his estate as *pauper* and speaks a lot about *paupertas* when he praises the superior quality of the *pauper* lover (I.5.61-6) but this is not hard evidence of anything. In I.5 he has been supplanted by a rich lover (*dives amator*) and is looking to distance himself from this man, and the word *pauper* often (in poetry at least) had the meaning 'modest' rather than denoting starvation-level penury. He did not, then, need food handouts but he did welcome the emotional and literary support which an eminent citizen could give to his work, and his patron was the great Roman general and statesman Marcus Valerius Messalla Corvinus (64 BC–AD 8), to whom the poet devotes a good deal of space (e.g. I.3, I.7, II.5).

As we saw above, Messalla had supported Brutus and Cassius after the assassination of Caesar in 44 BC, but then switched sides and backed first Mark Antony and then the eventual victor Octavian. It was on Octavian's side that he took part (as consul for that year) in the decisive battle of Actium in 31 BC and he later led two expeditions of his own. In the first of these (to the east) Messalla took Tibullus on his staff but the poet fell ill and only got as far as Corfu before returning to Italy (see I.3). Tibullus did manage to take a full part in the later expedition to Aquitania, where Messalla was putting down a Celtic rebellion, and the campaign was successful enough for Messalla to be awarded a triumph on 25 September 27 BC – the same year in which Augustus first began to rule Rome. Tibullus was (according to the short ancient biography of the poet) decorated for his achievements in this war, and yet the poet distances himself from military prowess on many occasions. At I.2.65–70, for instance, he criticises anyone who goes abroad on military campaign in preference to staying at home with his lover. We know that Messalla had literary interests and that he was a famous orator: but his main claim to literary fame now is the fact that he was the patron of Tibullus, Ovid, Lygdamus and (Messalla's niece) Sulpicia – the poetry of these last two is preserved in the third book of the manuscript of Tibullus. The *Panegyric of Messalla* – a lavish poem in epic hexameters comparing the great man to Odysseus and even Alexander the Great – has come down to us as poem III.7 in the Tibullan collection but is unlikely to be by Tibullus himself. Messalla, having been a glorious *triumphator* in his younger years, seems to have taken something of a back seat as the new emperor Augustus consolidated his control of the Roman empire. Not that he was a rebel – he was the man who in 2 BC proposed that Augustus should be given the title of 'father of the fatherland' and he made massive contributions to the improvement of Rome's infrastructure – but it cannot escape notice that whereas Maecenas' poetic clients Virgil and Horace make explicit (favourable) remarks about Augustus, the emperor as such finds no place in the text of Tibullus. In his magisterial work *The Roman Revolution* (1939) the great historian Ronald Syme states with acid disdain (p. 460) that 'Augustus' chief of cabinet, Maecenas, captured the most promising of the poets at an early stage and nursed them into the Principate.... Other patrons of literature were left far behind ... Messalla had to be content with the anaemic Tibullus.' Syme assumes that Tibullus was second-rate – a judgement which his contemporaries disagreed with as we shall see – and also that his poetry was lacking in poetic vigour. One purpose of this book is to ask the reader to question both these judgements.

It may in fact be unfair to say that Tibullus did not engage with the political milieu just because he did not name Augustus himself. Tibullus' promotion of peace over war sits well with the emperor's ostentatious closing of the temple of Janus in 29 BC – symbolising the end of war – after his triumph over his enemies. The rustic idyll we see in Tibullus is not too far from the world of Virgil's *Georgics* (29 BC) with their praise of the Italian countryside, or from Horace's idealised Sabine estate (and the setting in Tibullus I.5 is itself more imaginary than real), and the praise of Messalla is also praise of the emperor who appointed him. Other poets fell foul of Augustus: the influential love-poet Gallus enjoyed a distinguished career under Octavian in Egypt but was foolish enough to erect monuments to his achievements and was made to commit suicide in 27 BC. Ovid fell spectacularly from grace when he was banished by the emperor in AD 8, claiming that his disgrace was partly caused by a poem: there is no evidence that this popular and skilful poet Tibullus was ever silenced by the emperor.

Nor was this simply because Tibullus was an unknown and insignificant poet: Horace wrote two poems (*Epistles* I.4 and *Odes* I.33) to a certain 'Albius' who may have been the poet Albius Tibullus, although we cannot be certain of the identification. Ovid was certainly speaking of our Tibullus when he said (*Amores* I.15.28–9):

> So long as flames and the bow are the weapons of Cupid, your verses will be learned, elegant Tibullus.

Ovid also wrote an elegy on his death (*Amores* III.9) which begins with the personified spirit of Elegy in deep mourning for his loss, and all this proves that his poetry was admired by other poets of his day and thereafter. Quintilian (X.1.93), writing in the first century AD, placed him highly in his account of the genre of elegy:

> We (Romans) challenge the Greeks also in elegy. The most polished and elegant (tersus atque elegans) writer seems to be Tibullus: there are those who prefer Propertius. Ovid is more playful than either, and Gallus is harsher.

In recent years Tibullus has been surprisingly neglected and criticised. The eminent scholar Kenneth Quinn wrote him off (*Latin Explorations* 136) as 'the placid second-rater without the calibre to sense the dangerous inadequacies of the genre he has adopted but cannot revitalise'. He has been less often read and less highly valued when compared to Propertius, but there is no doubt that in ancient times he was regarded as outstanding in his field.

## Love elegy as a genre

Any poet in ancient Rome had a wide range of genres to choose from. There was obviously epic – the genre which began with the Greek poet

Homer and which was executed brilliantly by Ennius in his *Annales*, by Virgil in his *Aeneid* and by his successors Lucan, Statius and so on. Many poets of the Augustan era explicitly state that they choose *not* to write epic poetry about *reges et proelia* (as Virgil puts it (*Eclogues* 6.3)), and Tibullus also rejects the poetry of warfare at II.4.15–16. Horace wrote lyric, satire and hexameter epistles as well as the early *Epodes*, but always stated that military epic was not for him (see e.g. *Satires* II.1.10–20), and Ovid's only foray into epic was the gloriously anarchic mythological epic *Metamorphoses*. Tibullus chose to work in the genre of elegy and made it very much his own.

The word 'elegiac' in English often suggests a 'lament' or 'dirge', and the Greek word *elegos* can indeed refer to a poem sung in mourning. The metre of the 'elegiac couplet' (with its rising hexameter line followed by a falling pentameter) was to become very popular in ancient Greece, both in its public form (elegy) and in the static medium of the 'epitaph' such as Simonides' famous couplet on the dead soldiers at Thermopylae (*fragment* 531):

> *Wanderer, if you go to Sparta, tell them that*
> *we lie here, obeying their orders.*

There was also the 'epigram' in elegiacs, a poem which purported to be attached to a statue or dedication but which was elevated into its own (often scurrilous) genre perfected by many poets in Greek and in Latin and which expressed an emotion or an *aperçu*. This short form of epigram is to be distinguished from the longer elegy which dates back to at least the 650s BC and could deal with serious matters – such as politics in the elegies of the statesman Solon or warfare in the works of Tyrtaeus – as well as less serious ones such as the drinking party, where it is assumed that the text will be sung to the accompaniment of a musical instrument. The early Greek poet Theognis produced verse which was at times political and philosophical, as well as verses closer to what we might term satire and also love poems. Later elegies tended to tell stories such as that of the 'Lock of Berenice', which was narrated in Greek elegiacs by Callimachus (third century BC) and then in Latin elegiacs by Catullus (poem 66) or the four books of Callimachus' *Aetia*, albeit in a less exalted and more personal manner than epic. Callimachus' emphasis on the need to cultivate perfection of literary form and avoidance of long epics made this form highly suitable for him and for his successors, and the link between the world of mythology and the personal world of the poet is something of a new trend in Greek poetry which the Roman elegists (especially Propertius) were to make their own.

The Latin love elegy as we have it begins with Catullus (*c.* 84–54 BC): poems 65–116 of his collection are all written in elegiac couplets and range in length from the single couplet poem 85 to the 160 lines of poem 68. Catullus was one of a group (often called the 'new poets') who consciously rejected the demands of public and didactic poetry in favour of personal and subjective expression: in the elegiac poem 76, for instance, Catullus begs the gods to rid him of the 'plague' of love which has driven all joy from his heart after his betrayal by his lover, while poem 101 is a lament for his dead brother. Poem 68 combines both of these themes as it is both a love-poem about his meeting with his mistress and a meditation on the death of his brother, couched within a mythological version of the legend of Protesilaus. Catullus' poetry is deeply personal in tone but also highly polished and literary even when – especially when – it is most obscene as in the scathing abuse of Gellius in the short epigrams 88–91.

The missing link between Catullus and Tibullus is the poet Cornelius Gallus from the generation after Catullus, whose military career we met earlier on. His poetry was universally acknowledged by later poets as formative on their own work but of his text only a meagre 10 lines has survived. We learn from the ancient sources that Gallus composed four books of elegies to his mistress, the actress Lycoris, and clear citations of his work in Virgil's tenth *Eclogue* make it obvious that he made use of themes which later elegists continued: the longing for rustic life, the elevation of peace over war and abundant use of mythology.

The elegists whose work survives are Tibullus, Propertius and Ovid. Propertius (?57 BC–?AD 2) enjoyed the patronage of Maecenas, as did

Horace and Virgil. He wrote four books of elegies, the first three of which chart the ups and downs of his relationship with his mistress who ensnares him on the first line of the first poem of the first book:

> *Cynthia prima suis miserum me cepit ocellis* ('Cynthia first captured me, lovesick, with her little eyes').

Not that Propertius' life was unchanging misery: some of his poems (e.g. II.15) express the exuberant joy of his sexual relationship with Cynthia, for instance. He could compose an elegy (II.7) critical of Augustus' attempts to curb sexual misbehaviour and encourage marriage but also one (III.4) which seems to be backing Augustus' campaigns – so long as they do not involve the poet leaving town.

Ovid (43 BC–AD 17) composed several books in the elegiac metre: his early *Amores* (25–15 BC), the *Heroides* (fictional verse letters from women in love), the spoof didactic elegies *Ars Amatoria* ('the Art of Love) and *Remedia Amoris* ('Remedies for Love'). He also began to compose his elegiac *Fasti* (on the dates and legends of the Roman calendar) but was banished from Rome by the emperor for his literary and personal misdemeanours in AD 8. From there, in exile in Tomis on the Black Sea, he composed his moving and highly personal elegies the *Tristia* ('sad poems') and *Epistulae ex Ponto* ('Letters from Pontus'). His approach to love elegy was self-consciously ironic, often treating conventional themes in an unconventional way and drawing attention to the artifice and the artificiality of the genre. Where he re-enacts scenarios found in earlier poets, we have to wonder whether the life had gone out of the genre and it may not be an accident that Ovid's elegies were the last to be composed in this form.

One example of such a conventional theme which we can trace through all these poets is that of the 'serenade' poem, which we find in Tibullus I.2 and I.5. The Greek term for this form of poem (*paraklausithyron*) means something like 'song by the locked door' and we find it in Greek literature (such as Aristophanes *Ecclesiazousai* 952– 76, Theocritus *Idyll* 3, *Palatine Anthology* V.23, V.191) and also Roman comedy (e.g. Plautus *Curculio* 147–57). Lucretius, in his didactic poem *On the Nature of Things* (IV.1177–84) describes the phenomenon as part of his critique of infatuated lovers:

> *The locked-out lover, weeping, keeps on covering the doorway with flowers and garlands, anointing the arrogant doorposts with marjoram and planting kisses – the fool – on the door itself. If he were admitted, just one sniff of the air would shock him into seeking any decent excuse for leaving, his long-rehearsed and deeply conceived lament would fall flat and he would damn himself for his folly now that he sees that he has endowed her with more than is right to endow a mortal woman.*

Lucretius would not tilt at windmills, and this passage is seen by many scholars as evidence that such behaviour really went on in Rome, especially in the night-time antics of young men returning home from a revel: but its interest to us here is in the ways it was used and manipulated by Roman poets. Horace (*Odes* I.25) tells Lydia that young men do not knock on her door so often these days and one day will stop altogether, but in *Odes* III.10 he pleads from the doorway to the stubborn Lyce to let him in, pleading in terms similar to those of Tibullus I.2. The form had already been subverted in Catullus 67, where the door tells some of the gossip it has been privy to, and Propertius (1.16) continues this by letting the door speak for itself and parody the lovers' laments it has been forced to endure. Ovid (*Amores* 1.6) serenades the doorkeeper rather than the girl locked inside, and all these variations on the theme expect the reader to be familiar with the basic outlines of the genre. Tibullus I.2 purports to be a piece of persuasive rhetoric appealing to the girl's self-interest (I.2.73–6) and praying directly to Venus (I.2.81–8, 99–100). Poem I.5 also alludes to the same locked-out status (I.5.67–76) endured by himself and also by other unnamed rivals for the affections of his beloved.

Another common theme which Tibullus uses is that of the 'slavery of love' (*servitium amoris*) whereby the male lover is prepared to subject himself to the domination of his beloved. Tibullus tells us this right at the start, with the additional note of the locked-out lover:

*me retinent vinctum formosae vincla puellae*
*et sedeo duras ianitor ante fores* (I.1.55–6: 'the chains of a pretty girl hold me tied up and I sit as door-keeper in front of her door')

Propertius also states (II.23.24) roundly that 'nobody who is looking for love will be a free man' and the elegists' use of the word *domina* (meaning 'mistress' in both senses of the word) for the girl is telling. Tibullus takes this further: when he has misbehaved he asks for servile punishment (I.5.5–6) and in II.4 he gives his humiliation full throttle: he is now suffering *servitium triste* (bitter slavery), bids farewell to his ancestral freedom and is held in chains with no chance of remission (II.4.1–4).

## The life of love

Poets (of course) make things up all the time and these poems may well bear little or no relation to the real-life experiences of the writer. He might after all be simply writing what tickles his poetic fancy and what will win him a readership among his peers, assuming the mask of 'romantic poet' for the purposes of composition without giving away any of his own secrets. This dichotomy between the 'art' and the 'life' is well established and readers always need to beware of seeing poems such as those of Tibullus as crude confessions. Readers have always also wondered how realistic these poems are in the world of Augustan Rome. If (after all) their contents are ludicrously implausible then that would make them closer to the world of farcical Roman comedy and seriously affect the tone in which we read them.

Many things about the Roman 'life of love' remain unclear, not least because the vast majority of our sources on the matter were male writers and not female: and also because nobody goes around speaking in elegiac couplets, which removes these texts from anything like real life. The names of Tibullus' women were always regarded in antiquity as witty pseudonyms: Delia ('the woman from Delos') was (we are told by Apuleius) really called Plania – a bilingual joke as the Greek word *delia* means something like the Latin adjective *plana* and was also a reference to the god of poetry, Apollo, who was worshipped on the island of Delos. Nemesis as a Greek term denotes 'retaliation' and it has been speculated that this girl was his 'revenge' on the faithless Delia: equally the term might denote the personal havoc this girl caused in the lover's life as she was the poet's 'nemesis'.

Scholars often refer to both women as 'courtesans' or *demi-mondaines* – women who were neither enslaved nor married to Roman citizens and so were free to choose their lovers more freely than either of those classes of woman. If, however, Delia was really called Plania then she may well have been a citizen and her *coniunx* (I.2.43) in that case might be her husband, leaving her status similar to that of Clodia who allegedly (according to Cicero's invective against her in the *Pro Caelio*) conducted sexual affairs with young men after the suspicious death of her husband Metellus Celer. In the period when Tibullus was writing it was legal and common for Roman citizens to marry freedwomen (*libertinae*) who either had been slaves themselves or were the children of freed slaves: and so the *coniunx* mentioned in Tibullus (I.2.43) may have been the girl's legal husband or at least a man who exercised control over her movements (*domini* I.2.7) and in whose house she lived. Both Delia and Nemesis are said to be having a relationship with other men in preference to the poet, and Tibullus warns one such rival that yet more men are queuing up for her favours (I.5.71–6). Elsewhere we read that these women are only available to men who can pay for their time – Nemesis 'shuts out lovers by her prices' (II.4.39) and it takes cash to get past the security on her door (II.4.33–4), while Delia now entertains a 'rich lover' (I.5.47) and only opens her door when it is knocked by a 'hand full of cash' (I.5.68). Should we take this language seriously and conclude that these girls were prostitutes? Or see it as the bitterness of a rejected lover blaming his poverty for his lack of sexual success?

Things are further complicated when we read the sequence of poems in which Tibullus expresses passion for a young man whom he calls Marathus. Same-sex desire was not unusual as a theme of poetry in the ancient world – cf. Virgil *Eclogue 2*, Horace *Odes* IV.1 – and Catullus who was ardent in his desire for at least two women also describes (poems 24, 48, 81, 99) how he courted a young man he calls Iuventius. Juvenal (6.34-7) seems to take it as read that a Roman male could find sexual satisfaction with a boy as an alternative to a woman – as does Ovid (*Ars Amatoria* II.684) – and Catullus (61.134-42) mocks a new bridegroom for being reluctant to leave behind his boy-loves and reminds him that what was acceptable for a bachelor is not so for a married man, although it is clear that some married men did continue such homoerotic relationships after marriage. In the pages of Petronius we see the married man Trimalchio with his boyfriend Croesus still on the scene. Modern society has moved a long way from the heteronormative paradigms of the past: but the sexual world depicted in Tibullus is hardly the same as our own and the differences are instructive about both his world and ours.

## Reading the poems of Tibullus

Tibullus' Latin is generally simple but that does not mean that the poems are easy or childlike: indeed one recent scholar (Kennedy *Arts of Love* p. 13) has stated that these poems are 'tantalizingly elusive' and it is hard to find consensus among scholars on how these elegies are to be understood and read. One difficulty which readers experience is the way this poet darts from topic to topic: other poets take a theme and spend the entire poem working through it, as did Ovid with the idea of 'the lover as soldier' in *Amores* 1.9. The strength of doing this is that the poem has a beginning, a middle and an ending and wraps up the theme with unflinching coherence. The drawback to it is that there are times when the poet flogs the idea to death – as Seneca later commented (*Controversiae* IX.5.17: 'Ovid does not know when to stop'). Tibullus on the contrary moves from topic to topic within a single poem in a stream-of-consciousness manner, and this 'disorganised' style does not please everyone.

Even the context of the poem has to be inferred from hints in the text: so, for instance, poem I.5 begins with the poet looking back on his quarrel with Delia and expressing remorse, addressing himself to her in the second person (*te*) as if she were with him: he reminds her of how when she was ill he prayed successfully for her recovery. In the following lines, however, the poet speaks as if Delia is now absent. He speaks of her in the third person as he fantasises about the rustic bliss he hoped they would enjoy. Is this section addressed to the reader? Or to himself? He confesses to his failed attempts at easing his pain (37–40) and then relates how Delia (again in the third person (*facit... devovet* 43–4)) has bewitched him, before turning on the evil woman who (he thinks) is to blame for Delia meeting her rich lover. The poet curses this 'go-between' (or perhaps 'pimp') with venomous brutality (49–56, again in third person verbs as she is not present to hear it). The speaker then turns to address Delia again (*at tu* 59) begging her to shun the rich man in favour of the poor poet, who describes himself now in the third person (61–6). Up to this point we have had no hint as to where the poet is speaking from: but now (67–8) all is revealed as he complains that 'the door does not open, won over by my words' and so we are to imagine him outside her door as in the 'serenade' poem I.2. The poem ends with another twist, as the speaker now turns to the new man in her life (*at tu* 69) to warn him that his own days in her boudoir are numbered as there is 'somebody' already waiting in the street to take his place. Who is this somebody? Is it the speaker himself (who is outside the door)? Or a third person in the long line of potential lovers for his woman? There is no certain answer to these questions and we are left with a puzzle.

This is presumably deliberate on the part of the poet. If a writer fails to tell us things, then that is usually because the information we seek is not part of the text. When read backwards, the poem makes situational sense. The poet is at the door after being locked out, and fills in the backstory of her illness, her recovery, his wishes for their future together, her new man, his failed attempts to get over her: he then ends up venting his rage at the pimp and the rich man (but interestingly not at Delia, who may be responsible for her own choices but who equally may be under his constraint). The sudden revelation of the setting at 67 is a wonderful surprise, foiling the reader's expectations and casting the text in a new light. The poem's playing with the temporal sequence forces us to think it all out for ourselves, but is not done simply to furrow the readerly brow but rather because this is how most of us think most of the time. The speaker lets us eavesdrop on his mental processes and shows us the emotional turmoil reflected and configured in the disjunctions and confusions. The final scenario of the 'somebody' lurking in the shadows waiting for his turn with Delia is amazingly effective at showing the poet's feelings about the revolving door leading to her favours. It was the poet, then the rich man, then it will be somebody else who might be the poet again, or might be somebody else: Horace *Odes* III.9 has the same scenario, where a man and woman have split up and found other partners but end up together again. It won't last, despite the passionate pleas of eternal love with which the poem ends, and neither will Delia's current *amour*. The poet describes himself at the start of the poem as spinning like a top (3–4): the poem ends with Delia's love-life making the same gyratory movements. This might (and might well not) be factually accurate reportage of her amatory involvements, but that is not the point: what these poems give us is snapshots of the mental landscape of a man in love, in pain, and in confusion.

As with most poetry of this kind, the language is beautifully chosen to express the sentiments behind the words, and the great achievement of a poet like Tibullus is that he has transformed the disorder of the setting into a supremely ordered and harmonious set of words on the page. The confused switches of focus we have seen in I.5 might suggest that the text is a simple outpouring of feelings, but there is nothing simple or easy about this verse and its very simplicity conceals its artistry.

Look for instance at I.2.65–6, where the poet lashes out at a man who abandoned his lover to go off seeking fame and fortune in the army. The passage begins with *ferreus* – a brilliant choice of word denoting both 'clad in armour' but also 'tough as nails' and a pun which the poet liked enough to reuse at I.10.2. *ferreus . . . fuit* is a good example of the 'f' alliteration which the Romans found harsh, and the key word *stultus* ('stupid') is delayed until halfway through the next line for added emphasis, while also suggesting the stock figure of the *stultus* husband in the highly popular 'adultery' mime in which a husband is betrayed by his wife while he is out. The alternatives are laid out: he could have 'had' his girl – a coy euphemism for having sex with her – but chose to 'chase after' money and weapons.

The opening of II.4 has been roundly written off by Kenneth Quinn (*Latin Explorations* 153–4) as 'cliché rather than image … maudlin rather than moving' but this is to miss the artistry of an astonishing poem. In II.3. the poet has told us that his girl (Nemesis) has gone to the countryside with her new lover who is a rich ex-slave and the poet longs to be there with her, even if it means working the land under her orders:

> 'Take me away: I will plough the fields at the command of my mistress (*ad imperium dominae*): I am not refusing chains and whipping' (II.3.79–80).

Chains and whipping are modes of coercion used on rural slaves and II.4.1–2 at once continues this theme:

> 'Here I see slavery and a mistress lined up for me: farewell, then, o my ancestral freedom'

The nature of the slavery is metaphorical rather than real, as the 'chains' (*vincla*) are being fastened by 'Love' rather than by any human master, and the poet calls himself *misero*, which was a common term to describe a man racked by unrequited love. The crucial point here is that this man is now unable to determine his own future and even the grammar brings this out – notice the juxtaposed passive verbs *datur teneorque* (3). Line 3 is marked by strong dental alliteration of 't' and 'd', and line 4 tells that Love 'never slackens the chains'. He could have said something like 'love keeps me constantly in chains' but that word *numquam* ('never') even with the present tense (*remittit*) can connote a hopelessness about the future as well as a statement of the present. Line 5 opens up the possibility that the poet deserves punishment for some crime unknown even to himself, suggesting an almost Kafkaesque state of mind in which his punishment seems unrelated to his crimes. The *saeva puella* ('savage girl') – presumably Nemesis – is urged to take away the 'torches' (*faces*). This is a key image in much of Latin love-poetry – the blazing of the torch is akin to the blazing passion of the lover as well as being the way the nocturnal lover lit his way to the home of the beloved – but here has a more sinister sense of slave-burning as suggested in the word *ure* ('burn me') at I.5.5, a sense reinforced by the repetition of *urit/uror* across the line-division at 5–6 and also the word *io* which graphically enacts the howl of pain. The poet then wishes away his pain (*dolores*) with a striking analogy: he would prefer to be a rock on icy mountains or a cliff exposed to the battering sea-waves. The imagery is beautifully created: note the onomatopoeic repetition in *tunderet unda* as the waves beat the cliff, the unusual adjective *naufraga* which usually means 'shipwrecked' but here means 'ship-wrecking' and so suggests the imagery of love as a stormy sea (found at e.g. Horace *Odes* I.5.7, 13–16). The winds here are *insani* ('crazy' – like the love) and the mountains are 'ice-cold' like his lover's heart: even when he is opting out of his pain, he ends up using its language. There are further subtleties: the poet wishes to 'stand firm' (*stare*) like the rock, reminding us of how Catullus also told himself (8.11, 19) to 'stand firm' in the face of his unrequited love, and recalling the use of the same verb *stare* when Virgil (Tibullus' older contemporary) describes (*Aeneid* VI.470–1) how the betrayed queen Dido responds to her former lover Aeneas' protestations in the underworld with no more feeling 'than if she were hard flint or Marpesian rock standing there (*stet Marpesia cautes*)'. The comparison goes back even further in literary history: when Patroclus accuses Achilles of being unfeeling, he tells him: 'You hard-hearted man: Peleus the horseman was not your father, not Thetis your mother: the grey sea gave birth to you and the sheer rocks, since your mind is hard.' (Homer *Iliad* 16.33–5). The poet uses the store of literary texts available to him as he strives to express feelings, but then these feelings seem later to explode the very poetic form in which they are composed: he rejects the Muses (15–16) and is prepared to commit crime to avoid becoming the poetic stock figure of the locked-out lover (22) whom we met in I.2 and

I.5. The poem ends with the poet almost despairing of his sanity – 'my advice is true, but what is the point of truth to me?' (51) – and the poem ends with him willing to sell his home and drink any drugs if only Nemesis will look on him kindly. This ending is startling: this man is willing to render himself homeless and even become the pharmaceutical plaything of this woman. His submission to her dominion could not be more total or more terrifying.

## The metre

Latin poetry was written in a fairly rigid system of metres, all of which in turn relied on the 'weight' of each syllable as either 'heavy' or 'light'. A syllable is light if the vowel is short and not followed by two (or more) consonants, whereas syllables containing long vowels, or diphthongs, or in which a vowel is followed by a succession of consonants, are heavy. A syllable is reckoned to be a single vowel sound, followed either by nothing (an 'open' syllable) or by a consonant (a 'closed' syllable): usually a single consonant following a vowel is reckoned to be the first consonant of the following syllable (e.g. *ca-li-gi-ne*) and does not affect the weight of the syllable.

Where two or more consonants follow a vowel, the first one is included in the first syllable (*men-sa*) which is thus 'closed' and becomes heavy – the exceptions being combinations of mute and liquid consonants (b, c, g, p, t followed by r: and c, p, t, followed by l) where both letters are considered as belonging to the following syllable (*ma-tris*) and need not affect the rhythm of the line. Diphthongs (double vowels pronounced as a single sound such as ae, eu, au) are always long by nature: single vowels can in many cases change their quantity in different forms of a word: the final -a of *mensa* is long in the ablative case, short in the nominative, and the perfect tense of the verb *věnio* is *vēni*, for instance. This needs to be considered before any judgement is made about assonance – if the vowels have different quantities then there cannot be assonance and the only way to be sure is to scan the line.

In cases where a word ending with a vowel (or a vowel + m such as *rapacem*) is followed by a word beginning with a vowel or h, the two syllables usually merge ('elide') into a single syllable, as at I.5.1 where *asper eram et* (five syllables) is scanned *asper er~~am~~ et* (four syllables).

– indicates a heavy syllable
∪ indicates a light syllable
× indicates a syllable which may be either heavy or light
// indicates the caesura (the break in the line of a pentameter: word-end in the middle of a foot of a hexameter).

Tibullus composed in a metre known as the elegiac couplet, where each pair of lines was a hexameter followed by a pentameter. We will analyse each in turn.

In the **hexameter** the line is divided into six 'feet', each of which is either a dactyl (a heavy syllable followed by two light syllables (–∪∪)) or a spondee (two heavy syllables (– –)). The last foot is always dissyllabic, and the last syllable of all may be either heavy or light. The metrical analysis of a line is called 'scansion' and a typical hexameter line (I.5.43) may be scanned thus:

– ∪∪ / – – / – //∪∪/–∪∪ /– ∪∪ /– ×
*nōn făcĭt/ hōc vēr/bīs// făcĭ/ē těněr/īsquě lăc/ērtīs*

where the // sign shows the 'caesura' – the word-break in the middle of a foot – which occurs in the third foot (as here) or else in the fourth.

Latin also had a stress accent, whereby most words of more than one syllable were stressed on the penultimate syllable, or on the antepenultimate if the penultimate contained a short vowel. Thus, I.5.19 would be spoken:

*át míhi felícem vítam sí sálva fuísses*

but 'scanned' metrically as:

*a̱t mihi/ fe̱lic/e̱m vit/a̱m si/ sa̱lva fu/i̱sses*

Here we can see that the metrical beat or 'ictus' clashes with the speech 'accent' in some of the first four feet but coincides with it in the final two feet. This is common in all hexameter verse.

The word **pentameter** suggests that the line is divided into five feet but it is better read as two halves of 2.5 feet, thus (II.4.26):

–   ∪∪/ –   ∪∪ /– // – ∪∪/–∪   ∪/ ×
*dāt mĭhĭ/ sācrĭlĕg/ās // sēntĭăt/ īllă mă/nūs*

The feet are (as in hexameters) made up of dactyls or spondees but the central pause or caesura is invariable and marks the division of the line into its two constituent halves. The final single syllable may be either long or short and is marked here with 'x' to indicate this.

## Glossary of key literary terms

**Alliteration** – repetition of consonants in successive words as at I.2.20, where the girl's footsteps are suggested in the 'p' alliteration of *pedem . . . ponere posse*.

**Anaphora** – repetition of a key word, often for rhetorical effect, as in the repetition of *pauper* three times in initial position in I.5.61–5.

**Assonance** – repetition of vowel sounds such as the 'e' sounds at II.4.47 (*veteres veneratus*).

**Enjambement** – where the sentence runs over the end of the line and continues into the next line: see e.g. I.2.29–30, I.5.19–20, I.5.51–2.

**Framing** – where a key word or phrase both begins and ends a passage (as at I.5. 20 and I.5.35 (*fingebam*): or where a line begins and ends with reinforcing or contrasting terms, e.g. I.2.28 (*vulneret . . . petat*) or I.5.49 (*sanguineas . . . cruento*).

**Hendiadys** – where two separate terms are used together to describe a single thing: e.g. *caedem et facinus* ('bloodshed and a deed' II.4.21) for 'a deed of bloodshed'.

**Hyperbole** – exaggeration, such as when the poet wishes 'thunderbolts sent by Jupiter' to batter the door at I.2.8.

**Irony** – a device in which the style suggests that the words are not to be taken at face value (e.g. I.2.43–57) or the use of words to undercut their own form, as when the poet disclaims poetry at II.4.13–14.

**Metaphor** – a comparison which uses terms appropriate for one thing in describing another. At I.5.35–6 the poet's wishes are described as having been tossed away by the winds: at II.4.12 the times are 'soaked in bitter bile'.

**Metonymy** – the substitution of a name for a thing: the goddess Venus is often so used for love itself, and the poet speaks (I.2.3) of his head being struck with 'much Bacchus' (i.e. much wine, as Bacchus was the god of wine).

**Onomatopoeia** – where the sound of the words imitates their meaning: the beating waves are recreated in the repeated sounds of *tunderet unda* at II.4.10.

**Pathetic fallacy** – in which inanimate and insentient objects are described as if they had feelings: the door is addressed in the second person and cursed with suffering the beating of rain and thunderbolts (I.2.7–8), only then to be reminded of how the poet has been kind to it in the past (I.2.13–14).

**Rhetorical question** – a question not expecting an answer within the text such as at I.2.61–2 (*quid credam?*) or II.4.51.

**Simile** – a passage describing one thing as being like another: at I.5.3–4 the poet tells us that he is being driven like a toy top being whipped into swift motion by a child.

**Spondee** – two long syllables forming a single measure of the line (see metre).

**Synecdoche** – the use of a part or an aspect of a thing to denote the thing as a whole, or vice versa: at II.4.28 the word for 'sheep' (*ovem*) is used to refer to a fleece.

**Tricolon (crescendo)** – a group of three phrases of increasing emphasis, often beginning with the same initial word as at I.2.37–8 (*neu ... neu ... neu ...*).

# Further reading

## For more on the genre of Latin Love Elegy see:

Luck, G. *The Latin Love Elegy* (London, 1969)
Lyne, R. O. A. M. *The Latin Love Poets* (Oxford, 1980)

Sullivan, J. P. (editor) *Critical Essays on Roman Literature: Elegy and Lyric* (London, 1962)

## Translations of Tibullus include:

Postgate, J. P. *Catullus, Tibullus and Pervigilium Veneris* (Loeb Classical Library revised edition, 1962)
Lee, G. *Tibullus Elegies* (Introduction, Text, Translation and Notes: 2nd edition, 1982)

## Commentaries on Tibullus include:

Smith, K. F. *The Elegies of Albius Tibullus* (1913: reprinted Darmstadt, 1964)
Postgate, J. P. *Selections from Tibullus* (2nd edition, 1922)
Maltby, R. *Tibullus Elegies* (Text Introduction and Commentary, 2002)
Murgatroyd, P. *A Commentary on the First book of Elegies of Albius Tibullus* (Pietermaritzburg, 1980)
Murgatroyd, P. *Tibullus Elegies II* (Oxford, 1994)
Putnam, M. J. *Tibullus: a Commentary* (Oklahoma, 1973)

## For deeper discussion of Tibullus see:

Ball, R. J. *Tibullus the Elegist: a Critical Survey* (1983)
Bright, D. F. *Haec mihi fingebam* (Leiden, 1978)
Cairns, F. *Tibullus: a Hellenistic Poet at Rome* (Cambridge, 1979)
Elder, J. P. 'Tibullus: tersus atque elegans' in J. P. Sullivan (editor) *Critical Essays on Roman Literature: Elegy and Lyric* (London, 1962) pp. 65–105

## On the 'serenade' poem as a genre see:

Copley, F. O. *Exclusus Amator: a Study in Latin Love Poetry* (1956)

## For the social background to these poems see:

Griffin, J. *Latin Poets and Roman Life* (Duckworth, 1985), chapters 1,2,3,6.
Lilja, S. *The Roman Elegists' Attitude to Women* (Helsinki, 1965)

Lyne, R. O. A. M. 'Servitium Amoris' *Classical Quarterly* 29 (1979): 117–30

Murgatroyd, P. 'Militia Amoris and the Roman Elegists' *Latomus* 34 (1975): 59–79

Whitaker, R. *Myth and Experience in Roman Love Elegy* (Göttingen, 1983)

Williams, G. *Tradition and Originality in Roman Poetry* (Oxford, 1968)

Wyke, M. 'Mistress and Metaphor in Augustan Elegy' *Helios* 16 (1989): 25–47.

## For more trenchant criticism of Tibullus see:

Quinn, K. *Latin Explorations* (Routledge, 1963) pp. 136–7, 153–8

## Further reading on individual poems include:

### I.2

Kennedy, D. F. *The Arts of Love: five studies in the discourse of Roman love elegy* (Cambridge, 1993) pp. 18–21

Solmsen, F. 'Tibullus as an Augustan Poet' *Hermes* 90 (1962): 314–16

Trinacty, C. V. 'Tibullus' Comedy' *Mnemosyne* 70 (2017): 1051–8

Williams, G. *Tradition and Originality in Roman Poetry* (Oxford, 1968) pp. 496–501

### I.5

Myers, K. S. 'The Poet and the Procuress: The Lena in Latin Love Elegy' *The Journal of Roman Studies* 86 (1996): 1–21

Musurillo, H. 'Furtivus Amor: The Structure of Tibullus 1.5' *Transactions and Proceedings of the American Philological Association* 101 (1970): 387–99

Gaisser, J. H. '*Amor, rura* and *militia* in Three Elegies of Tibullus: 1.1, 1.5 and 1.10' *Latomus* 42 (1983): 58–72

## For a survey of recent work on Tibullus see:

Zimmermann Damer, E. 'Recent Work on Tibullus' *The Classical World* 107 (2014): 443–50

## For the turbulent times in which Tibullus lived see e.g.:

Holland, T. *Rubicon* (new edition, 2004, also available as an audiobook)
Syme, R. *The Roman Revolution* (Oxford, 1939)

## On Messalla and his circle see:

Davies, C. 'Poetry in the 'Circle' of Messalla' *Greece and Rome* 20 (1973): 25–35.
Syme, R. *The Augustan Aristocracy* (1986) pp. 200–26.

# Text

## I.2

adde merum vinoque novos compesce dolores,
    occupet ut fessi lumina victa sopor:
neu quisquam multo percussum tempora baccho
    excitet, infelix dum requiescit amor.
nam posita est nostrae custodia saeva puellae,      5
    clauditur et dura ianua firma sera.
ianua difficilis domini, te verberet imber,
    te Iovis imperio fulmina missa petant.
ianua, iam pateas uni mihi, victa querelis,
    neu furtim verso cardine aperta sones;      10
et mala siqua tibi dixit dementia nostra,
    ignoscas: capiti sint precor illa meo.
te meminisse decet quae plurima voce peregi
    supplice, cum posti florida serta darem.
tu quoque ne timide custodes, Delia, falle.      15
    audendum est: fortes adiuvat ipsa Venus.
illa favet seu quis iuvenis nova limina temptat,
    seu reserat fixo dente puella fores;
illa docet molli furtim derepere lecto,
    illa pedem nullo ponere posse sono,      20
illa viro coram nutus conferre loquaces
    blandaque compositis abdere verba notis.
nec docet hoc omnes, sed quos nec inertia tardat
    nec vetat obscura surgere nocte timor.
en ego cum tenebris tota vagor anxius urbe      25
\* \* \*
nec sinit occurrat quisquam, qui corpora ferro

vulneret aut rapta praemia veste petat.
quisquis amore tenetur, eat tutusque sacerque
    qualibet: insidias non timuisse decet.                                30
non mihi pigra nocent hibernae frigora noctis,
    non mihi, cum multa decidit imber aqua.
non labor hic laedit, reseret modo Delia postes
    et vocet ad digiti me taciturna sonum.
parcite luminibus, seu vir seu femina fiat                               35
    obvia: celari vult sua furta Venus.
neu strepitu terrete pedum neu quaerite nomen
    neu prope fulgenti lumina ferte face.
si quis et imprudens aspexerit, occulat ille
    perque deos omnes se meminisse neget:                                40
nam fuerit quicumque loquax, is sanguine natam,
    is Venerem e rapido sentiet esse mari.
nec tamen huic credet coniunx tuus, ut mihi verax
    pollicita est magico saga ministerio.
hanc ego de caelo ducentem sidera vidi,                                  45
    fluminis haec rapidi carmine vertit iter,
haec cantu finditque solum manesque sepulcris
    elicit et tepido devocat ossa rogo;
iam tenet infernas magico stridore catervas,
    iam iubet aspersas lacte referre pedem.                              50
cum libet, haec tristi depellit nubila caelo;
    cum libet, aestivo convocat orbe nives.
sola tenere malas Medeae dicitur herbas,
    sola feros Hecatae perdomuisse canes.
haec mihi composuit cantus, quis fallere posses;                         55
    ter cane, ter dictis despue carminibus.
ille nihil poterit de nobis credere cuiquam,
    non sibi, si in molli viderit ipse toro.
tu tamen abstineas aliis: nam cetera cernet
    omnia, de me uno sentiet ille nihil.                                 60
quid credam? nempe haec eadem se dixit amores

cantibus aut herbis solvere posse meos,
et me lustravit taedis, et nocte serena
concidit ad magicos hostia pulla deos.
non ego, totus abesset amor, sed mutuus esset, 65
orabam, nec te posse carere velim.
ferreus ille fuit qui, te cum posset habere,
maluerit praedas stultus et arma sequi.
ille licet Cilicum victas agat ante catervas,
ponat et in capto Martia castra solo, 70
totus et argento contextus, totus et auro
insideat celeri conspiciendus equo,
ipse boves mea si tecum modo, Delia, possim
iungere et in solito pascere monte pecus;
et te dum liceat teneris retinere lacertis, 75
mollis et inculta sit mihi somnus humo.
quid Tyrio recubare toro sine amore secundo
prodest, cum fletu nox vigilanda venit?
nam neque tum plumae nec stragula picta soporem
nec sonitus placidae ducere posset aquae. 80
num Veneris magnae violavi numina verbo,
et mea nunc poenas impia lingua luit?
num feror incestus sedes adiisse deorum
sertaque de sanctis deripuisse focis?
non ego, si merui, dubitem procumbere templis 85
et dare sacratis oscula liminibus,
non ego tellurem genibus perrepere supplex
et miserum sancto tundere poste caput.
at tu, qui laetus rides mala nostra, caveto
mox tibi: non uni saeviet usque deus. 90
vidi ego, qui iuvenum miseros lusisset amores,
post Veneris vinclis subdere colla senem
et sibi blanditias tremula componere voce
et manibus canas fingere velle comas,
stare nec ante fores puduit caraeve puellae 95

ancillam medio detinuisse foro.
hunc puer, hunc iuvenis turba circumterit arta,
    despuit in molles et sibi quisque sinus.
at mihi parce, Venus—semper tibi dedita servit
    mens mea. quid messes uris acerba tuas? 100

## I.5

asper eram et bene discidium me ferre loquebar,
    at mihi nunc longe gloria fortis abest.
namque agor ut per plana citus sola verbere turben,
    quem celer assueta versat ab arte puer.
ure ferum et torque, libeat ne dicere quicquam      5
    magnificum post haec: horrida verba doma.
parce tamen, per te furtivi foedera lecti,
    per Venerem quaeso compositumque caput.
ille ego, cum tristi morbo defessa iaceres,
    te dicor votis eripuisse meis,      10
ipseque te circum lustravi sulpure puro,
    carmine cum magico praecinuisset anus;
ipse procuravi, ne possent saeva nocere
    somnia, ter sancta deveneranda mola;
ipse ego velatus filo tunicisque solutis      15
    vota novem Triviae nocte silente dedi.
omnia persolvi: fruitur nunc alter amore,
    et precibus felix utitur ille meis.
at mihi felicem vitam, si salva fuisses,
    fingebam demens, sed renuente deo.      20
rura colam, frugumque aderit mea Delia custos,
    area dum messes sole calente teret,
aut mihi servabit plenis in lintribus uvas
    pressaque veloci candida musta pede.
consuescet numerare pecus; consuescet amantis      25
    garrulus in dominae ludere verna sinu.
illa deo sciet agricolae pro vitibus uvam,
    pro segete spicas, pro grege ferre dapem.
illa regat cunctos, illi sint omnia curae,
    at iuvet in tota me nihil esse domo.      30
huc veniet Messalla meus, cui dulcia poma
    Delia selectis detrahat arboribus;

et tantum venerata virum, hunc sedula curet,
   huic paret atque epulas ipsa ministra gerat.
haec mihi fingebam, quae nunc Eurusque Notusque          35
   iactat odoratos vota per Armenios.
saepe ego temptavi curas depellere vino;
   at dolor in lacrimas verterat omne merum.
saepe aliam tenui, sed iam cum gaudia adirem,
   admonuit dominae deseruitque Venus.                    40
tunc me discedens devotum femina dixit
   (a pudet) et narrat scire nefanda meam.
non facit hoc verbis; facie tenerisque lacertis
   devovet et flavis nostra puella comis.
talis ad Haemonium Nereis Pelea quondam                   45
   vecta est frenato caerula pisce Thetis.
haec nocuere mihi. quod adest huic dives amator,
   venit in exitium callida lena meum.
sanguineas edat illa dapes atque ore cruento
   tristia cum multo pocula felle bibat;                  50
hanc volitent animae circum sua fata querentes
   semper et e tectis strix violenta canat;
ipsa fame stimulante furens herbasque sepulcris
   quaerat et a saevis ossa relicta lupis;
currat et inguinibus nudis ululetque per urbes,           55
   post agat e triviis aspera turba canum.
eveniet—dat signa deus—sunt numina amanti,
   saevit et iniusta lege relicta Venus.
at tu quam primum sagae praecepta rapacis
   desere; nam donis vincitur omnis amor.                 60
pauper erit praesto tibi semper: pauper adibit
   primus et in tenero fixus erit latere;
pauper in angusto fidus comes agmine turbae
   subicietque manus efficietque viam,
pauper ad occultos furtim deducet amicos                  65
   vinclaque de niveo detrahet ipse pede.

heu canimus frustra, nec verbis victa patescit
    ianua, sed plena est percutienda manu.
at tu, qui potior nunc es, mea fata timeto:
    versatur celeri fors levis orbe rotae.　　　　　　　　　　70
non frustra quidam iam nunc in limine perstat
    sedulus ac crebro prospicit ac refugit,
et simulat transire domum, mox deinde recurrit
    solus et ante ipsas exscreat usque fores.
nescio quid furtivus amor parat. utere quaeso,　　　　　　75
    dum licet: in liquida nat tibi linter aqua.

## II.4

hic mihi servitium video dominamque paratam:
    iam mihi, libertas illa paterna, vale.
servitium sed triste datur, teneorque catenis,
    et numquam misero vincla remittit Amor,
et seu quid merui seu nil peccavimus, urit.     5
    uror, io, remove, saeva puella, faces.
o ego ne possim tales sentire dolores,
    quam mallem in gelidis montibus esse lapis,
stare vel insanis cautes obnoxia ventis,
    naufraga quam vasti tunderet unda maris!     10
nunc et amara dies et noctis amarior umbra est,
    omnia nunc tristi tempora felle madent.
nec prosunt elegi nec carminis auctor Apollo:
    illa cava pretium flagitat usque manu.
ite procul, Musae, si non prodestis amanti:     15
    non ego vos, ut sint bella canenda, colo,
nec refero solisque vias et qualis, ubi orbem
    complevit, versis luna recurrit equis.
ad dominam faciles aditus per carmina quaero:
    ite procul, Musae, si nihil ista valent.     20
at mihi per caedem et facinus sunt dona paranda,
    ne iaceam clausam flebilis ante domum.
aut rapiam suspensa sacris insignia fanis;
    sed Venus ante alios est violanda mihi.
illa malum facinus suadet dominamque rapacem     25
    dat mihi; sacrilegas sentiat illa manus.
o pereat, quicumque legit viridesque smaragdos
    et niveam Tyrio murice tingit ovem.
addit avaritiae causas et Coa puellis
    vestis et e rubro lucida concha mari.     30
haec fecere malas: hinc clavim ianua sensit,
    et coepit custos liminis esse canis.

sed pretium si grande feras, custodia victa est,
    nec prohibent claves, et canis ipse tacet.
heu quicumque dedit formam caelestis avarae, 35
    quale bonum multis attulit ille malis!
hinc fletus rixaeque sonant, haec denique causa
    fecit ut infamis nunc deus erret Amor.
at tibi, quae pretio victos excludis amantes,
    eripiant partas ventus et ignis opes; 40
quin tua tum iuvenes spectent incendia laeti,
    nec quisquam flammae sedulus addat aquam.
seu veniet tibi mors, nec erit qui lugeat ullus,
    nec qui det maestas munus in exsequias.
at bona quae nec avara fuit, centum licet annos 45
    vixerit, ardentem flebitur ante rogum,
atque aliquis senior veteres veneratus amores
    annua constructo serta dabit tumulo
et 'bene' discedens dicet 'placideque quiescas,
    terraque securae sit super ossa levis.' 50
vera quidem moneo, sed prosunt quid mihi vera?
    illius est nobis lege colendus amor.
quin etiam sedes iubeat si vendere avitas,
    ite sub imperium sub titulumque, Lares.
quidquid habet Circe, quidquid Medea veneni, 55
    quidquid et herbarum Thessala terra gerit,
et quod, ubi indomitis gregibus Venus afflat amores,
    hippomanes cupidae stillat ab inguine equae,
si modo me placido videat Nemesis mea vultu,
    mille alias herbas misceat illa, bibam. 60

# Commentary Notes

## I.2

The poet's mistress Delia has been locked in her house and the poet appeals to her to come out. The poet calls for wine as he appeals to the door to open up (1–14) and asks Delia to creep out to him (15–16). Venus helps lovers – at least the ones who deserve her help (16–24). Tibullus claims her protection (25–32) and asks passers-by not to interfere (33–40). He claims to have used a witch to cast a spell on Delia's husband so that he would not believe that she was unfaithful with the poet (41–66) and criticises the fool who would abandon a lover for warfare (67–72), as the poet would prefer the poor rural life with his Delia (73–80). He swears that he will atone for any wrong he has done to Venus (81–8) and threatens anyone who mocks him with a pathetic future as an old man (89-98) chasing girls and being a laughing-stock. The poem ends with a prayer to Venus (99–100).

The literary 'serenade' was often called a *paraklausithyron* – a Greek term for 'song at the closed door' – or else a *kōmos* ('revel'), and can be found in many corners of Greek and Latin poetry (see introduction). This poem is not however a trite version of an unoriginal formula: it is not delivered solely to the woman or to the woodwork, and the poet addresses a wide range of people and things: his slave (1), the door itself (7–14), Delia (who cannot hear him, presumably), himself, Venus, any passers-by, an unnamed mocker. Some scholars think the setting is the doorway, others think it is delivered at a drinking party, others that the poet could be in his house, possibly even dreaming it all. Furthermore, he is not locked out by his unfeeling mistress but rather by her husband/owner, as in Plautus *Curculio* 147ff.

The speaker tries everything and covers a wide range of elegiac themes in a single poem, showing his butterfly mind working through an impressive arsenal of persuasive tactics: he appeals to the door, the girl, to Venus and even to total strangers not to impede or mock his efforts. He denigrates the husband as unworthy of her (unlike himself) and says he has even resorted to witchcraft to get her love. The unstable character of the speaker is dramatized by his words, as he rants at (and then apologises to) the door: he brags of being immune to night-time crime and claims not to feel the cold either, but is most upset at the thought of being observed and mocked. He claims to be able to dupe the husband (with help from a witch, whose powers are described in sensational terms) but then admits that he was in fact asking for Delia's love to match his own obsession with her – something which his locked-out status makes dubious. He mocks the macho soldier off on campaign when he could have had Delia, but (given that the poet cannot now have Delia) this reflects back on the poet as the soldier at least made a choice which was not available to Tibullus. The rural idyll of the poet and Delia happy in each other's arms (71–4) is absurdly optimistic but the poet wonders whether he has annoyed Venus rather than facing obvious facts. The poem is (in other words) a speech put into the mouth of a lover, whose pain and delusion is clear to all except (possibly) himself.

**1 adde merum** – the poet orders more wine. The two imperatives (**adde** and **compesce**) are addressed possibly to a slave or else to himself. **novos** does not mean that this is a new girlfriend, but simply that her situation is newly altered now that she is under guard, or even that this is a new instance of an established pattern of her behaviour.

**2** Translate: *ut sopor occupet lumina victa fessi* [*mei*] ('so that sleep might overcome and possess my eyes, tired as I am'). The tiredness may be as a result of the **dolores** – or the wine, or the lateness of the evening.

**3–4** The speaker does not wish his sleeping 'unhappy love' to be disturbed. **neu** (=*neve*) **quisquam** means 'and let not anyone . . .'. Bacchus was the god of wine and his name is here used in metonymy for wine itself. **tempora** (here meaning 'temples' of the head) is an accusative of respect ('struck as to my temples').

**5** The beloved is under 'harsh' (**saeva**) house arrest and has been locked in by her 'master' (**domini** (7)). **nostrae . . . puellae** is a dative of disadvantage. Tibullus calls her 'my girl' even though she is married or at least controlled by another, and he blames the 'master' for her unavailability rather than herself.

**6** Scansion of the line shows that **durā** is ablative going with **serā** ('with a solid bolt').

**7–8 difficilis domini** probably go together in the genitive case and refer to the girl's husband/owner. The poet addresses the door (**te**) in the vocative, cursing this obstructive object with the sort of bad weather it may well have met regularly. Note the hyperbolic concept of 'thunderbolts sent by order of Jupiter' to batter the door. This is a pathetic fallacy, imagining that the inanimate door feels what the lover endures as he lies on the doorstep, as at Horace *Odes* III.10.3–8, Propertius I.16.23–4, II.9.41, Ovid *Amores* II.19.21–2.

**9 ianua** is again addressed in the vocative. The poet wants to enjoy sole rights to this girl (**uni** is dative of *unus*, agreeing with **mihi**). **pateas** is a jussive subjunctive (roughly equivalent to a command).

**10** The negative in **neu** (see 3n.) goes with **sones**: 'when opened (**aperta**) with the hinge turned (**verso cardine**) secretly (**furtim**), do not make a noise'.

**11 mala . . . dixit** are to be understood together: *mala dicere* is to 'curse'. The poet is apologising for any angry outburst of his towards the locked door, claiming it was 'madness' on his part. He is still speaking to the door.

**12 ignoscas** is another jussive subjunctive ('forgive me'). **sint** is subjunctive understanding *ut* in an indirect command, with **capiti** as a dative of disadvantage: 'I pray (that) those (curses) be on my head' – as indeed the bad weather would be on his head.

**13–14** The pathetic fallacy continues. The door is asked to recall how the poet has treated it kindly in the past – the poet is evidently a regular visitor to this threshold. **peregi** (from *perago*) means here something like 'utter [prayers]', using the 'suppliant voice' (**voce ... supplici**). Putting garlands on the doorpost was a regular feature of the serenade (Lucretius IV.1178: see introduction). These garlands were a gift for the girl, but here are given to the door – i.e. left there when the lover trudges sadly home unsatisfied.

**15** The poet now turns to his girl (Delia) and tells her to 'trick the guards'. **ne timide ... falle** all go together ('Do not be fearful when you trick the guards'). The **custodes** (picking up *custodia* from line 5) are presumably household slaves who would suffer if they did not keep her indoors (cf. 1.6.37–8).

**16 audendum est** is a gerundive of obligation. The proverbial expression 'fortune helps the brave' (*fortes fortuna adiuvat*) is here given a lover's twist with the substitution of Venus for Fortune: Venus gives the lover every reason to be brave as she will protect him from the dangers of the streets (27–30).

**17–22** Examples of Venus helping young lovers, with effective anaphora of **illa** in emphatic position to describe Venus in suitably religious tones.

**17–18 reserat** – 'unbolt'. Roman doors seem to have been locked at the base with a bolt (*pessulus*) pushed into the doorstep and also with a horizontal bar pinned into the wall on either side. **fixo dente** (literally 'with an inserted tooth') is an ablative absolute stating that the door has been bolted, with **dente** probably standing for the tooth-like bar which has secured it. The girl is to unlock the 'door with its fixed bolt'.

**19–22** Venus teaches lovers adulterous behaviour – there would be no need for stealth, silence and secrecy if this were not illicit sex.

**19–20** The girl learns how to escape a lover's bed without making a noise. **furtim** from *fur* ('thief') reminds us that adultery was thought of as a form of theft: cf. 1.2.36, 1.5.7, 65, 69, 75, Catullus 7.8, 68.136. **derepere** is to 'creep down'. *mollis* often connotes pleasurable softness and femininity (cf. 58): here it is applied to the bed. Note the 'p' alliteration to suggest the light footsteps and the heavy use of 'o' assonance in line 20.

**21–2** Understand *docet* from 19 as the main verb governing the infinitives. 'Speaking nods of the head' is a wonderful phrase to denote the articulate but silent gestures shared between lovers who may not speak openly. **coram** goes backwards with **viro** ('in the presence of her husband'). Notice the way the **verba** are literally hidden inside the **compositis ... notis**.

**23–4** Lovers held back by lethargy or fear will not be helped by Venus, who only helps the strong (cf. line 16). The dark night is when illicit lovers get to work – and where dangers lurk (27–30). A similar scenario is explored by Propertius (III.16).

**25** The poet admits to feeling nervous (**anxius**) as he wanders all over the city (**tota ... urbe**). There is clearly a gap of at least one line after 25 as the line following it in the manuscript is in the same hexameter metre as line 25: every other even-numbered line in the poem is a pentameter. Presumably the missing line said something like 'I am safe as Venus looks after me' as the following lines give examples of the dangers faced.

**27** The dangers of the Roman streets at night: wounding and robbery. **sinit** here has a final subjunctive (*occurrat*) without **ut** to mean: 'she (Venus) does not let anyone bump into me who ...'. **vulneret** is either a generic subjunctive ('the sort of man to injure ...') or else a potential subjunctive ('who might injure'). The mugging is not personally targeted as is plain from the plural **corpora** – the villain is looking for 'bodies' to attack.

**28** The line is framed with the key verbs. **rapta ... veste** is an ablative absolute.

**29–30** Love protects the lover. Note the rapid dactyls as the lover strides confidently onwards, with **eat** as a potential subjunctive ('may walk'). **tutus** indicates 'being watched over' (and so 'safe') while **sacer**

has the sense of 'enjoying inviolability': **-que . . . -que** here joins the two terms ('*both* **tutus** *and* **sacer**'). **qualibet** is enjambed at the end of the phrase and the start of a new line and widens the scope of the lover's safety to 'anywhere he wishes'. Poets of this era often used the perfect infinitive (**timuisse**) where we might expect the present tense form *timere* (cf. 1.2.96).

**31-2** The lover's immunity from harm extends to nature as well as thugs. Note the anaphora of **non mihi** to start successive lines (with **mihi** as the indirect object of **nocent**). *piger* means primarily 'sluggish, inert' and is commonly seen as appropriate to the numbing cold of winter, here amplified with the word **noctis** at the end of the line. The juxtaposed **imber aqua** sounds overdone – what else is **imber** going to use but **aqua**? – but the point is to extend the concept of 'rain-shower' with two words to indicate the protracted rain. **multa aqua** is ablative of attendant circumstances.

**33-4** The poet elaborates the point: none of this suffering (**labor**) hurts me – so long as Delia in fact opens the door to let me in out of the cold. **reseret** and **vocet** are both concealed conditionals with **modo**: '[if] only Delia unbars. . .'. **vocet taciturna** is good: she 'calls me' but does so quietly (cf. 21-2 *nutus . . . loquaces*), merely using the sound of a finger tapping.

**35-40** A warning to passers-by not to inquire and gossip about the lovers. This underlines the transgressive nature of the relationship in which the lover does not wish to be recognised or reported.

**35-6** **parcite luminibus** – 'spare the lamps' here means 'do not look' but also carries the literal sense of saving on the lamps themselves: *lumen* is a common metaphor for 'eye' but is used of literal 'lamps' in line 38. **seu . . . seu** means 'whether . . . or . . .'. **fiat / obvia** has the sense 'turns up in the street', with the feminine gender of **obvia** taken from **femina**.

**36 furta** (literally 'thefts') is often used of adulterous affairs (cf. 19-20n.). The **furta** here are described as **sua** as Venus is the goddess of love who inspires them. There may also be a covert reference to the story told in Homer's *Odyssey* (8.266–366) about the adultery of Venus (Aphrodite) and Mars (Ares) and how it was uncovered by her jealous husband Hephaestus: in that case Venus certainly wanted her own *furta* to be hidden.

**37** **neu** = *nēve* 'and do not…': notice the anaphora of **neu** introducing a rising tricolon of three phrases. The lover who a moment ago (26–30) was striding fearlessly is now warning against intimidation by footwear. Once again, the loud footsteps are suggested with the alliteration of 'p' and 't'.

**38** **fulgenti … face** ('with shining torch') is an ablative of description going with **lumina** (which here means 'lamps').

**39–40** **et** is concessive with **imprudens**: 'even out of carelessness'. The couplet forms a conditional sentence, with the protasis ('if' half) using a future perfect indicative (**aspexerit**, from *aspicio*) and the apodosis using a jussive subjunctive (**occulat**: 'let him hide it'). The witness is asked to deny having any recollection of what he has seen, and **per deos omnes** ('by all the gods') is a strong oath.

**41–2** If anyone speaks out of turn, then Venus will punish them. Venus was, according to the legend, born out of the foam which emerged in the sea when the genitals of Uranus fell into the waters after he was castrated by his son Kronos and so has her share of inherited cruelty. **rapido** has the sense of 'snatching up' (from *rapio*) as well as the primary sense of 'fast-flowing'.

**43–57** Tibullus now brings in a familiar figure from elegy (cf. 1.5.59, Propertius 1.1.19–24) – the witch who can help the lover in securing and keeping the favours of his beloved, and who in this case can bewitch the husband into ignorance of the liaison. Clearly there are layers of irony at work here and we are not necessarily meant to take this at face value: it may (after all) be simply another trick to make Delia trust that she can conduct an illicit affair safely.

**43–4** **huic** refers back to the loose-lipped *loquax* of 41–2. **magico … ministerio** – 'by her use of magic'. Magic has a firm presence in ancient literature and is usually the province of women such as Circe and Medea (II.4.55–6n.). **coniunx** ('husband' or 'partner') raises the question of the status of Delia: see introduction on this.

**45–6** Witches in ancient literature are usually credited with these two tricks: drawing down the stars/moon from the sky and turning rivers back on their source. The poet claims 'I have seen' (**vidi**) this to lend extra credence to what he describes (and therefore extra pressure on Delia). **carmine** shows that the means used by the witch were verbal rather than material (as at 62 below). Note the clever word-play whereby the river's reversal is mirrored in the words **vertit iter** and the word **rapidi** underlining the difficulty of the task.

**47–8** The more gruesome skill of necromancy makes use of both burial sites and cremation pyres. The witch splits open the ground and conjures up the dead from their tombs or else summons bones from the pyre while it is still warm (**tepido**). **devocat** ('summons down from [the pyre]') suggests that she may even be reviving the corpses and then making them move down from the fire. **manes** are usually the spirits of the dead rather than their corpses.

**49–50** Note the anaphora on successive lines of **iam** + verb, as of **cum libet** in lines 51–2 and then **sola** in 53–4. This repetition of words suggests the incantation of the witch and adds to the rhetorical persuasion of the poet. **magico stridore** ('with her magic shrieking') she 'holds' the 'platoons from the underworld' against their will and then 'orders' them to retreat when they have been sprinkled with milk – which was commonly used to draw the dead (as at Homer *Odyssey* 10.519). The witch does all this to demonstrate her power and the poet sees this as proof that if she can do all that then she will *a fortiori* be able to bewitch Delia's *coniunx*.

**51–2 cum libet** – 'when it pleases her' suggests that her weather-magic is whimsical more than targeted but is all part of her repertoire. The sudden scattering of clouds is not so odd: but this witch can produce snows in summer which is more impressive and is stressed by postponing the key word **nives** to the end of the line and the sentence. **tristi** refers to the 'overcast' sky.

**53** Her reputation (**dicitur**) is that she alone (**sola**) 'holds' the 'evil herbs' of Medea. Medea was the daughter of King Aeetes of Colchis who used her magic powers (taught to her by Hecate herself) to help the Greek hero Jason secure the golden fleece. Her mastery of the pharmacopeia was legendary and she could use it for good or (as here (**malas**)) for evil purposes.

**54** Hecate was the Greek goddess of the Underworld associated with witches and often accompanied by dogs. She was associated with the place where three roads meet (cf. 1.5.15–16) and accordingly entitled *Trivia*. Her power here is underlined by the juxtaposed **sola feros** and the intensifying prefix **per-**.

**55 quis** = *quibus*. **posses** is a subjunctive in a relative final clause ('with which you could …')

**56** Spitting was a way of averting bad fortune (see 97–8 below) and the act is enacted in the consonants: *ter … ter dictis despue*. Three is something of a magic number (cf. 1.3.11, 1.5.14, 1.5.16) often used in ritual.

**57–8** The spell bewitches the *coniunx* (here simply 'that man' (**ille**)) so that he will not be able to believe anyone talking about 'us' (**nobis**: i.e. poet and Delia). The second line takes this to the wonderfully paradoxical conclusion that he would not even believe himself (**sibi**) if he saw the two of them in bed together, a trope which takes the 'dolt of a husband' theme (also found in comedy and mime) to new levels. The lovers' bed is once again *mollis* (cf. 1.2.19). The sentence is a straightforward conditional with a future tense (**poterit**) in the apodosis and a future perfect (**viderit**) in the protasis.

**59–60** Tibullus clearly doubts Delia's fidelity and warns her not to use this charm as a license to stray elsewhere: 'the spell only works for you and me' (i.e. not for you with anybody else). He enjambs **omnia** to up the stakes ominously: 'for he will find out the rest ... all of it'. Line 61 is framed by **omnia ... nihil**.

**61-6 quid credam?** – 'Why should I believe her?' is a rhetorical question whose answer will (perhaps) reassure Delia, who would have reservations about trusting the witch. The words backfire: Tibullus describes a ceremony in which the witch claimed to be removing his love altogether, at which he tells her to make the love mutual rather than non-existent. Both wishes seem to have failed as he clearly loves her but there is little evidence of her sharing his feelings. **nempe** begins the explanation ('why she even ...').

**62 solvere** – to 'unbind' or 'untie' applies to the poet's love which was 'bound' by the initial bond of love.

**63-4** The ritual is elaborate, with fire (**taedis**), purifying sulphur (often used to coat the torch used in the fire-purification: cf. I.5.11–12) and animal sacrifice to invoke the gods of the underworld (**magicos ... deos**). Olympian gods were offered white animals, underworld gods had dark victims: this one 'fell to the earth' (**concidit**) when stunned by the witch. **nocte serena** suggests that the moon was out – commonly associated with witches, with magic and with Hecate: cf. Medea at Ovid *Metamorphoses* VII.180–1.

**65-6** Take all the subjunctives after **orabam** in an indirect command understanding *ut*: 'I was not praying [that] my love should disappear totally ... but I [was praying that] our love might be mutual and that I would not be willing to be able to live without her'. Line 66 is framed by the verbs.

**67-72** The poet now turns to the *coniunx*, who seems to be out of town on military campaign, fighting in Cilicia, and has locked Delia inside the house, like the *durus vir* in Ovid *Amores* III.4. Military service or trade overseas would be a problem for many a romantic lover as it removes him from his beloved and leaves her vulnerable to seduction (cf. Horace *Odes* III.7, Propertius I.6–8, III.12). Tibullus the lover is hoping to capitalise on her isolation while Tibullus the poet repeats the themes of the simple life at home over against the quest for money and glory abroad, as at I.1.41–52. Note here the binary opposition of the husband (unfeeling, stupid, seeking money abroad, camping with soldiers or sitting proud on a horse) and the lover (caring, wise, not caring about money and living on the land with his beloved in a state of detached inconspicuous poverty with his oxen).

**66–8** Tibullus would not wish to live without her (**posse carere**) whereas this dolt chooses to go away even though he could have her (**posset habere**): *habere* here has sexual overtones. **ferreus** does double duty: the soldier is 'clad in iron' but also 'hard as nails' and unfeeling. He is **stultus** both in his leaving his lover and also in his blind pursuit of booty and violence. Note the harsh alliteration of 'f'.

**69–70** **licet** + subjunctive (**agat**) has concessive force: 'let him drive …'. The 'long-haired' Cilicians were notorious for their toughness (see I.7.16), adding to the folly of the venture (who would want to face these brutes?) but also creating a potentially heroic achievement for the poet's rival, whose success is stated twice (**victas** … **capto**). Tibullus' patron Messalla went on campaign there, as I.7 describes. **Martia castra** – 'martial camp' (Mars was the god of war). The phrasing is mock-heroic, as is the following line.

**71–2** He was 'iron-clad' (**ferreus**) in 67: he is now woven (**contextus**, from *contexo*) from head to toe (**totus**, repeated in anaphora) in gold and silver, presumably from the booty: his conspicuous appearance would also make him stand out as a target and here has the effect of reducing the man to a heap of metal. **conspiciendus** is a gerundive of obligation.

**73–4** The sequence is: 'if only I myself could yoke oxen – with you, my Delia – and …'. **mea** and **Delia** are vocatives. The poet disclaims any desire for wealth and power, exchanging the soldier's horse for the farmer's oxen. **solito** – the 'usual' mountain – suggests the rejection of exotic excitement in favour of rural stability.

**75–6** The attractions are sexual as well as agricultural as at I.1.45–6. The poet has 'gentle' arms and 'soft' sleep in contrast to the tough-guy soldier sleeping out on campaign. **et inculta** is concessive ('even on the rough' [ground]) his sleep would be 'soft' if Delia were with him.

**77–80** The poet exalts happy poverty over unhappy wealth (cf. 1.1.51–2, 1.8.39–40), drawing on the contrast of his rural poverty and the soldier's acquisition of precious metals and picking up the topic of 'sleep' to broaden the thinking more generally as he does with his elevation of poverty in 1.5.61–66. The tone here is Epicurean, with imagery from Lucretius (II.34–36). Note the contrast of the lover's soft sleep on the grass (76) with the insomniac weeping on expensive bedclothes of the lovesick man.

**77–8** 'Tyrian purple' was a byword for expensive luxury: the people of Tyre in Phoenicia perfected the extraction of a deep red dye from shellfish which was used to colour cloth. **secundo** here means both 'reciprocated' but also 'blessed by the gods'. **věnit** (present tense: 'night is coming') adds a touch of painful anticipation of the unhappy lover's insomnia. **vigilanda** is a gerundive of obligation.

**79–80** The poet lists three aspects of the luxurious lifestyle in a tricolon crescendo of futility: **plumae** ('feathers') were stuffed into downy pillows, **stragula picta** were 'embroidered bedclothes' and the 'sound of calm water' refers to the use of fountains made to run inside the homes of the super-rich such as Pliny (*Letters* V.6.22–3).

**81–8** The poet changes tack abruptly in a fit of self-pity and self-recrimination. Clearly the door has not opened despite his pleadings, and Venus' lack of help makes him wonder whether he has offended her. If so, he is ready to abase himself to regain her help.

**81–2** **num** introduces a question expecting the answer 'no'. The poet assumes that his offence was verbal and so his 'wicked tongue' is now 'paying the penalty'. He butters up Venus with laudatory language – **magnae . . . numina . . . sanctis** (84) **. . . sancto** (88): but this is intended also for Delia's ears to assure her of his piety.

**83–4** He moves from blasphemy to outright sacrilege. *fero* can mean 'I report' and so here the passive form **feror** means 'am I said to . . .'. The offence imagined is of stealing garlands from the altars (**focis**) – presumably to give them to his girlfriend (cf. II.4.23) or to hang them on her door (as at 1.2.14).

**85–8** **dubitem** is a present subjunctive in a mixed conditional sentence with **si merui** ('if I have deserved [punishment], then I would not hesitate to …') followed by four infinitives listing his expiatory punishments over four lines and working up to the climactic head-banging of line 88. The god's sanctity is stressed throughout (**sanctis** … **sacratis** … **sancto**). Interestingly, the behaviour described is close to that of the locked-out lover himself who also lies prostrate (II.4.22, Horace *Odes* III.10.3) and kisses the doorway (Lucretius IV.1179). **templis** is locative dative ('at the temples').

**88** Head-banging is a sign of frustrated grief but here also one of self-punishment. Note how the poet is banging his head with the door-post and not vice versa. The act here serves a double purpose – to expiate his guilt and also attract her attention.

**89–90** **at tu** – the poet now turns to the *Schadenfreude* of an imaginary person, who is 'happily' (**laetus**) observing his 'misfortunes' (**mala**) and gives him a warning: **caveto** is an archaic 'future' imperative ('look out for yourself (**tibi**)'): cf. 1.5.69. Note the heavy spondees of line 89 as the poet utters his stern rebuke. **usque** has the sense of 'unceasingly' and goes with **uni** (dative (of disadvantage) from *unus*): the god will eventually change her focus from one man to another.

**91–2** **vidi ego** – as at 43, the poet appeals to his own experience to emphasise the truth of his words. Understand *eum* before **qui**. The contrast is between the **iuvenum** (whose love was mocked) and the **senem** (who ends up being mocked much worse for the same thing). **post** is adverbial ('later on'). The metaphor in **subdere colla** is of an animal putting its neck into the halter and being held in the 'bonds' of Venus (cf. II.4.3). The key word is **senem**, postponed until the end of the line. **colla** is plural for singular.

**93-6** Roman poets and writers of comedy often make fun of older women seeking young lovers (see e.g. Horace *Epode* 8, *Odes* III.15), but in this case the figure of fun is an old man courting young girls. The mocker is now the butt of mockery. Old men are supposed to be happily freed from the slavery of lust (according to (e.g.) Plato *Republic* 329b, Cicero *De Senectute* 47: a more negative view is voiced by Juvenal 10.204–9) and this old fool is easy prey. The mockery is enhanced by the comic details: his age is shown by his quavering voice (**tremula ... voce**), the earnest composition of his chat-up lines (**blanditias**), and his white hair (**canas ... comas**) which he tries (**velle**) to shape (**fingere**) into something youthful and attractive. His disgrace extends to being a locked-out lover himself: he 'was not ashamed (**nec ... puduit**) to stand in front of the door'. The maid was often used as a go-between to take and return messages between a lover and his mistress: **medio ... foro** shows that he is brazen enough to do this in public.

**97-8** A neat reversal: whereas he used to laugh at young people in love (91), he is now mocked by young men, the repetition of **hunc** placing the old man verbally in the middle of the **puer ... iuvenis**. **iuvenis** is singular for plural. **despuit**: spitting into one's bosom is supposed to ward off bad luck when confronted with the insane or the unclean (as in Theophrastus *Characters* 16.15), and this old man fulfils both categories. **molles** here denotes 'young'.

**99-100** The poem ends with a prayer to Venus for mercy and a plea to her self-interest. As he is her devoted servant, she would be ill advised to hurt him and so rob herself of his worship. The language is powerful: she must be bitter (**acerba**) to do this, and burning one's own harvest is an act of supreme folly.

## I.5

Tibullus and Delia have quarreled and the repentant poet wishes to be reunited with her (1–8). He reminds her of how he helped her recover from sickness (9–17) but tells us that Delia has since moved on and that her new man is rich (17–18). The poet's dreams of an idyllic life with her (19–34) are now in tatters (35–6). His attempts to divert his affections with wine and women have been useless (37–40). Delia has bewitched him by her beauty (41–6) but he blames a female pimp for introducing Delia to her new partner and curses this woman violently (47–58). He pleads that poor lovers are more attentive than rich ones (59–66), but her door remains shut (67–8). He ends the poem with a warning to her new lover that his days are also numbered (69–76).

The poem is an interesting exercise in self-recrimination. It also presents the anguished and tormented mental state of the rejected lover struggling to deal with his feelings towards his ex-lover, her new boyfriend, an (imaginary?) older woman who may have broken them up, and himself. As with I.2, the text is a psychological dramatization of a man in the throes of bitter remorse, jealousy and sexual passion.

**1** **asper** ('angry') is a character trait which he shows to the full in his curse at lines 49–56. **ferre** has either a future sense ('I would bear') or potential ('I could bear'). **discidium** here means 'splitting up' of a relationship. The imperfect tense of **loquebar** is important: the poet kept telling himself that he did not mind the separation (when he obviously did).

**2** **gloria fortis** ('macho bragging') shows the poet's former attitude as so much posturing.

**3–4** A simile comparing the emotional turmoil of the poet with the whirling of a child's spinning top (**turben**). Note the interlocking word order: take **per plana** with **sola** ('over the level ground') and **citus** with **turben**. The top was made to spin with a whip (**verbere**) and the speed is enhanced by the fact that this child is expert at it (**assueta ... ab arte**: 'with practised skill'). **ab** here indicates 'by means of'.

**5–6** The poet calls himself **ferum** ('uncouth') and issues orders for himself to be punished. Burning (**ure**) and torture (**torque** literally means 'twist' and suggests the rack) were used on slaves. Take **ne** before **libeat** as a purpose clause ('so that I may have no desire …'). The poet paints himself vividly in this choice of vocabulary: **magnificum** picks up *gloria fortis* from line 2, **doma** (singular imperative from *domo*) suggests the 'taming' of a wild animal, while **horrida** (literally 'shaggy') has the sense here of 'savage'.

**7–8** The poet addresses Delia, begging for her mercy. Take **te** with **quaeso** ('I beg you') and **per** with **foedera** ('by the bonds of our secret affair'). **lecti** literally means 'bed' but here is used in metonymy for the sexual affair, and **furtivi** (literally 'stolen') suggests 'secret, adulterous'. Venus was the god of love and her name is used in metonymy for 'love'. **compositum caput** ('the head laid next to [mine/yours]') indicates the shared pillow.

**9–10** The poet claims the credit for Delia's recovery from illness, with boastful language (**ille ego … te dicor … eripuisse** – 'I am the man who … is said to have saved you'). Note the accumulation of words to indicate Delia's sickness: **tristi morbo defessa iaceres**. A *votum* was a prayer, often accompanied by a vow to carry out an act of devotion to the god.

**11–12** **sulpure** – sulphur was used as a cleansing agent in purification rituals. **circum** is adverbial ('all around'). **puro** here means 'purifying'. The old woman (**anus**) had sung her 'magic spell' before (**praecinuisset**) the poet used the sulphur.

**13–14** The poet also claims to have used 'sacred meal' (**sancta … mola**: i.e. ground barley and salt) 'three times' (**ter**: cf. 1.2.56) to avert the evil dreams which would plague Delia in her illness. The key verb is **procuravi** ('I expiated') and **ipse** shows that the poet did this personally rather than entrusting it to a priest. **ne possent** is a negative final clause ('to prevent them being able to harm you').

**15–16** The narrative continues, with the poet (**ipse** again) dressed in ritual garb of a woollen head-dress and with his tunic undone. The woollen garland was worn by a priest conducting a sacrifice, where garments were also worn loose (cf. Ovid *Metamorphoses* VII.182). *Trivia* ('the crossroads deity') refers to Hecate, the goddess of the underworld also identified with the moon and with Diana: she was invoked nine times (which as a multiple of three has magic significance: see 1.2.56n.).

**17-18** After eight lines of detail, the poet sums up wistfully that his efforts just helped another 'lucky' (**felix**) man who now 'enjoys' (**fruitur**) her love, and is 'making use of' (**utitur**) Tibullus' prayers.

**19  felicem** picks up **felix** from the previous line and applies it to himself (**mihi**) in his former imagination (**fingebam**, emphasised in enjambement). **fuisses** is a pluperfect subjunctive in a conditional within reported speech: 'I imagined that my life [would be] happy, if you had been restored to health'.

**20**  The line is a damning summary of his failure: it was all in his mind (**fingebam**), he was mad to think it (**demens**) and the god said no (**renuente deo** – an ablative absolute). As in 1.2.79-82, the poet is quick to blame divine interference for his misfortune.

**21-34**  The poet itemises his own fantasy, couched in confident future indicatives or else jussive subjunctives.

**21  aderit** (from *adsum*) has the sense of 'will be with me': Delia is imagined as working to help the poet.

**22  area** – 'threshing-floor' – was the place where the farmer would 'thresh' (**teret**) the harvest (**messes**). **sole calente** (ablative absolute) reminds us that the threshing was done in the open air and the blazing sun.

**23-4  lintribus** – 'troughs' held the grapes to be trodden, while *mustum* is the rough grape juice produced by this process. **pede** is singular for plural, and **veloci** adds a touch of efficiency to the process.

**25-6**  Delia is imagined as needing time to learn the country ways, with anaphora of **consuescet**. Roman slaves could produce offspring and these 'home-bred' slaves were known as *vernae*. Here the chattering (**garrulus**) little slave 'will learn to play in the lap of his loving mistress' (Delia).

**27-8** Take **deo agricolae** together ('to the farming god'). Delia will know how to offer (**ferre**) grapes for the vines, ears of corn (**spicas**) for the crops, and a sacrificial meal (**dapem**) for the flock'. Keeping the gods on side was vital for the health and prosperity of the estate. Note the lengthening of the final 'e' of **segete** before the two consonants starting **s**picas.

**29-30** A pair of jussive subjunctives: 'let [Delia] direct everybody, and let everything be her concern'. **curae** is a predicative dative with **sint**. The subjunctive **iuvet** is again a wish: 'may it please me to be nothing in the entire house'. Tibullus is happy to take a back seat in the running of his farm, as shown in the antithesis of **tota** ... **nihil**.

**31-2 Messalla** – Tibullus' patron (see introduction): **meus** indicates affection. The subjunctive **detrahat** is in a relative final clause: 'for whom Delia is to ...'. The choice nature of the apples is stressed by the adjectives **dulcia** and **selectis**.

**33-4** The final syllable of **virum** would normally elide into the next word (*vir*um *hunc*) but this would spoil the scansion and so we have to posit a hiatus between the two words. Some editors have emended the words to remove this problem. **curet**, **paret** and **gerat** are all jussive subjunctives. Delia, who is by now in the poet's imagination the mistress of the household, is here acting as the servant of the distinguished guest at their 'feast' (**epulas**).

**35-6 fingebam** picks up the same word from line 20 to round off this section. **vota** is to be taken with **haec**. The metaphor of unfulfilled wishes and prayers being tossed away on the winds is common in Latin poetry. Armenia was a territory far to the east of Rome here used as a byword for oriental distance – an exoticism increased with the adjective **odoratos** referring to the spices and perfumes coming from the east.

**37-8** The commonplace that sad lovers drown their sorrows in drink (cf. 1.2.1) is here enlivened by the stark metaphor of the wine transformed into tears.

**39-40** **saepe** indicates that the poet attempted diversionary sex on a regular basis. **gaudia** here refers to 'orgasm' and **deseruit** ... **Venus** is a metonymic way of indicating that the poet suddenly became impotent as the goddess 'reminded me of my mistress'. **dominae** is crucial to this: he was still under the command of Delia.

**41-2** **devotum** – 'under a spell' (from *devoveo*: cf. **devovet** at 44). The **femina** who made this claim is presumably the **aliam** of 39: she is explaining his disappointing performance and telling people (**narrat**) to his embarrassment (**a pudet** is an exclamation: 'oh for shame!') that his '[mistress] knows wicked things' (i.e. is skilled in magic).

**43-6** Delia <u>has</u> bewitched him – but by her beauty and not by magic.

**43-4** There is a contrast between words (**verbis**) and physical charms, and the poet uses the verb **devovet** (usually connoting supernatural rituals) for the very natural assets which 'bewitch' him. **facie** here means 'beauty'. Beautiful women in Latin poetry are often described (however implausibly) as having blonde hair, although we also hear about hair dyes and wigs. Note here that Tibullus still regards Delia as 'my girl' (**nostra puella**).

**45-6** Unlike Propertius, Tibullus does not often use mythology as a source of exemplary material, but here he compares Delia to the sea-nymph Thetis who was given in marriage to the mortal Peleus: their meeting and idyllic marriage is described in Catullus (64.1-49, 265-408) but the comparison is not without its dark side. Thetis and Peleus had one son (Achilles) and split up shortly afterwards, leaving Peleus a byword for a lonely old man in Homer's *Iliad*. Peleus was from Thessaly (**Haemonium**), and Thetis is described as a **Nereis** ('sea-nymph', born from the sea-god Nereus). 'Rode on her bridled fish' refers to the tale later told in Ovid (*Metamorphoses* XI.237) that Thetis liked to ride naked on a dolphin.

**47-8** Delia's charms ('these things') have damaged (**nocuere**) the poet, but he is unwilling to blame her and chooses instead to blame an unnamed 'crafty pimp-woman' (**callida lena**) for losing his place to a rich lover. **quod** here means 'as to the fact that (a rich lover...)'. **huic** is dative with **adest** (he is 'there for her'). The **lena** is the female form of the male pimp (*leno*) who was a much more threatening figure and who often owned the house in which the girls entertained their lovers in exchange for 'gifts' (cf. 59-60, II.4.33-39).

**49-56** An exuberant and imaginative curse on the **lena**, conveyed in a string of jussive subjunctives (**edat ... bibat ... volitent ... canat ... quaerat ... currat ... ululet ... agat**). The aggressive language confirms that this poet can indeed be **asper** (cf. 1.5.1). The **lena** is cast in animal imagery throughout: she is to eat bloody meat, drink gall, go scavenging for food from sacrifices, and run naked howling like a wolf before being driven away by dogs.

**49-50** The line is framed with words denoting blood. **ore cruento** is the sort of language used of wild animals in epic poetry (e.g. a lion at Virgil *Aeneid* IX.341, XII.8). **tristia** often (as here) denotes 'bitter-tasting' and the sourness is increased with the adjective **multo**.

**51-2** Ghosts are to fly around her – take **circum** with **hanc**. These ghosts are not contented spirits but the sort of unhappy ghosts whom Aeneas meets in the underworld (Virgil *Aeneid* VI.426-476). They are roaming the earth and lamenting their lot 'constantly' (**semper**: stressed in enjambement). The **strix** was the 'screech-owl' and was said to have great magical significance not least because of its nocturnal screeching. When it perched on the roof it was a bad omen (as Virgil *Aeneid* IV.462-3) and **violenta** (nom. sing. agreeing with the **strix**) here alludes to the tale that they sucked the blood out of young children.

**53-4** **fame stimulante** is an ablative of cause with **furens**: 'driven mad by her raging hunger'. Note the lengthening of the final 'e' of **fam̄e** before the two consonants beginning s̄timulante (cf. 27-8n.). Her hunger is going to force her to seek out both (**-que**) grasses from tombs – an act of disrespect to the dead – and (**et**) bones which even wolves have turned down.

**55** Mention of wolves leads the poet to imagine the **lena** running and howling as if turned into a wolf: lycanthropy is memorably narrated in Petronius *Satyricon* 62, where the man-wolf 'howled and ran into the woods'. **inguinibus nudis** ('with naked groin') suggests that she is totally naked: if her groin is uncovered then we can assume that the rest of her is also. The phrase brings out her shame and degradation and is also fitting for this woman who meddled in sexual matters to have her own sexual parts exposed in disgrace.

**56** These dogs might be normal dogs: but the connection with the crossroads (**e triviis**) suggests that they are the hounds of Hecate the goddess of the crossroads (see 15–16n.). **post** is adverbial ('from behind') and the object of **agat** is the **lena**.

**57 eveniet** – a confident future indicative after the wishlist of the previous lines. Note here the staccato style of short snappy phrases. **amanti** is a dative of possession with **sunt**.

**58** Venus is savage (cf. 1.2.39–40) when abandoned and when her contract is broken (**iniusta lege**). So far, the poet has been cursing the **lena** and is perhaps still blaming her for invalidating his lovers' contract with Delia – but there is also scope to see the poet as warning Delia herself not to cross him.

**59–60 sagae:** *saga* means 'witch' but here alludes to the **lena**, who is here described as 'grasping' (**rapacis**) and who seems to have infected Delia with her own avarice. The cynical conclusion that 'all love is overcome with gifts' is one explanation for the poet's replacement with a wealthy lover. **quam primum** – 'as soon as possible'.

**61–6** Praise of an impoverished lover as more dependable and attentive than a rich one. The steadfast loyalty is brought out by **semper** and **fidus comes**. Note the anaphora of **pauper** beginning each successive couplet and the plosive alliteration in lines 61–2.

**61–2** *praesto esse* + dative is 'to be available' like an attendant.

**63–4** The lover will escort his beloved in the 'choking column of a crowd' – a function often performed by slaves. **subicietque manus** has the sense of using his hands to push aside the crowd.

**65–6** **furtim** suggests 'illicitly' (cf. 7–8n.) and the phrase 'private friends' could mean either his own friends or Delia's 'friends': in both cases this would be done behind the back of (**occultos ... furtim**) her husband/owner. The removing of sandals suggests a dinner-party and the job is again servile. Delia's feet are idealised as 'snow-white' (**niveo**) just as her hair is blonde (1.5.44).

**67–8** **heu canimus frustra** is an expression of grief and frustration as the focus switches to the door (**ianua**) which refuses to open to him and is emphasised in enjambement. The poet even seems to be rejecting his poetry (**canimus**). **plenā** is ablative going with **manu** which here means 'a hand full [of cash]' (cf. II.4.14): the *dives amator* wins again.

**69** The poet now rounds on this rich lover (**at tu**) with an ominous warning about his own position. **potior** denotes 'superior' or 'more capable'. **timeto** is a 'future' imperative (cf. *caveto* at 1.2.89), often found in laws enjoining public behaviour.

**70** 'Chance turns in a fickle way with a swift turn of the wheel'.

**71–2** Even now (**iam nunc**) somebody (**quidam**) is standing on the threshold, awaiting his chance to replace the current lover. The following lines are satirical in tone as the would-be lover tries both to hide and to show his affection for the girl.

**72** The new suitor's enthusiasm is stressed: note the enjambed **sedulus**, the adverbial **crebro** ('often'), the pair of parallel verbs **prospicit ac refugit** and the continuation of the sentence into the next couplet in his excitement. The present tenses warn the rich lover that these things are already happening.

**73–4** The would-be lover pretends to be walking past her house by chance if anybody sees him and quickly 'runs back' (**recurrit**) to his post. **exscreat** denotes the noisy clearing of the throat with spitting of phlegm to attract her attention.

**75–6** **nescio quid** (literally 'I know not what') means 'something or other'. **utere** (imperative singular from *utor*) means here 'enjoy [your good fortune]' (cf. 1.8.48). The poem ends (as does 1.2) with a fitting metaphor ('your boat sails on running water') to warn the poet's rival. His boat is only light (**linter**) and the running river will soon force him into the heavy seas.

## II.4

The poet is a slave to his mistress and is unhappy about it (1–12). Poetry is no use in securing the favours of his harsh mistress (13–20) and he considers turning to crime and sacrilege to acquire the gifts he needs for her (21–6). Luxury in female attire is the cause of female greed and infidelity, leading to lovers being locked out (27–38). The greedy mistress deserves to lose everything and will die a lonely death (39–44), whereas the good mistress will have a lover to attend her even if she lives to be 100 (45–50). The poem ends with a remarkable declaration of servitude: the poet would be willing to sell his house and even drink noxious potions if only it would make her look kindly on him (51–60).

The mistress in this poem is no longer Delia but a woman called (ominously) Nemesis who treats the poet badly, continuing the argument of the previous poem (II.3) which ended with the image of the poet going to plough fields under the orders of this same cruel mistress. She cannot be won by love but only by money and the poet is compelled to abandon any moral scruples (along with even poetry itself) in his pursuit of her: his addiction has made him helpless in her hands. Like Catullus in poem 76, the unhappy lover is caught in a relationship which is painful but which he cannot escape. The contrast with the earlier poems is deliberate: imagined torture (I.5.5–6) is now happening in real life at least in his mental state, and the anonymous woman's claim (I.5.41–2) that Delia was a witch is brought vividly to life in the closing line of this poem as Nemesis is imagined pounding the potions of witchcraft to feed to her ardent helpless lover for her amusement. The figure of the deluded and helpless male abused and exploited by his beloved is one which we find again and again in world literature: see for example Vladimir Nabokov's *Laughter in the Dark* and Heinrich Mann's *Professor Unrat*.

This poem also has self-aware and ironic touches: the rejection of poetry in a fine elegiac poem is deliberate and leaves the reader thinking that this text is itself part of the lost world which Tibullus now has to abandon in his servitude. The poet expresses his idealism both when decrying the venal state of society (with a curse (27–30) on the purveyors of wealth) and when imagining a happy free relationship extending even beyond death (45–50). These happy moments are just dreams, however, and the poem ends with the male's total subjection – body and soul – to his cruel venal mistress. Some have seen this poem as a desperate appeal to the girl's better nature, but it reads more plausibly as a howl of anguish and an appeal to the poet's friends bewailing his fate.

**1** **hic** – 'here'. **servitium** is 'slavery': Roman love poets often speak of the *servitium amoris* (see Introduction) and the girl is appropriately called his 'mistress' (**dominam**). **paratam** here means 'planned'.

**2** **libertas illa paterna** – 'that traditional freedom' of the Roman male citizen to do and speak as he pleased – is here addressed in the vocative case. **vale** – 'farewell'. **mihi** (like **misero** in line 4) is a dative of disadvantage, meaning 'as far as I am concerned'.

**3–4** Notice the two passive verbs juxtaposed (**datur teneor**) as the poet uses the language of slavery (**catenis … vincla**). The master enforcing the slavery is the god of love (**Amor**).

**5–6** **urit / uror** shows effective repetition over the line-end and line 6 is framed with words of fire, denoting both the physical burning with which slaves could be punished and also the metaphorical 'burning' of his passion. **io** here is a cry of pain, and **saeva puella** must refer to the mistress: the god of love (**Amor**) is the torturer.

**7** **o** is an exclamation and does not elide with the first vowel of **ego** (scan: ō ĕgŏ).

**7–10** The poet would prefer to be without any sensation at all than to suffer these pains of love. He uses powerful adjectives: the mountains are 'icy-cold' (**gelidis**), just as he wishes he were 'frigid' rather than on fire with love, the winds are 'mad' (**insanis**) like the love which torments him. Maritime imagery is elsewhere used of the stormy waters of sexual passion (cf. Horace *Odes* I.5.6–7), especially as Venus was born from the sea (cf. I.2.40): here the sea is 'vast' (**vasti**) and the wave is 'ship-wrecking' (**naufraga**).

**7–8** **ne possim** is a negative final clause ('so that I might not be able …') and **quam mallem** is a wish ('how I would prefer …').

**9–10** **vel** is to be taken first ('or to stand …'). **quam** is the relative pronoun picking up **cautes** from the line before. Line 10 reads: 'which the ship-wrecking wave of the vast sea battered'. **tunderet** is an imperfect subjunctive as the whole sentence is an extended wish. Here **tunderet unda** is pleasingly onomatopoeic for the waves battering the cliff (cf. Catullus 11.4).

**11–12** A powerful couplet, with repetition of *amarus* in different forms and a strong metaphor in **felle madent** – the times are 'soaked in gall' with **tristi** meaning 'bitter-tasting' as at 1.5.50. **nunc** means 'as things are', recalling the poet back to reality after his fantasy of lines 7–10.

**13–14** Ironically, this elegiac poet tells us in a poem that his elegies are of no use. Apollo was the god of poetry, prophecy, medicine and the sun; and his inspiration of the poets was legendary. This poetry may be divinely-inspired but is still of no value to the philistine Nemesis, who is constantly (**usque**) 'demanding money' (**pretium flagitat**) with 'open hand' like a beggar.

**15–16** Line 2 bade farewell to freedom: here the poet bids farewell to the Muses if they will not 'be of use to the lover' in what is a crudely utilitarian approach to literature. The Muses were the nine female deities of artistic inspiration. The poet here rudely tells them that he is not worshipping them in order to compose military epics or didactic poetry: such poetry was often regarded as 'useful' to the reader but this poet only has one (unfulfilled) use in mind for his poems. **canenda** is the gerundive from *cano*: the poet is not asking the Muses for 'wars to be sung about'.

**17–18** The reference here is to didactic epic such as was written by Lucretius: he scorns astronomical information as useless for this lover. Translate: 'nor am I reporting the paths of the sun and the way in which the moon, when she has filled out her disc, turns her horses around and returns'. Ironically, Tibullus in telling us what he is not going to write, does a very good job of writing excellent didactic Latin, with a vivid present indicative (**recurrit**) where we might expect the subjunctive in an indirect question. **versis ... equis** is an ablative absolute (literally: 'when her horses have been turned round').

**19-20** The only 'paths' which this poet is interested in are the ones leading to his mistress: if his poems do not secure him access to her, then it is farewell to the Muses. Line 20 repeats **ite procul, Musae** from line 15 in ring-composition. **nihil** is adverbial ('not at all') and **ista** (i.e. *carmina*) is contemptuous.

**21** He rejected 'wars' (**bella**) as poetic subject-matter in line 16, but here proposes using violence to get gifts for his mistress. **caedem et facinus** is a hendiadys ('bloodshed and deed' for 'deed of bloodshed'). **mihi** is the dative of agent with **sunt dona paranda** ('I must acquire gifts').

**22** Another ironic touch: Tibullus would prefer to commit violence than to end up lying outside a closed door as he was in previous poems (1.2, 1.5.67-8). The suggestion is that only gifts will secure the opening of the door (see 1.5.60). **flebilis** – 'weeping'.

**23-4** Temple-robbing is a heinous crime, involving both larceny and sacrilege (see 1.2.81-4). People would hang up objects in temples as ornamental thank-offerings to the god who had answered their prayer: here the poet proposes to steal these 'ornamental things' (**insignia**), and the word **sacris** underlines the sacrilege: line 24 delivers the punch-line as this frustrated lover will target Venus above all as she has obviously *not* listened to his prayers. **violanda** is a gerundive of obligation (she deserves violation).

**25-6** Venus is prompting him to commit this crime by making him love a greedy mistress – so she deserves his punishment: **facinus** picks up the same word from 21.

**27-8** **pereat** is a subjunctive expressing a wish ('may he die!'). Tibullus uses -**que ... et** here to mean the same as *et ... et* (cf. 17). Note that **quĕ**

remains a short vowel even before the two consonants *sm-*. Green emeralds were named as part of the romantic lover's expenditure in Lucretius (IV.1126) and Tibullus elsewhere (I.1.51) uses them as part of the rich man's gains from overseas commerce. Here they begin a bright sequence of colours continuing with the purple dye applied to a snowy-white fleece in 28.

**28** The *murex* was a shellfish which produced a purple dye (cf. I.2.75): here the word simply indicates the dye. **ovem** (literally 'sheep') by synecdoche simply means 'fleece': but the line when read literally has a suitably surreal quality ('dips a snowy sheep in Tyrian shellfish') which suits his comment on the unnatural nature of this luxury.

**29-30** **addit** is a singular verb with two subjects (**vestis** and **concha**). Coan garments were infamous for being expensive, chic and diaphanous (cf. II.3.53). **concha** (literally 'shell') here indicates the pearl inside the shell: note again the colour contrast of the red sea and the gleaming pearl. Tibullus is not referring to what we term the Red Sea but rather the Persian Gulf, which is rich in pearls.

**31-2** 'These things rendered [women] bad'. A sententious generalization, followed by the cynical remark that women now lock their doors to lovers unless those lovers bring gifts. **clavim** is the accusative singular of *clavis* ('door-key'): note the pathetic fallacy as the door 'felt' the key. Romans kept guard dogs in their houses: note here the barking alliteration of 'c'.

**33-4** **feras** – indefinite second person singular addressed to anyone who has money. The restrictions of the previous couplet are now magically undone – **custodia** picks up **custos**, **claves** picks up **clavim** and **canis** picks up **canis**. In a nice touch of humour, even the dog (**canis ipse**) has been corrupted by the gifts.

**35** Take **caelestis** with **quicumque** ('whichever god'). **caelestis** is an adjective ('heavenly') acting as a noun ('god'), just as **avarae** means 'to a greedy [girl]'.

**36** *multa mala* ('much suffering') is common in the elegists (cf. 1.8.64, 1.9.18, II.3.40, Propertius II.22.1-2) and the poet here laments that beauty (**formam**) has been added to their woes.

**37-8** **fletus** ('weeping') and **rixae** ('lovers' quarrels') are both noisy things (**sonant**) and arise from the greed which makes the greedy girl unsatisfied. **infamis** properly denotes a class of persons (such as prostitutes) who are regarded as unclean: love is personified here as 'wandering' (**erret**) in disgrace, although many editors read *esset* (from *sum*).

**39-40** The poet rounds on the greedy girl herself (**tibi**) in apostrophe, with a curse on her wealth. **pretio** (picking up *pretium* in 33) goes with **victos** ('defeated by the price'). **eripiant** is a jussive subjunctive whose subjects are 'wind and fire' and its object the 'wealth you have gained' (**partas** is from *pario* (here meaning 'to procure')). The wind would of course make the fire all the more fierce.

**41-2** **quin** adds a further thought ('why in fact, let ...') to add human mockery to the financial loss: the string of short words (**quin tua tum**) suggests excitement on the part of the speaker and **laeti** adds *Schadenfreude* to the mix. The normal response to a fire is to put it out: the poet hopes that nobody would do so with this one. **spectent** and **addat** are jussive subjunctives.

**43-4** The punishment continues after her death as the poet wishes her to have no funeral rites. **seu** = *sive* ('or if'). **erit qui** + subjunctive means 'there will be somebody to ...'. **nec ... ullus** means 'and not ... anyone'. Romans took funerals seriously and often spent lavishly on them, but this unloved woman has nobody to mourn or to make offerings. **munus** (literally 'gift') represents either money paid towards the cost of the funeral or gifts (of flowers for instance) for the funeral rites (**exsequias**): these are generally a sad occasion (**maestas**) but unlikely to be so for these laughing young men (**iuvenes ... laeti** 41). The first half of line 44 is marked by sombre heavy monosyllables (**nec qui det maestas**).

**45-6** **licet** + perfect subjunctive here means 'even though she has lived'. **bona** (when applied to a lover) indicates 'free with her favours' – i.e. not charging money for them – and is contrasted with the **avara**. **flebitur** is an impersonal passive (literally 'weeping will happen'): note that it does not specify the number of mourners. **ardentem** ('burning') is of course apt for a funeral pyre but also hints at the flames of passion as well as the house fire of 41–2.

**47-8** Note the juxtaposition of **senior veteres** and the assonance of **veteres veneratus**. The aged lover will place garlands (**serta**) every year (**annua**) on the 'built up' tomb – a tomb which he presumably has paid for. This respectful old man is faithful to his long-standing love and is nothing like the absurd gigolo of I.2.89–96.

**49-50** **discedens** is a present participle ('as he leaves'): **quiescas** (second person present subjunctive) and **sit** (third person present subjunctive) both express his wish ('may you rest ... and may it be'). Roman tombstones often bore the inscription STTL (for *sit tibi terra levis* ('may the earth be light on you')) and the old lover expresses the same sentiment verbally. The emphasis in his words is on peace and quiet (**placide ... securae**).

**51-2** Line 51 is framed by the word **vera** and the two verbs are centrally placed to form a powerful rhetorical question. **illius** refers to Nemesis and **lege** shows her to be the lawmaker in the relationship: 'I must worship love on her terms'. **colendus** is a gerundive of obligation.

**53-4** For **quin** see 41n. Roman homes were more than a building to sleep in: family property passed down the generations and had their own ancestral deities (*Lares* and *Penates*). For any Roman citizen to allow the family home to be sold would amount to him also selling the household gods. **sub imperium** denotes passing into the control of another, while the *titulus* was the label attached to goods up for sale.

**55-6** **veneni** and **herbarum** are both partitive genitives with **quidquid** ('whatever [of] poison ... whatever [of] herbs'). **Circe** was the witch who in Homer *Odyssey* 10 turned Odysseus' men into pigs with her 'wicked potions', while **Medea** (cf. 1.2.53n.) was the princess of Colchis who helped Jason secure the golden fleece and who was a skilled poisoner as shown memorably in Euripides' play *Medea* and also in Ovid *Metamorphoses* VII.224–33. Thessaly was famed as the home of witches. The nature of the potions is not clear: this besotted man does not need a love-potion as he is already in love, and so perhaps he is prepared to undergo any magical transformation to please his cruel mistress.

**57–8** A grotesque image: 'that *hippomanes* which (**quod**), when Venus breathes sexual passion into the unbridled herds, drips from the groin of the mare on heat'. **hippomanes** derives from Greek ('horse-madness') and was well known as an aphrodisiac as early as Aristotle.

**59–60 si modo** – 'if only ...'. After all these vows, the poet tells us what he wants and it is astonishingly little – a smile from this woman. **placido ... vultu** ('with serene countenance') is often used of gods and here raises Nemesis to that level of power over him: interestingly this is the first (and last) time that she is named in this poem. Her name in Greek means 'retribution' and the wording is calculated to display the absurdity of the poet's folly: she is not 'my girl' (**mea**) and her demeanour is anything but **placido** as the preceding 58 lines (and poem II.3) have shown. Even her name is ominous (see Introduction): and yet the speaker continues to hope. The syntax is also complex and distressed: we have a remote conditional with present tense subjunctives **videat** and **bibam** ('if she looked on me ... I would drink') but we also have a jussive subjunctive **misceat** ('let her mix a thousand other herbs') also. **bibam** is also ambiguous: it could be either present subjunctive or else future indicative, ending the poem on a defiant note of futile intent.

# Vocabulary

An asterisk * denotes a word in OCR's Defined Vocabulary List for AS, although the meanings given in this book are not necessarily the same as the ones in the DVL as this vocabulary is tailored to this text. This vocabulary lists every word in the text. Nouns are listed with their genitive singular, and verbs are listed with all their four principal parts. Adjectives are listed with the endings of the different genders (e.g. **cupidus -a -um**) except where the three genders are the same in the nominative where the genitive is listed (e.g.: **demens, dementis**). Short vowels are unmarked but long vowels are marked with macra (e.g. **rapax, rapācis**). Where a word has different meanings in different lines this is indicated with line-references.

| | |
|---|---|
| **a!** | Ah! |
| *****a, ab** (*preposition + ablative*) | by, from |
| **abdō, abdere, abdidī, abditum** | hide |
| **abstineō, abstinēre, abstinuī, abstentum** | keep away from |
| *****absum, abesse, āfuī** | disappear (I.2.65), be missing |
| **ac** | and |
| **acerbus -a -um** | ruthless, merciless |
| *****ad** (*preposition + accusative*) | to, towards, at (I.2.30) |
| **addō, addere, addidī, additum** | add |
| **adeō, adīre, adi(v)ī, aditum** | approach (I.2.83), draw near to (I.5.39), attend on (I.5.61) |
| **aditus -ūs** *m.* | access, path towards |
| **adiuvō, adiuvāre, adiūvī, adiūtum** | help, assist |
| **admoneō, admonēre, admonuī, admonitum** | remind (somebody (*acc.*) of something (*genitive*)) |
| *****adsum, adesse, adfui** | be present, be available |
| **aestīvus -a -um** | in summer |
| **afferō, afferre, attulī, allātum** | contribute, give |
| **afflō, afflāre, afflāvī, afflātum** | breathe on |

AS

| | |
|---|---|
| *agmen, agminis *n.* | throng, crowd |
| *agō, agere, ēgī, actum | drive |
| agricola -ae *m.* | farmer |
| *aliquis, aliquid | someone, something |
| *alius -a -um | another, other |
| *alter, altera, alterum | the other |
| amārus -a -um | bitter, harsh |
| amātor -ōris *m.* | lover |
| *amīcus -ī *m.* | friend |
| *amō, amāre, amāvī, amātum | love |
| *amor, amōris *m.* | love |
| Amor, Amōris *m.* | God of Love |
| *ancilla -ae *f.* | maidservant |
| *angustus -a -um | confined, narrow |
| anima -ae *f.* | spirit |
| *annus -ī *m.* | year |
| annuus -a -um | yearly |
| *ante (*preposition + accusative*) | before |
| ante (*adverbial*) | in front (I.2.69) |
| anus, anūs *f.* | old woman |
| anxius -a -um | troubled, anxious |
| apertus -a -um | opened |
| Apollo, Apollinis *m.* | Apollo |
| *aqua -ae *f.* | water |
| *arbor, arboris *f.* | tree |
| ardeō, ardēre, arsī, arsum | burn |
| ārea -ae *f.* | threshing-floor |
| *argentum -ī *n.* | silver |
| *arma -ōrum *n.pl.* | weapons, warfare |
| Armenius -ī *m.* | an Armenian |
| *ars, artis *f.* | skill |
| artus -a -um | close-packed, dense |
| asper, aspera, asperum | angry (I.5.1), savage (I.5.56) |
| aspergō, aspergere, aspersī, aspersum | sprinkle |
| aspiciō, aspicere, aspexī, aspectum | catch sight of, look at |
| assuētus -a -um | usual, accustomed |
| *at | but |
| atque | and |
| auctor -ōris *m.* | inspirer, source |

AS

| | |
|---|---|
| *audeō, audēre, ausus sum | to be bold |
| aurum -ī n. | gold |
| *aut | or |
| avāritia -ae f. | avarice, greed |
| avārus -a -um | grasping, greedy |
| avītus -a -um | ancestral, belonging to the family |
| | |
| bacchus -ī m. | wine |
| *bellum -ī n. | war |
| *bene (adverb from bonus) | well, happily |
| *bibō, bibere, bibī | drink |
| blanditia -ae f. | affectionate speech |
| blandus -a -um | affectionate |
| *bonum -ī n. | good thing |
| *bonus -a -um | generous (II.4.45) |
| bōs, bŏvis m./f. | ox |
| | |
| *caedēs, caedis f. | slaughter |
| caelestis -is m./f. | god |
| *caelum -ī n. | sky |
| caerulus -a -um | sea-blue |
| caleō, calēre, caluī | be hot |
| callidus -a -um | clever, crafty |
| candidus -a -um | gleaming |
| *canis -is m./f. | dog (I.2.54, I.5.56, II.4.32, II.4.34) |
| *canō, canere, cecinī, cantum | sing |
| cantus -ūs m. | song, singing |
| cānus -a -um | white (I.2.94) |
| *capiō, capere, cēpī, captum | capture |
| *caput, capitis n. | head |
| cardō, cardinis f. | hinge |
| careō, carēre, caruī, caritum | to live without, lack |
| carmen, carminis n. | singing (I.2.46, I.2.56, I.5.12), poetry (II.4.13, II.4.19) |
| *cārus -a -um | beloved |
| *castra -ōrum n.pl. | army camp |
| catēna -ae f. | chain |
| caterva -ae f. | platoon |
| *causa -ae f. | cause, explanation |

| | |
|---|---|
| cautēs -is f. | cliff face |
| caveō, cavēre, cāvī, cautum | be on guard |
| cavus -a -um | open |
| *celer, celeris, celere | swift, quick |
| *cēlō, cēlāre, cēlāvī, cēlātum | hide |
| centum | 100 |
| *cernō, cernere, crēvī, crētum | see, find out |
| *cētera -ōrum n.pl. | all the rest, everything else |
| Cilices, Cilicum m.pl. | The Cilicians |
| Circē, Circēs f. | Circe (II.4.55) |
| *circum (preposition + accusative) | around |
| circumterō, circumterere | press on all sides |
| citus -a -um | swift |
| claudō, claudere, clausī, clausum | close |
| clāvis -is f. (acc. sing. clavim) | key |
| *coepī, coepisse | begin, start |
| collum -ī n. | neck |
| *colō, colere, coluī, cultum | cultivate (I.5.21), worship (II.4.16, II.4.52) |
| coma -ae f. | hair |
| *comes, comitis m. | companion |
| compescō, compescere, compescuī | to check, restrain |
| compleō, complēre, complēvī, complētum | fill, complete |
| compōnō, compōnere, composuī, compositum | compose (I.2.55, I.2.93) lay beside (I.5.8) |
| compositus -a -um | pre-arranged (I.2.22) |
| concha -ae f. | shell |
| concidō, concidere, concidī | fall down (as sacrifice) |
| *conferō, conferre, contulī, collātum | exchange |
| *coniunx, coniugis m. | husband |
| *conspiciō, conspicere, conspexī, conspectum | look upon, gaze at |
| construō, construere, construxī, constructum | build up |
| consuescō, consuescere, consuēvī, consuētum | get in the habit of, become accustomed to |
| contexō, contexere, contexuī, contextum | weave together |
| convocō, convocāre, convocāvī, convocātum | summon |
| cōram (preposition + ablative) | close to |

## Vocabulary

| | |
|---|---|
| corpus, corporis *n.* | body |
| Cōus -a -um | from Cos |
| crēbrō (*adverb*) | frequently |
| crēdō, crēdere, crēdidī, crēditum (+ *dative*) | believe, trust |
| cruentus -a -um | bloody |
| *cum (*preposition* + *ablative*) | with |
| *cum (*conjunction*) | when |
| *cunctus -a -um | all |
| *cupidus -a -um | on heat (of a mare: II.4.58) |
| *cūra -ae *f.* | concern (I.5.29) anxiety (I.5.37) |
| *cūrō, cūrāre, cūrāvī, cūrātum | attend on |
| *currō, currere, cucurrī, cursum | run |
| custōdia -ae *f.* | security, guarding |
| *custōs, custōdis *m.* | guard, protector |
| | |
| daps, dapis *f.* | sacrificial meal (I.5.28) |
| *dē (*preposition* + *ablative*) | down from (I.2.45) about (I.2.57, I.2.60) from (I.2.84, I.5.66) |
| decet, decēre, decuit (*impersonal verb*) | it is right |
| dēcidō, dēcidere, dēcidī | fall down |
| dēditus -a -um | devoted |
| dēdūcō, dēdūcere, dēduxī, dēductum | escort |
| *dēfessus -a -um | exhausted |
| deinde | then |
| Dēlia -ae *f.* | Delia |
| dēmens, dēmentis | mad |
| dēmentia -ae *f.* | madness |
| *dēnique | in fact |
| dens, dentis *m.* | key (I.2.18) |
| dēpellō, dēpellere, dēpulī, dēpulsum | scatter (I.2.51) remove (I.5.37) |
| dērēpō, dērēpere, dērepsī | creep out of |
| dēripiō, dēripere, dēripuī, dēreptum | steal, snatch |
| dēserō, dēserere, dēseruī, dēsertum | leave behind, abandon (I.5.40) |
| dēspuō, dēspuere | spit |
| dētineō, dētinēre, dētinuī, dētentum | detain, hold back |
| dētrahō, dētrahere, dētraxī, dētractum | pluck from (I.5.32) remove (I.5.66) |
| *deus -ī *m.* | god |
| dēveneror, dēvenerārī, dēvenerātus sum | avert, repel |

| | |
|---|---|
| dēvocō, dēvocāre, dēvocāvī, dēvocatum | summon down from |
| dēvōtus -a -um | cursed |
| dēvoveō, dēvovēre, dēvōvī, dēvōtum | bewitch |
| *dīcō, dīcere, dixī, dictum | speak, say |
| *diēs, diēī f. | day |
| *difficilis -e | unyielding |
| digitus -ī m. | finger |
| *discēdō, discēdere, discessī, discessum | leave, depart |
| discidium -ī n. | separation |
| *dīves, dīvitis | wealthy |
| *dō, dare, dedī, datum | make (vows I.5.16), give |
| *doceō, docēre, docuī, doctum | teach, instruct |
| *dolor, dolōris m. | pain, grief |
| *domina -ae f. | mistress |
| *dominus -ī m. | master, husband |
| domō, domāre, domāvī, domātum | subdue, curb |
| *domus -ūs f. | house |
| *dōnum -ī n. | gift |
| *dubitō, dubitāre, dubitāvī, dubitātum | hesitate |
| *dūcō, dūcere, duxī, ductum | draw down (I.2.45), bring about (I.2.80) |
| dulcis -e | sweet |
| *dum | while, so long as (I.2.75) |
| *dūrus -a -um | firm, hard |
| | |
| *ē (preposition + ablative) | out of, from |
| edō, esse, ēdī, ēsum | eat |
| *efficiō, efficere, effēcī, effectum | carve out, create |
| *ego, meī | I, me |
| elegī -ōrum m.pl. | elegies |
| ēliciō, ēlicere, ēlicuī, ēlicitum | summon, draw out |
| ēn (interjection) | look! |
| *eō, īre, īvī, itum | go, move (plural imperative **ite**) |
| epulae -ārum f.pl. | feast |
| equa -ae f. | mare |
| *equus -ī m. | horse |
| ēripiō, ēripere, ēripuī, ēreptum | save (I.5.10), snatch away (II.4.40) |
| *errō, errāre, errāvī, errātum | roam, wander |
| *et | and, even (I.2.39) |
| *etiam | also |

## Vocabulary

| | |
|---|---|
| Eurus -ī m. | east wind |
| ēveniō, ēvenīre, ēvēnī, ēventum | happen, come about |
| *excitō, excitāre, excitāvī, excitātum | awaken, stir |
| exclūdō, exclūdere, exclūsī, exclūsum | shut out |
| *exitium -ī n. | destruction |
| exscreō, exscreāre, exscreāvī, exscreātum | cough noisily |
| exsequiae -ārum f.pl. | funeral rites |
| faciēs, faciēī f. | beauty |
| *facilis -e | easy |
| *facinus, facinoris n. | deed |
| *faciō, facere, fēcī, factum | achieve (I.5.43), render (II.4.31), bring about that (II.4.38) |
| *fallō, fallere, fefellī, falsum | deceive, trick |
| famēs -is f. | hunger |
| fānum -ī n. | temple, shrine |
| fātum -ī n. | fate, destiny |
| faveō, favēre, fāvī, fautum | favour, support |
| fax, facis f. | torch |
| fel, fellis n. | bile, gall |
| *fēlix, fēlicis | fortunate |
| *fēmina -ae f. | woman |
| *ferō, ferre, tulī, lātum | bring (I.2.38, II.4.33), endure (I.5.1) offer (I.5.28) |
| feror (passive of ferō) | be said to |
| ferreus -a -um | made of iron |
| *ferrum -ī n. | blade |
| ferus -a -um | savage (I.2.54), uncouth (I.5.5) |
| fessus -a -um | weary |
| fīdus -a -um | faithful |
| fīgō, fīgere, fīxī, fīxum | fix, insert (I.2.18) |
| fīlum -ī n. | woollen fillet |
| findō, findere, fidī, fissum | split |
| fingō, fingere, finxī, fictum | shape (I.2.94), imagine (I.5.20, I.5.35) |
| fīō, fierī, factus sum | turn up (I.2.35) |
| firmus -a -um | strong, sturdy |
| fixus -a -um | attached |
| flagitō, flagitāre, flagitāvī, flagitātum | demand, ask for |
| *flamma -ae f. | flame |

| | |
|---|---|
| flāvus -a -um | blonde |
| flēbilis -e | weeping, pathetic |
| fleō, flēre, flēvī, flētum | weep, mourn |
| flētus -ūs *m.* | weeping |
| flōridus -a -um | flowery |
| *flūmen, flūminis *n.* | river |
| focus -ī *m.* | sacrificial altar |
| *foedus, foederis *n.* | bond, contract |
| forēs -um *f.pl.* | door |
| forma -ae *f.* | beauty |
| fors, fortis *f.* | chance, fortune |
| *fortis -e | strong, brave (I.2.16), arrogant (I.5.2) |
| *forum -ī *n.* | forum, town square. |
| frēnātus -a -um | bridled |
| *frīgus, frīgoris *n.* | cold, frost |
| frūgēs, frūgum *f.pl.* | crops |
| fruor, fruī, fructus sum (+ *ablative*) | enjoy |
| *frustrā (*adverb*) | in vain, to no purpose |
| fulgeō, fulgēre, fulsī | gleam, blaze |
| fulmen, fulminis *n.* | thunderbolt |
| furens, furentis | raving, mad |
| furtim (*adverb*) | secretly |
| furtīvus -a -um | cheating, secret |
| furtum -ī *n.* | adulterous affair |
| | |
| garrulus -a -um | chattering |
| *gaudium -ī *n.* | orgasm (I.5.39) |
| gelidus -a -um | icy |
| genu, genūs *n.* | knee |
| *gerō, gerere, gessī, gessum | carry out (I.5.34), bear, produce (II.4.56) |
| glōria -ae *f.* | boasting |
| grandis -e | lavish, generous |
| grex, gregis *m.* | flock, herd |
| | |
| *habeō, habēre, habuī, habitum | have, possess |
| Haemonius -a -um | Thessalian |
| Hecata -ae *f.* | Hecate |
| herba -ae *f.* | herb, plant |
| heu (*interjection*) | alas! |

## Vocabulary 173

| | |
|---|---|
| hībernus -a -um | wintry |
| *hīc | here |
| *hic, haec, hoc | this |
| *hinc | as a result of this |
| hippomanes -is *n.* | hippomanes (see II.4.58n.) |
| horridus -a -um | savage, harsh |
| hostia -ae *f.* | sacrificial victim |
| *hūc | to this |
| *humus -ī *f.* | ground. |
| | |
| *iaceō, iacēre, iacuī | lie down |
| iactō, iactāre, iactāvī, iactātum | throw away |
| *iam | now (I.2.9, I.2.49–50), already (I.5.71), from now on (II.4.2) |
| iam cum | at the point when (I.5.39) |
| iānua -ae *f.* | door |
| *īdem, eadem, idem | the same |
| *ignis -is *m.* | fire |
| ignōscō, ignōscere, ignōvī, ignōtum | forgive |
| *ille, illa, illud | that |
| imber, imbris *m.* | rain |
| *imperium -iī *n.* | order, command |
| impius -a -um | wicked |
| imprūdens, imprūdentis | careless |
| *in (*preposition* + *ablative*) | in, on |
| *in (*preposition* + *accusative*) | into (I.2.98, I.5.38), for the purpose of (I.5.48, II.4.44) |
| *incendium -iī n | fire |
| incestus -a -um | wicked |
| incultus -a -um | uncultivated |
| indomitus -a -um | wild, untamed |
| inertia -ae *f.* | idleness, sloth |
| infāmis -e | having a bad reputation |
| infēlix, infēlīcis | unhappy |
| infernus -a -um | infernal, of the underworld |
| inguen, inguinis *n.* | groin |
| iniustus -a -um | unfair, harsh |
| insānus -a -um | raving, mad |
| insideō, insidēre, insēdī, insessum | sit upon |

| | |
|---|---|
| *insidiae -ārum f.pl. | ambush, trap |
| *insignis -e | ornamental (II.4.23) |
| iō (interjection) | ah! |
| *ipse, ipsa, ipsum | oneself |
| *is, ea, id | he, she, it |
| *iste, ista, istud | that |
| īte | see eo |
| *iter, itineris n. | journey |
| *iubeō, iubēre, iussī, iussum | command |
| *iungō, iungere, iunxī, iunctum | yoke together |
| Iuppiter, Iovis m. | Jupiter |
| *iuvenis -is m. | young man |
| iuvenis -e (adjectival) | young (I.2.97) |
| *iuvat (impersonal) | it pleases |
| | |
| *labor -ōris m. | toil, suffering |
| lac, lactis n. | milk |
| lacertus -ī m. | arm |
| lacrima -ae f. | tear |
| *laedō, laedere, laesī, laesum | harm, hurt |
| *laetus -a -um | joyful |
| lapis, lapidis m. | stone |
| Lar, Laris m. | household god |
| *latus, lateris n. | flank, side |
| lectus -ī m. | bed |
| legō, legere, lēgī, lectum | pick, gather |
| lēna -ae f. | procuress, female pimp |
| levis -e | light |
| *lex, lēgis f. | law, term |
| lībertās, -ātis f. | freedom |
| libet (impersonal) | it pleases one |
| *licet (impersonal) | it is allowed, one may |
| licet (conjunction) | although (I.2.69, II.4.45) |
| līmen, līminis n. | threshold |
| lingua -ae f. | tongue |
| linter, lintris f. | trough (I.5.23), boat (1.5.76) |
| liquidus -a -um | flowing, running |
| *longē (adverb) | far away |
| loquax, loquācis | meaningful (I.2.21) outspoken (I.2.41) |

| | |
|---|---|
| *loquor, loquī, locūtus sum | speak |
| lūcidus -a -um | gleaming |
| lūdō, lūdere, lūsī, lūsum | play (I.5.26), mock (I.2.91) |
| lūgeō, lūgēre, luxī, luctum | mourn |
| lūmen, lūminis *n.* | eye (I.2.2, I.2.35) light (I.2.38) |
| lūna -ae *f.* | moon |
| luō, luere, luī | pay, discharge (penalty) |
| lupus -ī *m.* | wolf |
| lustrō, lustrāre, lustrāvī, lustrātum | purify |
| | |
| madeō, madēre, maduī | be soaked |
| maestus -a -um | sad, sorrowful |
| magicus -a -um | magical |
| magnificus -a -um | boastful, bragging |
| *magnus -a -um | great |
| *mālō, mālle, māluī | prefer |
| *malus -a -um | evil (I.2.53), wicked (II.4.25, II.4.31) |
| mala dīcō, dīcere, dixī, dictum | curse |
| malum -ī *n.* | misfortune (I.2.89, II.4.36) |
| mānēs, mānium *m.pl.* | spirits of the dead (I.2.47) |
| *manus -ūs *f.* | hand |
| *mare, maris *n.* | sea |
| Martius -a -um | belonging to Mars (god of war) |
| Mēdēa -ae *f.* | Medea |
| *medius -a -um | central, in the middle of |
| meminī, meminisse | remember |
| *mens, mentis *f.* | mind |
| mereō, merēre, meruī, meritum | deserve |
| merum -ī *n.* | (undiluted) wine |
| Messalla -ae *m.* | Messalla (patron of Tibullus) |
| messis -is *f.* | harvest |
| *meus -a -um | my |
| *mīlle | thousand |
| ministerium -ī *n.* | service |
| ministra -ae *f.* | servant |
| misceō, miscēre, miscuī, mixtum | mix, mingle |
| miser, misera, miserum | unhappy, lovesick |
| mittō, mittere, mīsī, missum | release, fire (a thunderbolt: I.2.8) |
| *modo | only |

| | |
|---|---|
| mola -ae *f.* | salted meal |
| mollis -e | soft (I.2.19, I.2.58), gentle (I.2.76), youthful (I.2.98) |
| *moneō, monēre, monuī, monitum | urge |
| *mons, montis *m.* | mountain |
| *morbus -ī *m.* | sickness, disease |
| *mors, mortis *f.* | death |
| *mox (*adverb*) | in time, after that |
| *multus -a -um | much, many |
| *mūnus, mūneris *n.* | offering |
| mūrex, mūricis *m.* | shellfish, dye |
| Mūsa -ae *f.* | Muse |
| mustum -ī *n.* | (unfermented) grape juice |
| mūtuus -a -um | requited |
| | |
| *nam | for |
| namque | for |
| *narrō, narrāre, narrāvī, narrātum | tell the tale |
| *nascor, nascī, nātus sum | be born |
| naufragus -a -um | causing shipwreck |
| *nē | do not (I.2.15), so that ... not (I.5.5, I.5.13, II.4.7, II.4.22) |
| *nec | and not, nor |
| nec ... nec | neither ... nor (I.2.23–4, I.2.79–80, II.4.13, II.4.43–4) |
| nefandus -a -um | wicked, unspeakable |
| *negō, negāre, negāvī, negātum | deny |
| Nemesis, Nemeseōs *f.* | Nemesis (mistress of the poet in II.4) |
| nempe | indeed |
| *neque | and not |
| Nērēis, Nērēidis *f.* | a daughter of Nereus |
| nescio quis, nescio quid | someone, something |
| neu | and let not (I.2.3) and do not (I.2.10, I.2.37–8) |
| *nihil/nil | nothing, not at all (II.4.20) |
| niveus -a -um | snow-white |
| nix, nivis *f.* | snow |
| nō, nāre, nāvī | swim, float |
| *noceō, nocēre, nocuī, nocitum (+ *dative*) | hurt, harm |

| | |
|---|---|
| *nōmen, nōminis *n.* | name |
| *nōn | not |
| *nōs, nostrum | we, us |
| *noster, nostra, nostrum | our, my |
| nota -ae *f.* | sign |
| Notus -ī *m.* | south wind |
| *novem | nine |
| *novus -a -um | fresh, new |
| *nox, noctis *f.* | night |
| nūbilum -ī *n.* | cloud |
| nūdus -a -um | naked |
| *nullus -a -um | not any |
| *num? | surely ... not? |
| nūmen, nūminis *n.* | divinity (I.2.81), divine power (I.5.57) |
| numerō, numerāre, numerāvī, numerātum | count |
| *numquam | never |
| *nunc | now |
| nūtus -ūs *m.* | nod (of the head) |

| | |
|---|---|
| ō (*exclamation*) | oh |
| obnoxius -a -um | exposed to |
| obscūrus -a -um | dark |
| obvius -a -um | in the way |
| occulō, occulere, occuluī, occultum | conceal, hide |
| occultus -a -um | secret |
| occupō, occupāre, occupāvī, occupātum | take possession of |
| occurrō, occurrere, occurrī, occursum | run into, encounter |
| odōrātus -a -um | scented |
| *omnis -e | all, every |
| opēs, opum *f.pl.* | wealth |
| orbis -is *m.* | sky (I.2.52), circle (I.5.70), disc (II.4.17) |
| *ōrō, ōrāre, ōrāvī, ōrātum | pray, beg |
| *ōs, ōris *n.* | mouth |
| os, ossis *n.* | bone |
| osculum -ī *n.* | kiss |
| ovis -is *f.* | sheep (fleece: II.4.28) |

| | |
|---|---|
| *parcō, parcere, pepercī, parsum (+ *dative*) | spare |

| | |
|---|---|
| *pariō, parere, peperī, partum | procure, get |
| *parō, parāre, parāvī, parātum | prepare (I.5.34), devise (I.5.75) plan (II.4.1), get (II.4.21) |
| pascō, pascere, pāvī, pāstum | feed, pasture |
| pateō, patēre, patuī | be open |
| paternus -a -um | ancestral |
| patescō, patescere, patuī | open up |
| *pauper, pauperis | poor |
| peccō, peccāre, peccāvī, peccātum | do wrong |
| pecus, pecoris *n.* | herd, flock |
| Pēleus (*acc.* Pēlea) *m.* | Peleus |
| *per (*preposition + accusative*) | across, through (I.5.3, I.5.36, I.5.55) by (in oaths: I.2.40, I.5.7–8) by means of (II.4.19, II.4.21) |
| peragō, peragere, perēgī, peractum | utter (I.2.13) |
| percutiō, percutere, percussī, percussum | strike |
| perdomō, perdomāre, perdomuī, perdomitum | tame |
| pereō, perīre, periī, peritum | perish, die |
| perrēpō, perrēpere, perrepsī | crawl across |
| persolvō, persolvere, persolvī, persolutum | discharge (vows) |
| perstō, perstāre, perstitī, perstātum | remain standing |
| *pēs, pedis *m.* | foot |
| pedem referō | step back |
| *petō, petere, peti(v)ī, petītum | seek out |
| pictus -a -um | embroidered |
| piger, pigra, pigrum | numbing |
| piscis -is *m.* | fish |
| placidus -a -um | peaceful (I.2.80, II.4.49) serene (II.4.59) |
| plānus -a -um | level, flat |
| *plēnus -a -um | full |
| plūma -ae *f.* | feather |
| plūrimus -a -um | very many |
| pōculum -ī *n.* | cup |
| *poena -ae *f.* | penalty, punishment |
| *polliceor, pollicērī, pollicitus sum | promise |
| pōmum -ī *n.* | apple |
| pōnō, pōnere, posuī, positum | place, put |
| *possum, posse, potuī | be able |

# Vocabulary 179

| | |
|---|---|
| *post (*preposition + accusative*) | after (I.5.6) |
| *post (*adverbial*) | afterwards, later on (I.2.92) from behind (I.5.56) |
| postis -is *m*. | doorpost |
| potior, potius | superior, favoured |
| praeceptum -ī *n*. | advice, instruction |
| praecinō, praecinere, praecinuī, praecentum | sing first |
| *praeda -ae *f*. | booty |
| *praemium -ī *n*. | (financial) reward |
| praestō (*adverb*) | ready, available |
| precēs, precum *f.pl*. | prayers |
| *precor, precārī, precātus sum | pray |
| premō, premere, pressī, pressum | squeeze, press |
| *pretium -ī *n*. | money (II.4.14, II.4.33), price (II.4.39) |
| *prīmus -a -um | first |
| quam prīmum (*adverb*) | as soon as possible |
| *prō (*preposition + ablative*) | for |
| *procul (*adverb*) | far away |
| prōcumbō, prōcumbere, prōcubuī, prōcubitum | bow down |
| prōcūrō, prōcūrāre, prōcūrāvī, prōcūrātum | expiate |
| prohibeō, prohibēre, prohibuī, prohibitum | exclude, keep away |
| *prope (*adverb*) | nearby |
| prōspiciō, prōspicere, prōspexī, prōspectum | look about |
| prōsum, prōdesse, prōfuī (+ *dative*) | be of advantage |
| pudet, pudēre, puduit (*impersonal verb*) | it is embarrassing |
| *puella -ae *f*. | girl |
| *puer, puerī *m*. | boy |
| pullus -a -um | dark-coloured |
| pūrus -a -um | purifying |
| | |
| *quaerō, quaerere, quaesīvī, quaesītum | ask after (I.2.37), seek out (I.5.54), ask for (II.4.19) |
| quaesō, quaesere | pray for |
| quālibet (*adverb*) | wherever one likes |
| *quālis -e | of what kind |

AS

# 180 Tibullus: Elegies I.2, I.5, II.4

| | |
|---|---|
| *quam (exclamation) | how (II.4.8) |
| *-que | and |
| querēla -ae f. | lament, complaint |
| *queror, querī, questus sum | lament |
| *quī, quae, quod | who, what |
| quīcumque, quaecumque, quodcumque | whoever, whatever |
| quid? | why? (I.2.61, I.2.100) |
| *quīdam, quaedam, quoddam | someone |
| *quidem | indeed |
| quiescō, quiescere, quiēvī, quiētum | rest |
| quīn | in fact, furthermore |
| *quis, quis, quid | who, what |
| nescio quid | something or other (I.5.75) |
| *quisquam, quicquam | anyone, anything |
| *quisque, quaeque, quidque | each |
| *quisquis, quidquid | whoever, whatever |
| *quod (conjunction) | because, as to the fact that (I.5.47) |
| quondam | in the past |
| *quoque | also |
| | |
| rapax, rapācis | grasping, greedy |
| rapidus -a -um | fast-flowing |
| *rapiō, rapere, rapuī, raptum | steal |
| recubō, recubāre, recubuī | lie down |
| recurrō, recurrere, recurrī, recursum | run back |
| *referō, referre, rettulī, relātum | report, recount (II.4.17) |
| *referō pedem | step back (I.2.50) |
| refugiō, refugere, refūgī | run away |
| *regō, regere, rexī, rectum | control, order |
| *relinquō, relinquere, relīquī, relictum | leave behind (I.5.54) abandon (I.5.58) |
| remittō, remittere, remīsī, remissum | slacken, untie |
| removeō, removēre, remōvī, remōtum | put aside |
| renuō, renuere, renuī | refuse, deny |
| requiescō, requiescere, requiēvī, requiētum | lie dormant |
| reserō, reserāre, reserāvī, reserātum | unbolt |
| *retineō, retinēre, retinuī, retentum | hold |
| rīdeō, rīdēre, rīsī, rīsum | laugh at |
| rixa -ae f. | quarrel |

AS

# Vocabulary

| | |
|---|---|
| rogus -ī *m.* | funeral pyre |
| rota -ae *f.* | wheel |
| ruber, rubra, rubrum | red |
| *rūs, rūris *n.* | countryside |
| | |
| sacer, sacra, sacrum | untouchable (I.2.29), sacred (II.4.23) |
| sacrātus -a -um | hallowed, holy |
| sacrilegus -a -um | sacrilegious |
| *saepe | often |
| saeviō, saevīre, saeviī, saevītum | rage, be furious |
| *saevus -a -um | harsh (I.2.5), cruel (I.5.13, II.4.6), savage (I.5.55) |
| sāga -ae *f.* | witch |
| salvus -a -um | healthy, safe |
| sanctus -a -um | sacred, holy |
| sanguineus -a -um | bloody |
| *sanguis, sanguinis *m.* | blood |
| *sciō, scīre, scīvī, scītum | know |
| *sē, suī | himself, herself, itself, themselves |
| *secundus -a -um | reciprocated, mutual (I.2.77) |
| sēcūrus -a -um | free from care, tranquil |
| *sed | but |
| *sēdēs -is *f.* | abode (I.2.83) house (II.4.53) |
| sēdulus -a -um | diligent (I.5.33), attentive (I.5.72, II.4.42) |
| seges, segetis *f.* | corn |
| sēligō, sēligere, sēlēgī, sēlectum | pick out, choose |
| *semper | constantly |
| *senex, senis *m.* | old man |
| senior, senius | older |
| *sentiō, sentīre, sensī, sensum | be aware of (I.2.42, I.2.60), feel (II.4.7, II.4.26, II.4.31) |
| sepulcrum -ī *n.* | tomb |
| *sequor, sequī, secūtus sum | follow after |
| sera -ae *f.* | door-bolt |
| serēnus -a -um | peaceful, calm |
| serta -ōrum *n.pl.* | garlands |
| serviō, servīre, servīvī, servītum | serve |
| servitium -ī *n.* | slavery |
| *servō, servāre, servāvī, servātum | keep, tend |

| | |
|---|---|
| seu | or if |
|    seu... seu | whether... or |
| *sī | if |
| sīdus, sīderis *n.* | star |
| *signum -ī *n.* | sign |
| silēns, silentis | silent |
| simulō, simulāre, simulāvī, simulātum | pretend |
| *sine (*preposition* + *ablative*) | without |
| *sinō, sinere, sīvī, situm | allow |
| sinus -ūs *m.* | bosom |
| sī quī, sī qua, sī quod | if any |
| sī quis, sī quid | if anybody, if anything |
| smaragdus -ī *m.* | emerald |
| *sōl, sōlis *m.* | sun |
| solitus -a -um | accustomed, usual |
| solum -ī *n.* | land, earth |
| *sōlus -a -um | alone |
| *solvō, solvere, solvī, solūtum | release (I.2.62) untie, undo (I.5.15) |
| somnium -ī *n.* | dream |
| *somnus -ī *m.* | sleep |
| sonitus -ūs *m.* | sound |
| sonō, sonāre, sonuī, sonitum | make a sound (I.2.10), re-echo (II.4.37) |
| *sonus -ī *m.* | sound |
| sopor, sopōris *m.* | sleep |
| *spectō, spectāre, spectāvī, spectātum | look at |
| spīca -ae *f.* | ear of corn |
| stillō, stillāre, stillāvī, stillātum | drip |
| stimulō, stimulāre, stimulāvī, stimulātum | goad, drive on |
| *stō, stāre, stetī, statum | stand |
| strāgulum -ī *n.* | coverlet |
| strepitus -ūs *m.* | noise |
| strīdor, strīdōris *m.* | shrieking |
| strix, strigis *f.* | screech-owl |
| *stultus -a -um | stupid |
| suādeō, suādēre, suāsī, suāsum | prompt, urge |
| *sub (*preposition* + *accusative*) | under |
| subdō, subdere, subdidī, subditum | place under, subordinate |
| sūbiciō, sūbicere, sūbiēcī, sūbiectum | push from underneath (I.5.64) |

## Vocabulary

| | |
|---|---|
| sulpur, sulpuris *n.* | sulphur |
| *sum, esse, fuī | be |
| super *(preposition + accusative)* | above, over |
| supplex, supplicis *(adjective)* | supplicating, pleading (I.2.14) |
| supplex, supplicis *m.* | suppliant |
| surgō, surgere, surrexī, surrectum | get up |
| suspendō, suspendere, suspendī, suspensum | hang up |
| *suus -a -um | one's own, their own |
| | |
| taceō, tacēre, tacuī, tacitum | be silent |
| taciturnus -a -um | silent |
| taeda -ae *f.* | torch |
| *tālis -e | of such a kind |
| *tamen | however |
| *tantus -a -um | so great |
| tardō, tardāre, tardāvī, tardātum | slow down, impede |
| *tēctum -ī *n.* | roof |
| *tēcum | with you |
| tellus, tellūris *f.* | earth |
| *templum -ī *n.* | temple |
| temptō, temptāre, temptāvī, temptātum | make an attempt on (I.2.13), try (I.5.37) |
| tempus, temporis *n.* | temple (of the head: I.2.3) |
| *tempus, temporis *n.* | time (II.4.12) |
| tenebrae -ārum *f.pl.* | darkness |
| *teneō, tenēre, tenuī | hold firm (I.2.29, II.4.3), control (I.2.49, I.2.53), hold in an embrace (I.5.39) |
| tener, tenera, tenerum | soft |
| tepidus -a -um | warm |
| ter | three times |
| terō, terere, trīvī, trītum | thresh |
| *terra -ae *f.* | earth (II.4.50), land (II.4.56) |
| *terreō, terrēre, terruī, territum | frighten |
| Thessalus -a -um | Thessalian |
| Thetis, Thetidis *f.* | Thetis |
| *timeō, timēre, timuī | fear, be afraid |
| timidus -a -um | fearful |
| timor, timōris *m.* | fear |
| tingō, tingere, tinxī, tinctum | dye, stain |

| | |
|---|---|
| titulus -ī m. | label |
| torqueō, torquēre, torsī, tortum | twist, torture |
| torus -ī m. | bed |
| *tōtus -a -um | whole, all |
| transeō, transīre, transi(v)ī, transitum | walk past |
| tremulus -a -um | tremulous, quavering |
| *tristis -e | overcast (I.2.51) grim (I.5.9, 2.4.3) bitter (I.5.50, II.4.12) |
| Trivia -ae f. | Trivia, Hecate (I.5.16) |
| trivium -ī n. | crossroads |
| *tū, tuī | you (singular) |
| *tum | then |
| tumulus -ī m. | tomb, mound |
| tunc | at that moment |
| tundō, tundere, tutudī, tunsum | beat, batter |
| tunica -ae f. | tunic |
| *turba -ae f. | crowd (I.2.97, I.5.63) pack (I.5.56) |
| turben, turbinis m. | spinning-top |
| *tūtus -a -um | safe |
| *tuus, tua, tuum | your |
| Tyrius -a -um | Tyrian |
| | |
| *ubi | when |
| *ullus -a -um | any |
| ululō, ululāre, ululāvī, ululātum | howl |
| umbra -ae f. | shadow, darkness |
| *unda -ae f. | wave |
| ūnus -a -um | one, alone |
| *urbs, urbis f. | city |
| ūrō, ūrere, ussī, ustum | burn |
| *usque | continuously |
| *ut (+ subjunctive) | so that (I.2.2, II.4.16, II.4.38) |
| *ut (+ indicative) | as (I.2.43) like (I.5.3) |
| *ūtor, ūtī, ūsus sum (+ ablative) | use |
| ūva -ae f. | grape |
| | |
| vagor, vagārī, vagātus sum | wander, roam |

# Vocabulary

| | |
|---|---|
| vale! | farewell (II.4.2) |
| *valeō, valēre, valuī | have power, be effective |
| vastus -a -um | vast |
| *vehō, vehere, vexī, vectum | carry, transport |
| *vel | or else |
| vēlō, vēlāre, vēlāvī, vēlātum | veil, cover |
| vēlōx, vēlōcis | nimble, swift |
| vendō, vendere, vendidī, venditum | sell |
| venēnum -ī n. | drug |
| veneror, venerārī, venerātus sum | respect |
| *veniō, venīre, vēnī, ventum | come |
| *ventus -ī m. | wind |
| Venus, Veneris f. | Venus |
| vērax, vērācis | truthful |
| *verbum -ī n. | word |
| verber, verberis n. | blow, whipping |
| verberō, verberāre, verberāvī, verberātum | lash, beat against |
| verna -ae m./f. | house-slave |
| versō, versāre, versāvī, versātum | spin (I.5.4) whirl around (I.5.70) |
| *vertō, vertere, vertī, versum | turn |
| *vĕrus -a -um | true |
| *vestis -is f. | clothing |
| *vetō, vetāre, vetuī, vetitum | prevent |
| *vetus, veteris | old |
| *via -ae f. | path |
| *videō, vidēre, vīdī, vīsum | see, look on |
| vigilō, vigilāre, vigilāvī, vigilātum | stay awake |
| vinclum -ī n. | chain (I.2.92, II.4.4), fastening (I.5.66) |
| *vincō, vincere, vīcī, victum | overcome |
| vīnum -ī n. | wine |
| violentus -a -um | fierce, savage |
| violō, violāre, violāvī, violātum | violate, assault |
| *vir, virī m. | man (I.2.35, I.5.33) husband (I.2.21) |
| viridis -e | green |
| *vīta -ae f. | life |
| vītis -is f. | vine |
| *vīvō, vīvere, vīxī, vīctum | live |

| | |
|---|---|
| *vox, vōcis f. | voice |
| *vocō, vocāre, vocāvī, vocātum | call |
| volitō, volitāre, volitāvī, volitātum | fly |
| *volō, velle, voluī | want |
| *vōs, vestrum | you (*plural*) |
| vōtum -ī n. | prayer, vow |
| *vulnerō, vulnerāre, vulnerāvī, vulnerātum | injure |
| *vultus -ūs m. | face |

# Ovid

## Metamorphoses *VII.1–227*

A Level

# Introduction

## What is this book about and why should we read it?

*Metamorphoses* VII is a wonderful narrative, full of twists and turns and all told in witty and elegant Latin. The section prescribed for study in Latin (1–227) tells the tale of the sorceress Medea and her love for Jason (the leader of the Argonauts) who had come to Colchis to retrieve the Golden Fleece and claim the throne of his home city of Iolcus from his uncle Pelias. Medea helps Jason to surmount the impossible challenges imposed on him by her father King Aeetes: with her magic he forces fire-breathing bulls to plough a field, he sows dragon's teeth which at once grow into fully-armed warriors, and he overcomes the unsleeping dragon which guards the Golden Fleece. Medea and Jason then go to Greece with the Golden Fleece and hand it triumphantly to Pelias, only for him to refuse to give up the throne. Medea uses her magic further to rejuvenate Jason's old father Aeson and then tricks Pelias' daughters into killing their own father by convincing them that she could similarly restore *his* youth and has them boil the old man in a cauldron instead. Jason and Medea settle in Corinth, but Jason abandons Medea for Glauce, the daughter of the king. Medea takes her revenge by sending Glauce a poisoned dress which burns her and her father to death, before fleeing on a chariot drawn by dragons. Medea then goes to Athens and marries King Aegeus to provide him with the son he craves as he thinks that he is childless. When his real son Theseus appears, Medea tries to kill him, but Aegeus recognises Theseus just in time and Medea makes a sharp exit from her husband.

The book continues with the war waged by Minos king of Crete against the Athenians in revenge for the Athenians' killing of Minos' son Androgeos. Minos tries to secure help from the island of Aegina but the Aeginetans refuse, wishing to help the Athenians instead. Aeacus (the Aeginetan king) entertains the Athenian ambassadors with an account of the plague at Aegina, which decimated the population, and tells the tale of how he asked for help from Jupiter – at which a new race of men (the 'Myrmidons') was born from ants. One of the Athenians (Cephalus) then narrates the sad tale of how the goddess Dawn, having failed to seduce him, had persuaded him that he needed to test the chastity of his new bride Procris: disguised as a stranger he finds her fidelity lacking – and she leaves him to join a band of women devoted to Diana. Cephalus begs her to return to him and eventually she does so, only for him to end up killing her accidentally with the magic spear which Procris had given him.

The book is thus framed by love-stories: Medea's ultimately unhappy passion for Jason at the beginning and Cephalus' tragic union with Procris at the end. There are passages of suspense (such as Jason's and Theseus' brushes with death) and there are passages of wonder and awe such as the taming of the bulls and the birth of the Myrmidons. Moral issues are explored: should Medea follow her feelings for Jason rather than her filial duty to her father? Is it ever a good idea to test the fidelity of one's beloved? Deeper ethical concerns are raised when Medea states (20–1) that she knows what is the better course of action but still does the opposite: if virtue is a matter of knowing what is good for us (as Plato had stated) then how does this even make sense?

Ovid also plays with earlier texts, including his own. Most of his readers would have been familiar with Euripides' wonderful play *Medea* (431 BC), in which Medea's dark psychology is tested to the limit and allows her to murder her own children in cold blood. Readers would also be familiar with the earlier epic treatment of the legend by the third-century BC Alexandrian poet Apollonius of Rhodes whose *Argonautica* told the legend in glorious detail and in a novel form of epic language. Ovid had already ventriloquised Medea by putting the twelfth of his *Heroides* into her eloquent mouth and readers familiar with that earlier text will recognise elements from it in this poem. In this book Ovid dispatches Medea's murder of her children in a single line (396) as he had told a tale of infanticide in the previous book and (anyway) he liked to foil readerly expectations rather than delivering predictable narratives: but he indulges his taste for the wonderful world of mutability which is the theme of the entire poem: old men become young again, seeds become warriors, ants become people after a plague wipes out a whole nation, reality trumps appearance and appearance defies reality. Time after time women emerge as superior to men – Medea, Dawn, Procris – while men who think they run things are shown to be inferior and even pathetic. Like all great literature, this text forces us to question our values and our beliefs while also keeping us gripped by the sheer power of the narrative which itself shifts and changes in style and register along with the tales it tells.

## Ovid and his times

Publius Ovidius Naso was born on 20 March 43 BC in a small town called Sulmo (modern Sulmona) about 80 miles east of Rome. We know more about his upbringing than we do about that of other poets as he left a substantial body of autobiographical works, and he tells us that his family was well-off but not politically active. He, along with his brother, was sent to school in Rome – one of the signs of wealth in an age where there was no free schooling – and he studied public speaking (with a view to a legal and/or political career) although he was more drawn to the writing of poetry than to the composition of speeches. He was born into turbulent times: by the time of his birth Julius Caesar had been dead almost a year and when he was twelve Caesar's great-nephew and heir Octavian defeated Mark Antony in the crucial battle off Actium, leaving the Roman republic in the hands of a young man who was soon to change his name to Augustus and become the first of the emperors of Rome. The Roman republic which had stood ever since the last of the kings – the infamous Tarquinius Superbus – was expelled in 510 BC was now subverted into a 'Principate' in which supreme power rested in the hands of the *princeps* (emperor) and freedom of speech and free elections came to be increasingly circumscribed and sanctioned. Ovid's choice of a career as a writer rather than as a lawyer or politician (or both, as Cicero had been) is therefore not totally surprising seeing that he was born in an age when the scope for a lively-minded man to find the outlet for his talents in politics was inevitably limited by the regime in power. Ovid hardly ever refers explicitly to politics as such in his works, although it is clear from some of his less guarded lines that he might not have survived long as a politician in the imperial court.

As a young man he did what we could call the 'Grand Tour', travelling to Greece, Sicily and Asia Minor, and it is clear from his work that he, like most educated Romans, understood and read Greek literature in the original. His training as a lawyer would have encouraged him to compose *suasoriae* – artificial exercises in which the student composes a speech to try to 'persuade' (*suadere*) a historical figure about to make some momentous act, such as Sulla about to invade Rome, or Hannibal after the battle of Cannae. This sort of imaginative work did him no harm at all as a writer and we can see the fruit of his youthful labours in speeches such as that of Medea (11–71) where she shows how she can argue both sides of the moral question of how she can follow her love for Jason without betraying her family, before (temporarily) siding with 'Right' rather than 'Love'.

Ovid's political career did not, then, last long and he soon devoted himself to writing poetry. He may well have enjoyed the private means which other poets such as Horace did not have: or he may have continued with some business interests alongside his literary output. Literature was clearly, however, the focus of his life.

He began by writing love poetry in elegiac couplets: three books of *Amores* ('Loves' or 'Love-affairs') which are fully in the tradition of love-elegy as practised by Catullus, Tibullus, Gallus and Propertius. He published three books of these elegies, purporting to be love-poetry told in the first person: he followed this with the *Heroides*, which are fictional verse letters written by famous women of legend, such as Dido writing to Aeneas or Penelope to Ulysses. One of these (*Heroides* 12) is a fictional letter from Medea to Jason and it is fascinating to see how the poet made use in *Metamorphoses* VII of points and language which he had used in this earlier poem, as well as points drawn from the wonderful character assassination of Medea which we find put into the mouth of Jason's former lover Hypsipyle (*Heroides* 6.75-164).

Ancient literature only survived by being copied out by hand, and inevitably much of it did not make it. We know, for instance, that Gallus wrote wonderful elegies, but only possess a tantalising few lines today. Equally sad for readers of this book is the loss of Ovid's tragedy *Medea* which was praised by the Romans: the later orator and scholar Quintilian (X.1.98) pointedly said of it: 'Ovid's *Medea* shows what Ovid could have achieved if he had controlled rather than indulged his talent' – which suggests that it was regarded as superior to his elegies and other poems – and Tacitus (*Dialogus* 12.6) mentions it as one of the two great plays of the Augustan age.

Much of ancient literature was 'didactic' in that it claimed to 'teach' its readers lessons of one sort or another. Sometimes it was explicitly so, as in Nicander's poem *On Venomous Reptiles*, Lucretius' poem *De Rerum Natura* or Virgil's *Georgics*; and sometimes it was simply a feeling that poetry ought to educate young and old. Ovid next produced two works which pretended to be didactic literature, but composed them in the elegiac metre of love poetry rather than the hexameters of the traditional didactic epic. The *Medicamina Faciei Femineae* ('Medical Treatments for Women's Appearance') looked at how women could maintain their appearance with drugs and potions – very much in the style of the didactic poet Nicander. We only have 100 lines surviving of this poem, but the *Ars Amatoria* (the first two books of which were published in 1 BC) was a sustained experiment in applying the form of didactic poetry to the elegiac content of the life of love, instructing young men on seduction techniques and using abundant material from literature and legend as well as some vivid descriptions of such features of ancient Roman life as the Circus Maximus and its races. This was followed by the 'Antidotes to Love' (*Remedia Amoris* (1 BC–AD 2) which is clearly a sequel to the successful *Ars Amatoria*. Successful – but also disastrous for the poet as he was exiled from Rome in AD 8 by the emperor Augustus because of an unspecified poem (usually regarded as the *Ars Amatoria*) and a mysterious 'crime' which seems to have consisted in the poet witnessing something secret and which was scandalous enough to have him banished to remote Tomis (modern Constanza on the Black Sea coast of Romania) for the rest of his life.

The *Metamorphoses* ('Transformations') was written before this catastrophe and we will examine this poem in more detail in the next section of this introduction. Before his exile he had also begun to write the *Fasti* – a poem on the feasts and tales associated with the Roman calendar, with one book for each of the months of the year.

Once stranded in exile in Tomis he composed the *Tristia* ('Sad Things') published between AD 9–12. These are poems expressive of Ovid's misery in his banishment, as well as the *Epistulae ex Ponto* and the mysterious curse-poem *Ibis* (AD 10–11?). For all his poetic pleading, Ovid never returned to Rome and died at the age of sixty in AD 17.

## The *Metamorphoses*

Epic in the ancient world begins with Homer, whose *Iliad* and *Odyssey* – poems of enormous length composed in dactylic hexameters – framed the conventions of the genre for ever after. Homer's poems concern themselves with warriors and gods and contain speeches and elaborate similes, and this is very much what 'epic' meant to the ancient reader. Homer was imitated widely in the centuries after his death by writers such as Apollonius Rhodius (whose *Argonautica* is a major influence on this book of the *Metamorphoses*) and many others whose works have not survived. The influential writer and critic Callimachus, who lived and worked in the great library at Alexandria in Egypt, led something of a revolt against the predominance of epic ('I detest epic' is one of his pithier fragments) and promoted the idea of literature as miniature gems of stylistic perfection rather than the broad brush of the epic narrative. His own surviving works show this tendency to give us the unexpected rather than to follow the well-trodden path of Homeric imitation, to produce small-scale poems rather than long tales – and Roman poets found themselves under the conflicting sways of both Homer and Callimachus. The last generation of the Roman republic saw the emergence of the so-called 'Neoteric' poets (such as Catullus) who followed Callimachus' production of 'art for art's sake' and produced such small-scale masterpieces as Catullus' short epic on Peleus and Thetis (poem 64). Then came Virgil.

Virgil's debt to Homer is obvious: the very opening words of his great Roman epic *The Aeneid* salute his Greek predecessor, with the *arma* ('weapons') of *arma virumque cano* representing the *Iliad* and the *virum* being a nod towards Odysseus who is the 'man' mentioned in the first word of Homer's *Odyssey*. Virgil's epic breaks into two halves, an 'Odyssean' (Books I–VI) and an 'Iliadic' half (VII–XII) and his debt to Homer in terms of storyline, language, style are all immediately obvious. Virgil however created his own very Roman style of national epic which also helped itself to some less Homeric ingredients such as the extended exploration of Dido's love for Aeneas in Book IV.

Clearly when Ovid decided to write his own epic he was not just going to imitate Virgil but needed to find his own way. The result is the *Metamorphoses*, a continuous poem (*carmen perpetuum* as he calls it in *Metamorphoses* I.4) in fifteen books, containing roughly 250 tales of 'transformations' or 'shape-shifting'. Not for Ovid the concentrated narrative of the *Iliad*, dealing with a short period of time in the final year of the Trojan War, or the *Aeneid* with its movement in the direction of the foundation of Rome and her glorious future – although the *Metamorphoses* does begin with creation and ends with the deification of Julius Caesar. Ovid's poem jumps from time to time and place to place, and the links between the stories are at times tenuous. He keeps his readers on their toes by sometimes putting stories within other stories – as in this text where the tale of Procris (as told by Cephalus) is part of the tale of the embassy to Aegina. Homer's *Iliad* is dominated by the major theme of 'anger' and a group of characters in two opposing groups of Greeks and Trojans, whereas the *Metamorphoses* has a huge list of characters from a whole world of different times and places.

The obvious 'subject' of the poem is stated in its title ('changes of shape') which is what the Greek word *metamorphosis* means. In Book

VII we see people created from seeds and ants: elsewhere we see people turned into trees (Baucis and Philemon in VIII), flowers (e.g. Narcissus in III), the opposite sex (Tiresias in III), stars (Julius Caesar in XV) and even gods (Augustus' deification is prefigured at the end of the poem). This suits Ovid the writer perfectly as his blend of epic poetry and 'magic realism' is ideal for these tales of 'shape-shifting' which make up the poem.

It also suits Ovid the literary stylist who can change one literary genre into another as we see in this book. What starts out as 'straight' epic narrative (with the Harpies plaguing poor old Phineus) soon becomes something out of love elegy as Medea pours out her feelings in language which we could find in the love-poet Tibullus. Later on, Aeacus gives an account of the plague in Aegina which could have walked straight off the pages of Lucretius' didactic poem *De Rerum Natura* – which ends with a very similar account of the plague in Athens. Material from tragedy is used – Oedipus makes a surprise appearance at 759–61 and of course Ovid makes full use of tragedies by Euripides and by himself in telling the tale of Medea. The courtship of Cephalus and Procris contains a lot of material which could come out of pastoral poetry: Cephalus is undone by the sort of pastoral whimsy (he addresses words of love to the cool breezes) which we find in Theocritus and in Virgil's *Eclogues*. The scene where the dog Laelaps ('Storm') is chasing the huge fox which is terrorising the neighbourhood is both reminiscent of the epic tale of Meleager and the boar-hunt (Homer *Iliad* 9.529–99) and also oddly close to one of Virgil's most effective similes (XII.749–57). All these disparate materials in a variety of forms – tragedy, comedy, elegy, lyric, rhetoric and so on – find themselves metamorphosed into this highly sophisticated hexameter poetry. On the outside it all looks the same – but read the poem and you find yourself taken on something of a tour of ancient literature as well as a long voyage through the seas of myth and history.

Ovid also loves creating irony which has the effect of distancing the text from the reader and preventing excessive emotional involvement. The artistry shown dampens our engagement with the text but enhances our admiration for the poet. In this book, for instance, we know that the terrifying bulls and dragons are mere paper tigers after Medea has applied her magic balm to Jason, and the element of fear is thus reduced when he walks into their midst – although Ovid later (134–8) uses this as a way of stressing Medea's passion when he admits that even *she* doubts her own skill and starts to add words to reinforce the pharmacology. Conversely, the enemies facing Medea (the forces of Right and Duty towards her father) are also paper tigers which her love swats like flies in a few short lines (72–7). When Cephalus is silly enough to address the wind in language appropriate to a lover this is a comedy of errors but soon ends in tragedy when his beloved doubts *his* fidelity as he had earlier doubted hers.

This ironic manner makes Ovid a pleasure to read but has in the past made him seem a difficult poet to take seriously. Critics felt that he was just a clever wordsmith when set next to the gravity of a Virgil or a Homer. More recently, however, with the post-modernist emphasis on the textuality of literature and the self-conscious relationship which all writers have with their work and the life it reflects, Ovid has come more into fashion, and his tales of shape-shifting no longer seem so silly in the age of 'magic realist' writers such as Gabriel Garcia Marquez and Jorge Luis Borges and films such as the *Twilight* franchise.

## Book VII

There are nine major storylines in this book:

1 Medea's love for Jason
2 Jason's successful execution of the challenges ordered by Aeetes (bulls and dragon)
3 Medea's rejuvenation of Aeson
4 Medea's proxy murder of Pelias
5 Medea's union with Aegeus and foiled attempt to kill his son Theseus
6 Minos' war against Athens

A Level

7 The plague in Aegina
8 The birth of a new race of men from ants
9 Cephalus and Procris

A poem like this walks the tightrope of maintaining variety without losing unity. It is immediately obvious that these stories are not simply a ragbag of tales plucked out of nowhere and stitched together at random. The tales link together neatly and allow the book to fall into two halves: the first 5 tales (1–424) all concern Medea, while the rest of the book (425–865) is set in the run-up to the war which will start in earnest in Book VIII. The book is framed by tales of love, while the central tales vary the emotional landscape with stories of suspense and excitement. The book begins with what may seem to be a pointless thumbnail sketch of Phineus, but this is of course anything but pointless as it signals the theme of female power (those 'virginal birds' the Harpies) over pathetic men – a theme which will be amplified time and again in Medea (who plays old Aegeus like a virtuoso), in the goddess of the Dawn (who manipulates Cephalus into his tragic spiral of doubt and deceit) and in Procris herself who obsesses Cephalus in death as she did in life. Parents and children dominate many of the stories – Aeetes and Medea, Aeson and Jason, Pelias and his daughters – and yet the story we expect him to tell (of Medea killing her children) is barely mentioned.

It is also remarkable that (as part of a poem called *Metamorphoses*) there is very little obvious shape-shifting. Clearly the notion of 'metamorphosis' is being stretched to include the change wrought on old Aeson when his youth is restored to him, the devastating changes brought about by the plague in Athens which reduced a populous city to a deserted landscape, or the psychological change which sees Medea going from impressionable ingenue to accomplished witch. There are also changes of perspective – shown when both Procris and Cephalus alter their impression of each other with disastrous consequences.

Variety is provided in the way the tales are told. Some are reported by the omniscient narrator, others are the personal and highly partial accounts told by a character within the story, and these different speakers are characterised by their different ways of speaking, from the gushing passion of a Medea to the greybeard musings of Aeacus describing the plague.

## Ovid at work

The narrative style is never anything but inspired. The ants, for example, turn into men in a scene worthy of a Hollywood horror-film or Kafka's *Metamorphosis* (624–42):

> I saw a long train of food-gathering ants, carrying vast loads in their tiny mouths, and forging their own way over [the tree's] corrugated bark. Astonished at their numbers, I said 'Best of fathers, give me this many citizens and fill the city's empty walls'. The tall oak-tree quivered, and its branches filled with sound, even though no wind was blowing. I shivered, my limbs quaked with fear, and my hair stood on end. I kissed the oak-tree and the earth, without admitting my hopes – and yet I did hope, and cherished longings in my heart. Night fell, and sleep seized hold of our bodies, worn out with anxiety. There before my eyes appeared the same oak-tree, with the same branches, and the same insects on its branches, shaking with similar motion, and seeming to scatter its grain-bearing line [of ants] on to the ground below. Bigger and bigger they suddenly seemed to grow, they reared up from the soil, and stood upright, they lost their skinny physique, their many feet, and their black colouring, and their limbs took on human shape. Sleep left me. Wide awake, I dismissed my dreams and complained that I had no help from the gods: but there was a great noise in the palace, and I thought I could hear human voices which I was by then getting used to. I thought these too were dreams, when Telamon came running out and threw open the door, shouting 'Father, come and see something way in excess of anything you could hope for or even believe. Come now!'

The narrative voice could not be more first-person, and yet (once again) the narrator plays tricks on us: telling us it was all a dream and then telling us that it was all true, giving his fantasy free rein and then saying that the truth was even weirder than the dream, and adding an extra

**A Level**

layer of magic in the form of this revelatory dream to accompany and comment on the 'real' magic being performed. A similar effect is achieved in the description of Jason's yoking of the bulls (100–14):

> postera depulerat stellas Aurora micantes:     100
> conveniunt populi sacrum Mavortis in arvum
> consistuntque iugis; medio rex ipse resedit
> agmine purpureus sceptroque insignis eburno.
> ecce adamanteis Vulcanum naribus efflant
> aeripedes tauri, tactaeque vaporibus herbae     105
> ardent, utque solent pleni resonare camini,
> aut ubi terrena silices fornace soluti
> concipiunt ignem liquidarum aspergine aquarum,
> pectora sic intus clausas volventia flammas
> gutturaque usta sonant; tamen illis Aesone natus     110
> obvius it. vertere truces venientis ad ora
> terribiles vultus praefixaque cornua ferro
> pulvereumque solum pede pulsavere bisulco
> fumificisque locum mugitibus impleverunt.

The passage starts with a conventional epic way of saying 'dawn broke' but the phrasing is one of violence and witch-like magic: 'Dawn had driven off the stars', just as Medea can also move celestial bodies (207–9), and this sets the tone for what is to follow (as well as dropping the first hint of the power Dawn will reveal when she sets out to seduce Cephalus later). The two sides gather in the plain of Mars: scholars wonder if this is an anachronistic reference to the Campus Martius in Rome, but it may simply be another hint that the god of war will have a hand in the battle which is about to begin. King Aeetes sits in the middle in all his pomp and finery (102–3) with robes of purple and sceptre of ivory: pomp which is ironic in this case as his apparent power will be shown up as worthless when Jason sets to work and the apparent victim (Jason) becomes the real victor. The bulls are now pointed out (*ecce*) as they come into focus 'breathing out Vulcan from their adamantine noses': the poet could have used the common word for 'fire' as that is what was actually coming out of their nostrils, but using the name of the god of fire (after naming the field after the god of war) instead adds a level of power and intensity and makes this a battle of man vs gods as well as man vs beasts. Why does Ovid call the noses 'adamantine'? The obvious answer is that they would burn their own faces off if they did not have some sort of added protection, but the word *adamanteis* also has a good Greek pedigree going back to the earliest poetry which adds a layer of authority to the tale. The bulls are 'bronze-footed' (*aeripedes*) which adds auditory imagery (metal hooves make more noise than natural hooves) which the alliteration of line 105 (*tauri tactae*) enhances, and also (again) adds epic authority as the compound adjective (*aeripedes*) gives archaic grandeur to these mythical beasts. Just as when a conjuror is about to perform a trick, the audience have to be shown that the fire here is real: Ovid tells us that grass burns up when it is just 'touched' (*tactae*) by their *vaporibus* – a perfect word to connote both 'breath' and also 'heat' and elsewhere (*Metamorphoses* III.152, X.126) used of the destructive heat of the sun. The result is sudden and stressed: the single verb *ardent* ('burn up') is placed in enjambement at the end of the phrase and the start of the following line. We expect the poet to move straight onto Jason's encounter with the bulls but he keeps us in suspense for three lines while he describes the fire-breathing bulls in terms of two similes drawn from real Roman life: the furnace and the limekiln. Some scholars have suspected that Ovid is using these 'humble' analogies as a way of downplaying the legend: if these mythical beasts can be adequately described in terms of what is down the end of the Roman street then perhaps they are not so special after all. This is to miss two points. Firstly, the point of epic similes is often to make us imagine what we have never seen by pointing to something we have all seen: when, for example, Homer (*Odyssey* 5. 51–4) describes the god Hermes as being like a cormorant, this is because we all know what cormorants look like but most of us have never seen a flying god. In the second place, one of Ovid's sources for this tale, the *Argonautica* of Apollonius Rhodius also likes to use similes which can at times give us vignettes of very humble everyday life: at

*Argonautica* 4.1062–5, for instance, the lonely Medea is compared to a poor widow who has to work all night to support herself and her children. When Apollonius is telling this same story he uses an almost identical simile to illustrate it (*Argonautica* 3.1299–1304) and this was clearly Ovid's inspiration:

> Just as when in the case of perforated melting pots, the leather bellows of the blacksmiths at one moment shine brightly, kindling the lethal flame, at other times stop their breathing; a dreadful roar comes out of the fire when it rushes up from underneath – in this way the pair of bulls blew out swift fire from their mouths with a great noise …

Note, however, how Ovid alters Apollonius' terminology to fit Roman bellows, adding the scientific touch that (contrary to expectation) the contact with water *causes* rather than inhibits ignition. He also moves from the general (*camini*) to the very specific Roman limekiln with very specific *silices* being melted: and note how Ovid smoothly brings back the 'tenor' (the bulls) from the 'vehicle' (the bellows) of his simile by focussing on the mechanics at work, their panting throats well conveyed in the assonance of *gutturaque usta* and the mingling of the flames deep inside their chests well suggested by the interlocking word order of *pectora sic intus clausas volventia flammas* (literally: 'chests thus inside enclosed rolling flames'). After all this build-up over seven lines, Jason simply strides towards them (*obvius it*). All he needs to do is not to be destroyed and in this case that is just a matter of facing them. Their features are still terrifying (*terribiles*) and their iron-tipped horns are still lethal, to bring home the bravery of Jason's approach: Ovid then adds more auditory imagery in the beating of the earth with plosive alliteration (*pulvereumque solum pede pulsavere*) and even olfactory imagery as their bellowing raises smoke (*fumificis*). The metre assists the meaning: the rapid dactyls of *pulvereumque solum pede* give way to a thumping spondee in *pūlsāvēre* and the following line goes even further with that rarest of Ovidian line-endings, the fifth foot spondee. Note the concentration of heavy syllables in *īmplēvērūnt* as the bellowing of the beasts echoes around the plain. Roman poets always had to assert originality while also being faithful to the literary tradition which they inherited, and Ovid's use of traditional epic material – the similes, the patronymics, the story itself – is tinged with his own ironic touch. These bulls had to be terrifying if Jason's task was to be heroic, but we know (as Jason does but the watching crowds do not) that the dangers they pose are trivial after his anointing by Medea. The crowd's response is genuine: but the reader is let in on the trick and can smile at these monsters as our hero strides towards them and ends up stroking their necks as if they were domestic animals. Does this diminish Jason's heroism? Not necessarily, since heroism is about more than just brutality and bravery, and (after all) the hero of Homer's *Odyssey* (Odysseus) owes his survival to his arts of persuasion and intelligence at least as much as to his strong right arm. Jason, like Odysseus, has the brains to overcome the insuperable foes against him and we can enjoy the vivid artistry (and the dramatic irony) of these lines without engaging our emotions too much, safe in the knowledge that he will survive in triumph. That said, Jason is not characterized with excessive subtlety in this book. He says little – a few words reported in indirect speech (89–91) and a short plea at 164–8 – and comes across as a man who gets on with the task without too much questioning of anything. By contrast, about 100 lines of lines 1–227 are direct quotation of Medea speaking to herself or to others. Her personality is drawn by what she does and by what she says, and readers may well wonder where this most formidable of women came from.

## Who was Medea and what does Ovid do with her story?

Medea in Greek legend was the granddaughter of the Sun God Helios and the daughter of King Aeetes of Colchis. Early accounts (such as Hesiod *Theogony* 992–1002 and Pindar *Pythian* 4.11) show that her divine origins made her more than mortal – she was a 'heroine' who lived and died among men but went to Elysium after her death and may even have married Achilles there. In this she resembled other 'heroes' such as Hercules – who was born of the god Jupiter and the woman Alcmene: he died as a man but was given immortality after this death. There was, however, no hard-and-fast rule: Aeneas was the son of a goddess (Venus) and the mortal Anchises but lived (and died) a totally human existence, whereas Dionysus (born of Jupiter and the mortal woman Semele) was a 'full' god from birth onwards. Helios also fathered the sorceress Circe who is treated by Homer as very human in her psychology and emotion but divine in her abilities. Medea shares this same existential ambivalence, being human enough to suffer pain and to arouse empathy from audiences from ancient times to the present day, but also supernatural in her power to manipulate people and the world around her.

This is seen most clearly in Euripides' *Medea* from 431 BC – a play which continues to be performed all over the world to great acclaim but which did not please the original Athenian audience who voted it into last place in the dramatic competition of that year.

In Euripides' play, Medea begins in a state of apparent emotional collapse as her husband Jason has left her and their children to secure an advantageous marriage with the daughter of Creon, the king of Corinth. Medea is to be exiled that very day. As the play proceeds she persuades Creon to allow her to stay one more day and (against his better judgement) he agrees. She pretends to accept Jason's decision in a crucial scene with him, throwing him off his guard, and she secures a place of refuge by doing a deal with Aegeus (king of Athens) who needs her help to produce an heir and offers her refuge in Athens in exchange. She now exacts a grisly revenge on Jason by murdering his new bride, and also his new father-in-law Creon. Some earlier versions of the legend had it that the Corinthians then killed Medea's children as punishment for her murder of their royal family, but Euripides raises the ethical and emotional temperature through the roof by having Medea kill her own children to punish Jason further, and this version of the legend is the one which stuck. She (as a semi-divine being) escapes scot-free on a chariot drawn by dragons. She began the play in a state of

**A Level**

collapse and ends the play literally looking down with righteous scorn on her errant husband as she makes her triumphant escape.

Euripides' play is certainly unusual. It can be performed by two actors rather than three: it does not feature the three-way dialogues which are so prominent in plays such as Sophocles *Oedipus the King*, and this has the effect of giving Medea dramatic dominance as she manipulates man after man (Jason, Creon and then Aegeus) with speeches which are masterpieces of dissembling hypocrisy. In the course of the play, Medea coins some of the most famous lines in tragedy as she bemoans the lot of women in ancient Greece:

> *Men say that we live a safe existence at home while they fight wars: well they are wrong. I would rather stand in the battle-line three times than bear a single child.*
>
> 248–51

In response, Jason comes across as an unfeeling chauvinist who trots out stereotypical prejudices against women as sex-mad feeble-minded people who should be grateful for all they receive from men like him. The moral side of the argument is loaded – to most readers at least – in that there is no doubt who is in the wrong in terms of the betrayal of a woman who has given up everything to help this selfish Greek: but the moral landscape swiftly changes when Medea begins to plot the murder of her children.

She does not kill them lightly but agonises at great length about the deed to the audience, to the chorus (whom she has sworn to secrecy), and to her own heart in a moment of searing indecision (1236–50, ending with the line '*I am an unfortunate woman*'). Her decision is framed in heroic terms – she cannot bear her enemies laughing at her and getting away with it (1049–50), just as Sophocles' Ajax has to commit suicide after his humiliation before his fellow-Greeks and Homer's Achilles cannot fight for a commander who has humiliated him. In the heroic world, status was everything; and Medea is more heroic than the puny men with whom she has to deal, who underestimate her to their cost. Her divine origins make this even more important as

A Level

Medea is not a million miles away from the scorned Aphrodite who punishes Hippolytus for his rejection of her in Euripides' *Hippolytus*, and the slighted god Bacchus who humiliates and then arranges the murder of that 'despiser of the gods' Pentheus in Euripides' *Bacchae*.

This short summary does not do justice to the psychological depth of this play, however. If Medea were simply a cold-hearted child-killer then the audience would find her simply repugnant. What Euripides achieves is to make his Medea both heroic and demonic, both terrifying and pathetic, both feminine and masculine. She lets *us* into the secret workings of her heart while also tricking the men on stage with her careful dissembling. Euripides shows us the forces which drive a woman to commit the most heinous of crimes. By the end of the play, we understand how the murder has come about, just as we understand by the end of Aeschylus' *Agamemnon* why its hero had sacrificed his daughter and been in turn murdered by his wife on his return. We understand how it has happened but we still cannot fathom what would make a loving mother behave like that.

Medea's place in the legend of the Argonauts was already known, and the Hellenistic epic poet Apollonius of Rhodes (third century BC) created the finest Greek account of Medea and her involvement in the venture in books 3 and 4 of his epic poem *Argonautica*. This account tells some of the tales which Ovid later picks up: the fire-breathing bulls, the dragon's teeth and the acquisition of the fleece. He adds further details not found in Ovid, such as Medea's murder of her brother Apsyrtus (see 51–2n.) and the need for her and Jason to be purified for this crime by her aunt Circe. He does not take the story past the return of the married couple, and his Medea is a frightened girl who thinks of taking her own life (3.766–9, 4.11–25) rather than the spine-chilling murderess of Euripides' play – although Euripides' heroine does begin the play in a state of anorexic despair. She feels pity for Jason at first and only gradually falls in love with him – no romantic love-at-first-sight here. The poet explores the clash of reason and passion in her heart with deft and cogent skill, putting into her mouth speeches of expressive unclarity which reveal the deep uncertainty within her heart.

Roman dramatists took up the tale, and it is a great pity that many of their versions do not survive. Ennius and Accius both wrote tragedies called *Medea*, based on plays by Euripides and Sophocles respectively, but of these only fragments survive: in the Neronian period Seneca composed a wonderful version in his play *Medea*.

Ovid clearly found Medea a congenial subject for his poetry: her ability to transform the world around her made her an obvious character to use in the *Metamorphoses*, but before that he had explored her character and her psychology in his much-admired but lost drama *Medea* and also in his early work *Heroides*.

The *Heroides* purport to be first-person elegies in the mouths of great women of ancient legend, and two of these poems (6 and 12) are highly relevant to this book. In poem 6 we read the lament of Queen Hypsipyle of Lemnos who had formed a close relationship with Jason when he visited her island on his way to Colchis. He has promised to return once he had secured the fleece, but never came back, and Hypsipyle has now heard about Medea who was the new woman in his life – gossip travels fast even in the ancient world. She is filled with righteous indignation at being rejected in favour of this 'barbarian mistress' (*barbara paelex* (6.81)) who has won his heart by her magic rather than any personal merits (83–4). Medea is a frightening bedmate:

> *Can you embrace this woman? Can you be left alone in a bedroom with her and still enjoy a peaceful night's sleep? She must have made you bear the yoke as she made the bulls do so and she clearly pacifies you with the same means as she pacifies savage serpents.*
>
> 6.95–8

Hypsipyle in this poem is troubled by the apparent triumph of Medea in taking her place in Jason's affections – only for this to be nicely overturned in poem 12 where the same Medea, now herself abandoned, utters the same sort of reproaches as her predecessor to the same faithless lover. Medea in this poem reminds Jason of what she has done for him and also stresses how terrified she was for him:

> When I went to bed, sorely hurt (by love), I spent the night in tears, and what a long night it was. Before my eyes stood the bulls and the unspeakable harvest, before my eyes was the unsleeping serpent. On one side love, on the other side fear; and the fear only increased my love.
>
> 12.57–61

Medea casts herself as a diffident lover with a close relationship to her sister and a gullible heart which was easily taken in by this devious Greek. Jason swears his oath of fidelity to her and only now does she smell a rat:

> These words (and many more like that) moved the heart of a simple girl, as did his right hand joined to mine. I also saw his tears – or was that too just part of the scam? I was a girl who was quickly overcome by your words.
>
> 12.89–92

She has thrown everything away and now regrets it:

> My father has been betrayed. I abandoned his kingdom and my fatherland. My reward was to be allowed a life in exile. My virginity was made the spoil of a foreign bandit, my excellent sister has been abandoned along with my dear mother.
>
> 12.109–12

Bad enough, but worse is to follow as she hesitantly reminds Jason of their murder of her brother and wishes she had been torn limb from limb in his place (113–14). Medea's life has been one of criminal subservience to Jason and she now harbours retrospective thoughts of suicide, wishing she and Jason had perished on the sea-voyage. She thinks she has lost the use of her powers since her magic cannot control this man, or her love for him:

> I was able to subdue serpents and savage bulls, but could not subdue this one man. I who repelled wild fires with my skilled medicines do not have the power to escape the fires of my own passion.
>
> 12.163–6

A Level

Ironically – to the reader of *Heroides* 6 – Medea refers (12.173) to Jason's new wife as a 'mistress' (*paelex*), which was the term Hypsipyle used of Medea (6.81). Hypsipyle had complained (6.75) that Medea would enjoy what should have been hers, and Medea says just the same:

> *A mistress embraces the limbs which I saved, and she now has the benefit of my trouble*
>
> 12.173–4

Chickens have come home to roost, but the difference is that Medea (unlike Hypsipyle) has the power to take decisive revenge on Jason's new bride (12.180–2). There is one last flickering of hope in Medea – and the great advantage of the epistolary setting of the *Heroides* is that the thoughts are frozen in time and space as are those of any other letter. She has not totally given up on him (12.191–4) and pleads by their shared children to restore her to his marital bed – only to return to her former wrath and end the poem on a note of dark menace:

> *I will follow where my anger leads me. Perhaps I will regret my actions, but I already regret that I acted out of regard for a faithless man. Let god see to that – the god who is now at work in my heart. My mind is without doubt stirring up something serious.*
>
> 12.209–12

Neither in the *Heroides* nor in *Metamorphoses* 7 does Ovid spell out Medea's murder of her children: the tale was so well known (cf. Propertius III.19.17–18, Horace *Ars Poetica* 185) that he could allude to it in the briefest of terms without explanation. Neither text gives Jason anything other than contempt and hatred – in the *Metamorphoses* the only crumb of moral goodness is found in Jason's offer to exchange years of life with his old father. Throughout the two poems, Medea is the dominant personality and the character whom the poet explores in depth: Jason is the soldierly, dutiful man who does what is expected of him and uses whatever – and whoever – is to hand to help him. He does not agonise – he does not really have a choice about what he is to do – whereas Medea self-consciously articulates her choices and takes us deep into her thought-processes, just as she did in Euripides' play.

In exploring Medea's behaviour Ovid is not excusing or justifying anything. He tells the story and leaves us to do the rest. Euripides had been mocked by the comic playwrights for filling the stage with wicked women, and Ovid also sails close to the wind at times in his depictions of the extremes of human nature in his treatment of such matters as incest. He does not do so in a spirit of prurience, however, but uses human psychology as yet another part of the amazing world around him which can delight but which can also appal us in equal measure. The poet's role is to be faithful to the subject matter and to use it to recreate the finest verse he can.

## Literary terms used in the commentary

***ab urbe condita*** construction: the completed action is described in a past participle: e.g. 56 *servatae pubis* ('saved youth') here means 'saving the youth' (cf. also 159).

**Anaphora**: rhetorical repetition of a word, often (but not always) at the start of successive phrases e.g. *tum ... tum* (32–3).

**Chiasmus**: parallel clauses where the order of items in the second is inverted from the order in the first (ABBA) such as *nimium dura ... dura nimis* (14–15) or *aliud cupido mens aliud* (19–20).

**Enjambement**: 'running on' of a sentence into the following line, often allowing the final word of the sentence to be stressed at the start of the following line as with *conscelero* (35) or *ardent* (106).

**Epic periphrasis**: an elevated way of describing a person or a thing in arch and stilted language such as *curvamine falcis aenae* ('the curve of a bronze sickle' 227) to mean 'a curved bronze sickle'.

**Golden line**: a line in which a central verb is framed by two adjectives before it and two nouns following it (aavnn) such as line 117 *pendulaque audaci mulcet palearia dextra*.

**Juxtaposition**: creating emphasis or contrast by setting words next to each other, as when Medea (205) emphasises her power over nature with the juxtaposed verbs *moveo iubeoque* or the chiasmus in line 75 which juxtaposes the key adjectives *umbrosum secretaque*.

A Level

**Metaphor** is the description of one thing in terms of another, using of words which cannot literally be true: for example 210 'you blunted (*hebetastis*) the flames of the bulls'.

**Metonymy**: 'changing names' such as by using (104) the name of the god of fire (Vulcan) to mean simply 'fire', a device which here enhances the imagery of the terrifying power of these bulls.

**Onomatopoeia**: where the sound of the words matches or even imitates their meaning, such as *mugitibus* ('bellowing' 115) or *ululatibus* ('howlings' 190).

**Oxymoron**: a sharp contrast in meaning of adjacent terms, such as *rapidas limosi* ('swift-flowing muddy') in line 6.

**Pathetic fallacy**: endowing inanimate things with human feelings. *miris ripantibus* in 199 supposes that the river-banks are 'amazed' at the reverse-flowing river.

**Patronymic**: naming a person simply by calling them 'child of' their father. Jason is thus *Aesonides* (60), Medea is *Aeetias* (9).

**Pleonastic** language over-eggs the pudding by using excessive and/or unnecessary terms: *muta silentia* ('dumb silences' 184) or the 'liquid waters' at 108.

**Polyptoton**: the repetition of a word in different grammatical forms as with *concussaque sisto/ stantia concutio* (200–1).

**Polysyndeton**: creating a list with excessive use of connective terms as with Medea's list of natural forces at 197 (*aurae**que** et venti montes**que** amnes**que** lacus**que***)

**Rhetorical question**: a question which does not expect an answer and which is used to vary the tone. Medea asks many such rhetorical questions in her speech to herself (11–71): e.g. *quae tanti causa timoris?* ('what is the reason for so much fear?' 16)

**Synecdoche**: alluding to a thing by mentioning one part or aspect of it: 'wedding-torch' for 'marriage' (49), 'poop-deck' for 'ship' (1), 'bed' for 'marriage' (91).

**Synizesis**: the merging of separate vowels into a single metrical syllable, as at *praeacutae* (scanned *prae(a)cutae*) at 131 or *aureae* (scanned *aur(e)ae*: 151)

**Tricolon**: a sequence of three phrases which may become successively longer ('tricolon crescendo' as at 35–6) or progressively shorter ('tricolon decrescendo' as at 201–2).

**Zeugma**: one verb governing two objects, with one of them literal and the other metaphorical, as at 133 where *demisere ... vultumque animumque* means 'they lowered their faces and their spirits'.

## The metre of the poem

Latin poetry is written in a fairly rigid system of metres, all of which in turn relies on the pattern of heavy and light syllables, and the metre of the *Metamorphoses* is the 'hexameter' which is a line of six 'feet'. The first four of these 'feet' can be either 'dactyls' (-∪∪) or 'spondees' (--), where the symbol - indicates a heavy syllable and the symbol '∪' a light one. It is usually assumed that a heavy syllable is equivalent to two light ones. The fifth foot of a hexameter is almost always a dactyl (line 114 is the exception in this text) and the final foot is always one of two syllables, and so it is either a spondee or else a trochee (-∪).

Syllables which contain a diphthong (i.e. a pair of vowels pronounced together such as *au*, *ae*) or else a long vowel are heavy syllables, and syllables where a short vowel is followed by two (or more) consonants are also made heavy – although not necessarily if the second consonant is 'l' or 'r', such as in the word *proboque* at the end of line 20 where the final syllable of *meliora* preceding it is not lengthened. The two consonants do not have to be in the same word as the vowel for this to take place (e.g. 136 *et subito* where the (short) 'e' of *et* is followed by initial 's' which creates a heavy syllable).

Single vowels may be long or short by nature and may vary with inflection (e.g. the final -*a* of *mensa* is long by nature in the ablative case, short in the nominative) and one must be aware that the letter 'i' may be a vowel in some places (*nix*) and a consonant in others (*iam*). The quantity of long vowels is marked with a '-' symbol in the vocabulary at the end of this book.

In cases where a word ending with a vowel (or a vowel + m) is followed by a word beginning with a vowel or *h*, the two syllables usually merge ('elide') into a single syllable, as at 79 where *alimenta assumere* is scanned as *aliment' assumere*.

**A Level**

Thus a 'typical' hexameter line (149) will run:

— UU/— U U /– // –/ – –/–U U /– -
*pervigil/em super/est// her/bis sop/ire drac/onem*

where the // sign shows the 'caesura' – the word-break in the middle of a foot within the line. This usually happens in the third foot after the initial heavy syllable but can also come in the middle of the two short syllables in a dactyl, where it is usually accompanied by a caesura in the fourth foot, as in line 42

*si facere hoc aliamve potest// praeponere nobis*

Lines varied in length: the maximum number of dactyls would give a line of 17 syllables, as at line 57 where an excited Medea is chattering to herself:

*nōtĭtĭ/āmquĕ sŏ/lī// mĕlĭ/ōrĭs ĕt/ ōppĭdă/ quōrŭm*

The shortest lines have only 13 syllables, as at line 152 where Jason is drugging the snake into sleep:

*hūnc pōst/quām spār/sīt// Lēth/āeī/ grāmĭnĕ/ sūcī*

Latin words also have a natural stress accent (which works as in the same way as English words such as táble, spectátor, fúrniture), whereby most words were stressed on the penultimate syllable, or on the antepenultimate if the penultimate were a short vowel. Thus the final line of the book would be spoken:

*Túraque dánt sánctasque cólunt Isménides áras*

but 'scanned' metrically as:

*Túraque dánt sanctásque colúnt Isménides áras*

Quite how the two ways of reading Latin verse blended or competed is unclear: one notes that in hexameters there is a tendency for the stress accent and the metrical ictus to collide in the earlier and middle parts of the line but to coincide at the end – a tendency which is however

A Level

abruptly broken when the line ends with monosyllables as at 12 (*nisi hoc est*).

# Further reading

The text printed in this book is based on that of the most recent Oxford Classical Text of the poem by Richard Tarrant (Oxford, 2004), but I have followed the spelling of the *Oxford Latin Dictionary* in assimilated prefixes, printing (for instance) *submisso* rather than *summisso* at 191. I have also printed third declension accusative plural endings as *-es* rather than *-is*.

There are several accessible **translations** of the whole of the *Metamorphoses*:

Stephanie McCarter (Penguin Classics, London, 2023)
Allen Mandelbaum (Everyman Library, London, 2013)
Stanley Lombardo (Indianapolis, 2010)
A. D. Melville (Oxford World Classics, Oxford, 2008)
David Raeburn (Penguin Classics, London, 2004)

There are no single-book editions of Book VII but the following larger **commentaries** deal with this text:

W. S. Anderson *Ovid's Metamorphoses Books 6-10* (text and commentary, Oklahoma, 1972)

F. Bömer *Metamorphosen Buch VI-VII* (commentary in German, Heidelberg, 1976)

D. E. Hill *Metamorphoses 5-8* (edited with translation and brief commentary, Oxbow Books, 1992)

## For general books on the *Metamorphoses* see:

Fantham, E. *Ovid's Metamorphoses* (London, 2004)
Feldherr, A. *Playing Gods: Ovid's Metamorphoses and the Politics of Fiction* (Princeton, 2010)
Galinsky, K. *Ovid's Metamorphoses: an Introduction to the Basic Aspects* (Oxford, 1975)
Janan, M. *Reflections in a Serpent's Eye* (Oxford, 2009)
Otis, B. *Ovid as an Epic Poet* (Cambridge, 1966)

## For more general discussions of Ovid see:

Hardie, P. *Ovid's Poetics of Illusion* (Cambridge, 2007)
Hardie, P. (ed.) *The Cambridge Companion to Ovid* (Cambridge, 2002)
Morgan, L. *Ovid – A Very Short Introduction* (Oxford, 2020)
Knox, P. E. *A Companion to Ovid* (Blackwell Companions to the Ancient World, 2009)
Wilkinson, L. P. *Ovid Recalled* (Cambridge, 1955)

## Articles analysing the content and the techniques of *Metamorphoses* 7 (available on JSTOR) include:

Hinds, Stephen 'Medea in Ovid: Scenes from the Life of an Intertextual Heroine' *Materiali e discussioni per l'analisi dei testi classici* 30 (1993): 9–47
Libatique, Daniel 'A Narratological Investigation of Ovid's Medea: *Met.* 7.1–424' *The Classical World* 109 (2015): 69–89
Rosner-Siegel, Judith A. 'Amor, Metamorphosis and Magic: Ovid's Medea (*Met.* 7.1–424)' *The Classical Journal* 77 (1982): 231–43
Segal, Charles 'Black and White Magic in Ovid's *Metamorphoses*: Passion, Love, and Art' *Arion* 9 (2002): 1–34

## For Medea in Apollonius Rhodius' *Argonautica* see:

Apollonius of Rhodes *Argonautica* Book 3 edited Richard Hunter (Cambridge, 1989)
Apollonius of Rhodes *Argonautica* Book 4 edited Richard Hunter (Cambridge, 2015)

## For more information on the metre of Latin hexameter poetry see:

Kennedy, B. H. *The Revised Latin Primer* (London, 1962) pp. 204–5

# Text

iamque fretum Minyae Pagasaea puppe secabant,
perpetuaque trahens inopem sub nocte senectam
Phineus visus erat, iuvenesque Aquilone creati
virgineas volucres miseri senis ore fugarant,
multaque perpessi claro sub Iasone tandem 5
contigerant rapidas limosi Phasidos undas.
dumque adeunt regem Phrixeaque vellera poscunt
lexque datur Minyis magnorum horrenda laborum,
concipit interea validos Aeetias ignes
et luctata diu, postquam ratione furorem 10
vincere non poterat, 'frustra, Medea, repugnas:
nescioquis deus obstat,' ait, 'mirumque, nisi hoc est,
aut aliquid certe simile huic, quod amare vocatur.
nam cur iussa patris nimium mihi dura videntur?
sunt quoque dura nimis! cur, quem modo denique vidi, 15
ne pereat, timeo? quae tanti causa timoris?
excute virgineo conceptas pectore flammas,
si potes, infelix. si possem, sanior essem.
sed trahit invitam nova vis, aliudque cupido,
mens aliud suadet: video meliora proboque, 20
deteriora sequor. quid in hospite, regia virgo,
ureris et thalamos alieni concipis orbis?
haec quoque terra potest, quod ames, dare. vivat an ille
occidat, in dis est; vivat tamen! idque precari
vel sine amore licet: quid enim commisit Iason? 25
quem, nisi crudelem, non tangat Iasonis aetas
et genus et virtus? quem non, ut cetera desint,
ore movere potest? certe mea pectora movit.
at nisi opem tulero, taurorum afflabitur ore
concurretque suae segeti, tellure creatis 30

hostibus, aut avido dabitur fera praeda draconi.
hoc ego si patiar, tum me de tigride natam,
tum ferrum et scopulos gestare in corde fatebor.
cur non et specto pereuntem oculosque videndo
conscelero? cur non tauros exhortor in illum              35
terrigenasque feros insopitumque draconem?
di meliora velint! quamquam non ista precanda,
sed facienda mihi. prodamne ego regna parentis,
atque ope nescioquis servabitur advena nostra,
ut per me sospes sine me det lintea ventis                40
virque sit alterius, poenae Medea relinquar?
si facere hoc aliamve potest praeponere nobis,
occidat ingratus! sed non is vultus in illo,
non ea nobilitas animo est, ea gratia formae,
ut timeam fraudem meritique oblivia nostri;               45
et dabit ante fidem, cogamque in foedera testes
esse deos. quid tuta times? accingere et omnem
pelle moram! tibi se semper debebit Iason,
te face sollemni iunget sibi, perque Pelasgas
servatrix urbes matrum celebrabere turba.                 50
ergo ego germanam fratremque patremque deosque
et natale solum ventis ablata relinquam?
nempe pater saevus, nempe est mea barbara tellus,
frater adhuc infans; stant mecum vota sororis.
maximus intra me deus est! non magna relinquam,           55
magna sequar: titulum servatae pubis Achivae
notitiamque loci melioris et oppida, quorum
hic quoque fama viget, cultusque artesque locorum,
quemque ego cum rebus, quas totus possidet orbis,
Aesoniden mutasse velim, quo coniuge felix                60
et dis cara ferar et vertice sidera tangam.
quid quod nescioqui mediis concurrere in undis
dicuntur montes ratibusque inimica Charybdis
nunc sorbere fretum, nunc reddere, cinctaque saevis

Scylla rapax canibus Siculo latrare profundo?    65
nempe tenens quod amo gremioque in Iasonis haerens
per freta longa ferar; nihil illum amplexa verebor
aut, si quid metuam, metuam de coniuge solo –
coniugiumne putas speciosaque nomina culpae
imponis, Medea, tuae? – quin aspice, quantum    70
aggrediare nefas, et, dum licet, effuge crimen!'
dixit, et ante oculos Rectum Pietasque Pudorque
constiterant, et victa dabat iam terga Cupido.

ibat ad antiquas Hecates Perseidos aras,
quas nemus umbrosum secretaque silva tegebat,    75
et iam fortis erat pulsusque resederat ardor,
cum videt Aesoniden exstinctaque flamma reluxit.
erubuere genae, totoque recanduit ore,
utque solet ventis alimenta assumere, quaeque
parva sub inducta latuit scintilla favilla    80
crescere et in veteres agitata resurgere vires,
sic iam lenis amor, iam quem languere putares,
ut vidit iuvenem, specie praesentis inarsit.
et casu solito formosior Aesone natus
illa luce fuit: posses ignoscere amanti.    85
spectat et in vultu veluti tum denique viso
lumina fixa tenet nec se mortalia demens
ora videre putat nec se declinat ab illo;
ut vero coepitque loqui dextramque prehendit
hospes et auxilium submissa voce rogavit    90
promisitque torum, lacrimis ait illa profusis:
'quid faciam, video: nec me ignorantia veri
decipiet, sed amor. servabere munere nostro,
servatus promissa dato!' per sacra triformis
ille deae lucoque foret quod numen in illo    95
perque patrem soceri cernentem cuncta futuri
eventusque suos et tanta pericula iurat:

creditus accepit cantatas protinus herbas
edidicitque usum laetusque in tecta recessit.

postera depulerat stellas Aurora micantes: 100
conveniunt populi sacrum Mavortis in arvum
consistuntque iugis; medio rex ipse resedit
agmine purpureus sceptroque insignis eburno.
ecce adamanteis Vulcanum naribus efflant
aeripedes tauri, tactaeque vaporibus herbae 105
ardent, utque solent pleni resonare camini,
aut ubi terrena silices fornace soluti
concipiunt ignem liquidarum aspergine aquarum,
pectora sic intus clausas volventia flammas
gutturaque usta sonant; tamen illis Aesone natus 110
obvius it. vertere truces venientis ad ora
terribiles vultus praefixaque cornua ferro
pulvereumque solum pede pulsavere bisulco
fumificisque locum mugitibus impleverunt.
deriguere metu Minyae; subit ille nec ignes 115
sentit anhelatos (tantum medicamina possunt!)
pendulaque audaci mulcet palearia dextra
suppositosque iugo pondus grave cogit aratri
ducere et insuetum ferro proscindere campum:
mirantur Colchi, Minyae clamoribus augent 120
adiciuntque animos. galea tum sumit aena
vipereos dentes et aratos spargit in agros.
semina mollit humus valido praetincta veneno,
et crescunt fiuntque sati nova corpora dentes,
utque hominis speciem materna sumit in alvo 125
perque suos intus numeros componitur infans
nec nisi maturus communes exit in auras,
sic, ubi visceribus gravidae telluris imago
effecta est hominis, feto consurgit in arvo,
quodque magis mirum est, simul edita concutit arma. 130

quos ubi viderunt praeacutae cuspidis hastas
in caput Aesonii iuvenis torquere parantes,
demisere metu vultumque animumque Pelasgi;
ipsa quoque extimuit, quae tutum fecerat illum.
utque peti vidit iuvenem tot ab hostibus unum, 135
palluit et subito sine sanguine frigida sedit;
neve parum valeant a se data gramina, carmen
auxiliare canit secretasque advocat artes.
ille gravem medios silicem iaculatus in hostes
a se depulsum Martem convertit in ipsos: 140
terrigenae pereunt per mutua vulnera fratres
civilique cadunt acie. gratantur Achivi
victoremque tenent avidisque amplexibus haerent.
tu quoque victorem complecti, barbara, velles:
[obstitit incepto pudor, at complexa fuisses,
sed te, ne faceres, tenuit reverentia famae.] 145
quod licet, affectu tacito laetaris agisque
carminibus grates et dis auctoribus horum.
pervigilem superest herbis sopire draconem,
qui crista linguisque tribus praesignis et uncis 150
dentibus horrendus custos erat arboris aureae.
hunc postquam sparsit Lethaei gramine suci
verbaque ter dixit placidos facientia somnos,
quae mare turbatum, quae concita flumina sistunt,
somnus in ignotos oculos sibi venit et auro 155
heros Aesonius potitur spolioque superbus
muneris auctorem secum, spolia altera, portans
victor Iolciacos tetigit cum coniuge portus.

Haemoniae matres pro natis dona receptis
grandaevique ferunt patres, congestaque flamma 160
tura liquefaciunt inductaque cornibus aurum
victima vota cadit; sed abest gratantibus Aeson
iam propior leto fessusque senilibus annis,

cum sic Aesonides: 'o cui debere salutem
confiteor, coniunx, quamquam mihi cuncta dedisti 165
excessitque fidem meritorum summa tuorum,
si tamen hoc possunt (quid enim non carmina possunt?)
deme meis annis et demptos adde parenti.'
nec tenuit lacrimas: mota est pietate rogantis,
dissimilemque animum subiit Aeeta relictus; 170
nec tamen affectus tales confessa 'quod' inquit
'excidit ore tuo, coniunx, scelus? ergo ego cuiquam
posse tuae videor spatium transcribere vitae?
nec sinat hoc Hecate, nec tu petis aequa; sed isto,
quod petis, experiar maius dare munus, Iason. 175
arte mea soceri longum temptabimus aevum,
non annis renovare tuis, modo diva triformis
adiuvet et praesens ingentibus adnuat ausis.'
tres aberant noctes, ut cornua tota coirent
efficerentque orbem; postquam plenissima fulsit 180
ac solida terras spectavit imagine luna,
egreditur tectis vestes induta recinctas,
nuda pedem, nudos umeris infusa capillos,
fertque vagos mediae per muta silentia noctis
incomitata gradus: homines volucresque ferasque 185
solverat alta quies, nullo cum murmure saepes,
immotaeque silent frondes, silet umidus aer,
sidera sola micant: ad quae sua bracchia tendens
ter se convertit, ter sumptis flumine crinem
irroravit aquis ternisque ululatibus ora 190
solvit et in dura submisso poplite terra
'Nox' ait 'arcanis fidissima, quaeque diurnis
aurea cum luna succeditis ignibus astra,
tuque, triceps Hecate, quae coeptis conscia nostris
adiutrixque venis cantusque artisque magorum, 195
quaeque magos, Tellus, pollentibus instruis herbis,
auraeque et venti montesque amnesque lacusque,

dique omnes nemorum, dique omnes noctis adeste,
quorum ope, cum volui, ripis mirantibus amnes
in fontes rediere suos, concussaque sisto, 200
stantia concutio cantu freta, nubila pello
nubilaque induco, ventos abigoque vocoque,
vipereas rumpo verbis et carmine fauces,
vivaque saxa sua convulsaque robora terra
et silvas moveo iubeoque tremescere montes 205
et mugire solum manesque exire sepulcris.
te quoque, Luna, traho, quamvis Temesaea labores
aera tuos minuant; currus quoque carmine nostro
pallet avi, pallet nostris Aurora venenis!
vos mihi taurorum flammas hebetastis et unco 210
impatiens oneris collum pressistis aratro,
vos serpentigenis in se fera bella dedistis
custodemque rudem somni sopistis et aurum
vindice decepto Graias misistis in urbes:
nunc opus est sucis, per quos renovata senectus 215
in florem redeat primosque recolligat annos,
et dabitis. neque enim micuerunt sidera frustra,
nec frustra volucrum tractus cervice draconum
currus adest.' aderat demissus ab aethere currus.
quo simul ascendit frenataque colla draconum 220
permulsit manibusque leves agitavit habenas,
sublimis rapitur subiectaque Thessala Tempe
despicit et certis regionibus applicat angues:
et quas Ossa tulit, quas altum Pelion herbas,
Othrysque Pindusque et Pindo maior Olympus, 225
perspicit et placitas partim radice revellit,
partim succidit curvamine falcis aenae.

# Commentary Notes

## 1–158

Jason meets Medea and persuades her to help him in his quest of the golden fleece in defiance of her father Aeetes, king of Colchis.

Book VI ended with the happy tale of the love of the god of the North wind (Boreas) for the Athenian princess Orithyia, resulting in the birth of twin sons who are blessed with wings inherited from their father. These boys grow up and the last lines of the book read: 'and so, when their period of boyhood gave way to that of being young men, they joined the Minyans in going over an unknown sea in the first ship ever, to seek the bright gleaming fleece'. Book VII joins them as the Argonauts are well into their voyage.

**1 Minyae** refers to the Argonauts, many of whom were said to be descended from King Minyas who ruled over the Minyae tribe in Boeotia in Greece. Pagasa was the town in Thessaly where the Argo was built: **puppe** properly means just the 'poop deck' of the ship but stands as often for the whole vessel in synecdoche. The imperfect tense **secabant** starts the book at a time when the narrative is already (**iam**) well advanced – a common device in ancient epic.

**2–3 Phineus** was a prophet who was blinded by Jupiter, when he revealed the gods' plans, and then forced to live on the Thracian coast. He is used here almost as a landmark – showing that the Argo has left the Mediterranean for the Black Sea – but also to introduce an element of horror into this book right at the start. Phineus was tormented by the Harpies – winged scavengers who stole his food or else befouled it and made it inedible – until the 'Boreads' (sons of the North Wind (**iuvenes Aquilone creati**) Calais and Zetes, who were members of the crew and whose birth ended Book VI) drove these creatures away in exchange for his advice on their route. Ovid brings out Phineus' blindness with

A Level

**perpetua ... sub nocte** and his hunger both with **inopem** and with the word **ore** (which can mean 'face' but also 'mouth').

**4** Ovid does not need to name the Harpies, simply calling them 'virgin birds' and expecting the reader to know the details. **fugarant** is the syncopated version of the pluperfect tense (*fugaverant*).

**5 perpessi** is the past participle from the deponent verb *perpetior*. **claro** highlights Jason's heroic status right at the start of the book: other versions of the Medea legend depict him in less flattering terms and it is possible that Ovid is being sarcastic. **tandem** expresses the length of the voyage.

**6** The river Phasis shows that we are in Colchis, in what is now Western Georgia. The epithet 'muddy' (**limosi**) may possibly be an allusion to the theory that iron oxide in the river water which the sheep drank caused the fleece to turn gold in colour. Note the oxymoronic juxtaposition of **rapidas limosi**.

**7–9** The use of conjunctions is telling: **dum** ('while') subordinates the primary purpose of the voyage (the acquisition of the fleece) to the passion (**ignes**) of the girl who is the main focus of this text. The **regem** is Medea's father Aeetes, king of Colchis. **Phrixēa**: Phrixus and his sister Helle were children of Athamas of Thebes: to escape their hostile stepmother Ino they were transported over the sea on a winged ram with a golden fleece. Helle fell into the sea (later called the Hellespont) while Phrixus made it to Colchis, where the ram was sacrificed and its wonderful fleece hung up and guarded by the dragon which Jason has to subdue (149–58).

**8 magnorum ... laborum** is a genitive going with **lex** ('a condition involving great toils'). The passive verb **datur** reinforces the weakness of the Argonauts and the term **horrenda** (the gerundive of *horreo*) adds that the condition was 'dreadful'. Without Medea's help it would have been impossible.

**9 Aeetias** is 'the daughter of Aeetes' i.e. Medea: epic poetry likes to refer to characters by naming their parent (a device known as the 'patronymic': Jason is three times called *Aesonides* ('son of Aeson') in this text for instance). This device requires readers to know the family background of the characters. The line is framed with the key words: **concipit** ... **ignes** literally means 'she catches fire' but her 'fire' is one of passion, as often in Roman love poetry (e.g. Catullus 35.15). The wording is recalled at line 17.

**10-11**   **luctata**: literally 'having wrestled', from *luctor*. Medea has been 'wrestling' with herself, pitching her 'reason' (**ratione**) against her 'passion' (**furorem**) and seeing her passion win.

## 11-71

Medea expresses her feelings in a fine speech of self-recrimination and self-justification, exploring her emotions and letting us eavesdrop on her as she agonises about her dilemma: Scylla has a similar speech in very similar circumstances in VIII.44-80.

**11-12**   Resistance is pointless as 'some god or other' (**nescioquis deus**) is in the way (**obstat**). Medea uses strong present tense indicative verbs expressing her certainty of what can in fact only be conjecture, although it was not uncommon for characters in epic to assume the help or hostility of gods when they encountered unexpected success or failure.

**12-13**   'and it is amazing if this – or else something very similar to it – is not what 'love' is called'. The infinitive **amare** is used as a neuter noun.

**14**   **nam** introduces the reason for her supposition that she is in love – her father's orders have not seemed excessively (**nimium**) harsh (**dura**) in the past. Medea now begins a series of rhetorical questions to herself.

**15**   Note how the verb **videntur** ('appear') at the end of 14 is changed at once to the adamant **sunt** and how Medea uses chiasmus when she repeats **nimium dura** as **dura nimis**.

**15–16** **modo denique** here means 'only just recently'. **ne** + subjunctive (**pereat**) is a clause of fearing with **timeo**. Note how Medea repeats the word 'fear' from **timeo** in **timoris** with indignant alliteration and in a further rhetorical question. **quae** is from the interrogative *qui* ('what is the reason for such great fear?').

**17** Medea uses the language which the poet had used of her at line 9, ordering herself to 'knock out' the flames of passions from her breast. **virgineo** (going with **pectore**) reminds us that she has never been in love before (cf. 12–13 and **nova vis** in line 19).

**18** A neat line, falling into two halves at the caesura, the second half rebutting the first. **possem** and **essem** are imperfect subjunctives in remote conditionals in present time ('if I were able, I would be less crazy'). **infelix** and **sanior** show that her feelings are not those of joy but rather of disturbed unhappiness craving fulfilment through Jason.

**19** **nova vis** ('power I have not felt before': i.e. love) is another expression of the innocent girl's inability to understand what is happening to her. **trahit invitam** go well together to denote the force pulling the reluctant girl along: cf. Seneca's dictum (*Letters* 107.11) that the forces of destiny *ducunt volentem*, *nolentem trahunt* ('lead the willing man, drag the reluctant one').

**19–20** **aliud ... aliud** means 'one thing ... another' (with chiasmus of **aliudque cupido mens aliud**) and the verb **suadet** is to be taken with each of the two subjects **cupido** and **mens**, picking up the contrast of *furorem* and *ratione* in line 10.

**20–1** Some of the most famous lines in Latin poetry: 'I see what is better and I approve of it – but I follow what is worse'. This inner psychological conflict is at the heart of the speech.

**21–2** Medea tries to argue herself out of a humiliating marriage with one who is beneath her and who would take her away from her kingdom. The juxtaposition of **hospite regia virgo** is pointed (he is only a guest in the house while she is a princess) and **alieni ... orbis** (literally '[belonging to] another person's world') exaggerates the trip to Greece which she will undertake in a single line at 158. **ureris** (from *uror*) is another example of 'love as fire' imagery, while **thalamos** (literally 'bedroom', another case of synecdoche) here means 'marriage' but the use of the Greek term hints at the exotic quality of the wedlock envisaged.

**23   ames** is a relative final subjunctive ('something to love'). Medea picks up the pace of her words with the maximum number of dactyls permitted in a hexameter.

**23-4   in dis est** is the main clause ('it is in the hands of the gods') and [*utrum*] **vivat an . . . occidat** are the alternative outcomes ('whether he lives or dies'), with the verbs in the subjunctive as they are indirect questions. The notion of divine responsibility for individual fates is common from Homer onwards (e.g. *Iliad* 17.514, 20.435, *Odyssey* 1.267) and picks up her opening remarks at line 12.

**24-5   vivat tamen**: the verb here is a jussive subjunctive ('let him live!'). She then offers an ethical reason for her prayer based on the man's innocence which is undeserving of pain, although **vel sine amore** gives away her true feelings.

**26-7   tangat** is a potential subjunctive and the singular verb has several subjects, suggesting that **genus** and **virtus** are afterthoughts – clearly it is Jason's youth (**aetas**) which is uppermost in her mind, rather than his nobility and courage.

**27-8   ut cetera desint**: 'even though he lacked the rest' (i.e. youth, nobility and courage). The subject of **potest** is now Jason who can stir anybody with his 'face' (**ore**) – i.e. beauty. Note the rhetorical repetition of the same verb in different tenses (**mŏvere . . . mōvit**).

**29-31**   Medea feels that she has to save him from certain death. The sentence is a simple future conditional with future perfect (**tulero**) in the protasis ('if' section) followed by confident future indicative verbs for what will happen otherwise. The terms of the **lex horrenda** as drawn up by Aeetes are envisaged in her fretful mind: he will be 'breathed on' (**afflabitur**) by the mouth of the bulls which he has to yoke and then use to plough a field. Next he will have to 'run at his own crop' (**concurretque suae segeti**) when he sows the dragon's teeth and faces the warriors which will spring up fully-formed. The last step is to get the fleece and risk being fed (as 'a savage piece of prey' (**ut ... fera praeda**)) to the 'greedy' dragon. Ovid reminds the readers of the key stages of the story while also revealing Medea's anxious state of mind.

**30-1** **tellure creatis/ hostibus** are in explanatory apposition to **suae segeti**. The adjectives **avido** and **fera** might seem otiose but they indicate her feelings: Medea pictures with horror her beloved being treated as a piece of meat and fed to this enthusiastic predator.

**32** **patiar** is future indicative. **tigride**: Medea makes use of a common trope in ancient poetry, that cruel people must be born from the sea, from rocks or from wild animals rather than humans – cf. Homer *Iliad* 16.33–5: Scylla makes similar points at VIII.120–1 where the bestial parent is a tiger as here: there may also be an ironic allusion to Euripides' play *Medea* in which Jason calls (1342) Medea a 'lioness' when denouncing her at the end of the play. Note the anaphora of **tum ... tum** in 32–3. **natam**: understand *esse* as this is the perfect infinitive of *nascor* in indirect speech ('I will admit that I was born from a tigress').

**33** 'Having iron in one's heart' is another way of saying 'cruel' and 'unfeeling': it goes back to Homer (*Odyssey* 23.103) and found its way into love poetry (Tibullus I.1.63–4, Propertius I.16.29–30). **fatebor** has the sense of 'admit to'.

**34-5** Following on from the idea of inhumanity, Medea challenges herself to watch Jason die – why can she *not* do this? – and answers her own question with the enjambed verb **conscelero** at the end of the sentence and the start of the next line: watching his suffering would 'defile' her eyes. This is interesting in a culture which enjoyed the sight of animal and human suffering in the arena. Note the emphasis on 'seeing' in 34 (**specto . . . oculosque videndo**) and the present participle **pereuntem** to indicate that she would be watching him 'as he dies'.

**35–6** Not content with passive viewing, Medea takes things further and imagines herself encouraging the lethal beasts, here depicted in a rising tricolon of horror: (a) **tauros** (b) **terrigenasque feros** (c) **insopitumque draconem**. **terrigenas** is a compound noun ('earth-born creatures') while **insopitum** ('unsleeping') seems to be a coinage of the poet. Medea is speaking in grand epic language.

**37  di meliora velint** – literally 'may the gods wish better things [than this]', with **velint** a jussive subjunctive. As in line 24, the assumption is that the gods control our destiny. **di** is the contracted form of *dei* here and in 198.

**37–8** Medea at once changes tack from fatalistic hope in divine providence to decisive action by herself. **precanda** and **facienda** are both gerundives of obligation ('things to be prayed for' and 'things to be done') and **mihi** takes the stress at the end of the sentence as the onus falls on Medea to act.

**38  prodam . . . parentis**: Medea at once sees the moral problem – helping Jason will betray her own father.

**39** A neat line in ABCBA sequence: **ope** goes with **nostra**, **nescioquis** with **advena**, and the main verb **servabitur** is central.

**40–1** Medea cynically but realistically speculates on what is likely to happen: Jason will use her to get the fleece and then flee. He will marry somebody else while she faces punishment for her treachery. The unfairness is brought out by the juxtaposition of **per me . . . sine me** and the large number of monosyllables suggest that she is jabbing her finger as she speaks. **det lintea ventis**: 'so that he may offer his sails to the winds' means 'so he can set sail'. The end-result is marriage with Jason for 'somebody else' (**alterius**) while she is abandoned to her punishment: **poenae** is in the dative case and **Medea** is the subject of the verb **relinquar**.

A Level

**42–3** If Jason is so heartless, then let him die! **occidat** is a jussive subjunctive.

**43–5** Medea argues (most implausibly) that so attractive a man cannot be unfaithful: a good example of deluded psychology which is more revealing of her passion than of her reason. She lists his attractions in a tricolon of phrases (cf. 26–7) each introduced by the demonstrative use ('that') of the third person pronoun (**is . . . ea . . . ea**). The sentence is a consecutive clause: these are not 'such as to make me fear . . .'. **meriti . . . nostri** is an objective genitive going with **oblivia** ('forgetfulness of my service').

**46–7** Medea compounds her naiveté with a pious belief that this Greek would not break an oath. Jason duly swears a complex oath at lines 94–7 and still ends up abandoning her (394–7). **ante** here is adverbial ('beforehand').

**47 tuta** could be either feminine nominative singular (agreeing with the speaker) or else neuter plural as the object of **times**. **accingere** (from *accingo*) is the passive imperative in a 'middle' sense of 'gird yourself [for action]'. The abrupt staccato style of this and the following line is suggestive of her agitated state of mind.

**48 se . . . debebit**: *debeo* primarily means 'I owe' and so the phrase here means 'Jason will owe his life to you'. Note the emphatic sibilant alliteration and the assonance of 'e' in **se *se*mper *de*bebit**.

**49 te . . . sibi** chiastically picks up **tibi se** from line 48. A *fax* was a fiery torch which was burnt at weddings, and so **face solemni** (ablative of manner) is synecdoche for 'in solemn marriage'. Ovid's readers will probably know that the only such solemn marriage was the one Jason conducted with his new bride Creusa when he abandoned Medea and their children in Greece.

**49–50 Pelasgas**: the Pelasgi were a tribe who lived in what is now Greece and in poetry the term means 'Greek'. The word goes with **urbes** in line 50. **celebrabere** is the second person singular of the future passive of *celebro* and **turba** is an ablative of agent ('you will be hailed by a crowd of mothers'). Medea rightly (see 159–62) envisages herself as saving the sons of these mothers – i.e. the Argonauts who will return safely home.

**51–2** Medea at once sees that fame abroad will be more than matched by the vilification she deserves at home. Medea's sister is called Chalciope in Apollonius, who has her positively helping Medea. Her brother Apsyrtus also 'helps' Medea and Jason in their flight as the pair dismember him and throw him overboard to delay the pursuing Colchians (who have to pick up the severed limbs from the water). **ablata** is nominative singular agreeing with Medea ('carried off by the winds').

**53–5** Medea answers her qualms with rhetorical repetition of **nempe** which here means 'yes, since . . .'. **saevus**: her father Aeetes is a harsh man (see 14–15) who has imposed a lethal *lex horrenda* (8) on Jason in his quest. **barbara** means 'uncivilised': Jason in Euripides' *Medea* (536–8) claims credit for bringing her from a 'barbarian' land to Greece. Medea's use of the term here is ironic: she is cast as the 'barbarian woman' in Greece and her exotic mastery of drugs and magic is also part of her image throughout antiquity (see e.g. Tibullus I.2.53, II.4.55).

**54** The line is framed by her siblings, with both being dismissed as obstacles. **vota** are prayers, often accompanied by vows to perform an act of homage if the prayer is answered. **stant mecum** ('they are firmly on my side') shows great confidence in her sister's unwavering support.

**55** The 'greatest god' here is the god of love who motivates her actions: note how the superlative **maximus** leads to the repeated simple form **magna** as she recasts her treacherous flight as honourable ambition.

**56–61** Medea's list of her goals is framed in terms of her happiness and her reputation. A *titulus* was usually a label attached to a statue recording the name and achievement of the person being honoured: here the achievement is that of 'saving the youth of Greece': and at the end of the passage she sees herself as being 'regarded as loved by the gods' (**dis cara ferar**) and 'touching the stars with her head' – all suggestive of divine felicity and fame.

**56  servatae pubis** is in the *ab urbe condita* construction where the completed action in a past participle is used for the action itself: 'saved youth' here means 'saving the youth'. **Achivae** (like *Pelasgas* at 49) here means 'Greek'.

**57–8**  Medea now lists the benefits awaiting her in Greece, whose reputation (**fama**) has reached even the land of Colchis (and which explains how she knows about Greece: 'even here' **hic quoque**). **loci melioris** is an objective genitive with **notitiam** ('knowledge of a better place'). **cultus** here means 'civilised culture' as at Virgil *Aeneid* VIII.316, while **artes** are 'fine arts'.

**59–60**  Medea crowns her list of attractions with Jason himself, whom she wants more than all the world. **quem** here must mean '[the man] whom' and is only identified in the following line with the distinguished epic patronymic (see line 9) **Aesoniden** ('son of Aeson' i.e. Jason). The construction is: 'whom I would be willing to have in exchange for [all] the things which the earth possesses'. **velim** is a potential subjunctive and **mutasse** is the syncopated form of *mutavisse* (perfect infinitive of *muto*).

**60–1**  **quo coniuge** is an ablative going with **felix** ('happy with him as my husband'). The resulting happiness is stated three times: (a) **felix** (b) **dis cara ferar** (c) **vertice sidera tangam**. **felix** indicates requited love (cf. Tibullus I.5.18–19), **dis cara** also suggests requited love (divine opposition is enough to thwart romantic happiness as at Catullus 76.12) while 'touching the stars with one's head' can denote 'being world-famous' (as in Homer *Odyssey* 9.20) but also suggests sharing divine felicity: Horace *Odes* I.1.36 uses similar phrasing in both senses. **ferar** here means 'I shall be deemed'.

**62–5**  Medea has (it seems) read Homer's *Odyssey* and Apollonius' *Argonautica*, and knows the perils of seafaring – in this case the dangers of the clashing rocks, Charybdis, and Scylla.

A Level

**62 quid quod**: 'what of it that ...'. The 'peaks' (**montes**) which are said to run together (**concurrere**) are the Symplegades or 'Clashing Rocks' which crush any vessel trying to pass between them. Jason was famed for getting through them with advice from Phineus and the help of a dove: see Homer *Odyssey* 12.59-72, Apollonius 2.317-340, 5.922-81. Medea distances herself from the threat with **dicuntur**.

**63-5** Charybdis was a whirlpool which sucked ships down to the depths of the sea. The alternating withdrawal and regurgitation of water is well conveyed in the parallel phrases **nunc sorbere... nunc reddere**. Scylla, with her twelve feet, six heads, three rows of teeth, voice of a dog (**latrare**) and dogs attached to her waist, was a monster who lived on the opposite side of the channel from Charybdis and the pair are commonly used of equal and opposing threats. Scylla snatched up sailors from their ships and so could only take six at a time, whereas Charybdis could destroy the whole ship. For a graphic account of both threats in action see Homer *Odyssey* 12.235-59. The two were commonly located in the Straits of Messina (**Siculo ... profundo** 'in the Sicilian seas').

**66** Medea will fear nothing if she is holding (**tenens**) Jason and clinging to his embrace (**gremio...haerens**). Her excitement is stressed with the run of rapid dactyls in 66-7.

**67-8 ferar** (passive of *fero* in the sense of 'travel') could either be future indicative or else a jussive subjunctive. **amplexa** repeats her image of his embrace and allows her to admit that any fear she has will be for him and not for herself, neatly stressed with the repetition of **metuam**.

**69-71** Medea ends the speech with a sharp self-correcting u-turn. **coniuge** in 68 reminds her that Jason is not her **coniunx** (but only a visitor) and she then chides herself with words drawn almost straight from Virgil's *Aeneid* (IV.172): Dido the queen of Carthage has fallen in love with Aeneas and Virgil comments drily '*coniugium vocat; hoc praetexit nomine culpam*' ('she calls it marriage and with this name

A
Level

conceals her wrongdoing'). **quin** emphasises the imperative **aspice** ('take a good look …'). The present subjunctive **aggrediare** is in an indirect question after **quantum**. Her final words are poignant: instead of fleeing the country (with Jason), flee the wrongdoing itself.

**72-3** Medea sees the personifications of good moral qualities standing before her and Cupid is portrayed as a defeated enemy. **Rectum** is 'correct behaviour', **Pietas** is behaving well towards her family and the gods of the state, while **Pudor** is feminine modesty which would resist throwing away her honour on a *hospes*. We know from lines 20-1 that Medea is unlikely to follow her moral instincts: four lines later she is back in love.

**74** Medea is often linked with Hecate – goddess of the moon, the underworld and of witchcraft – in ancient literature (cf. Tibullus 1.2.53-4) and it is Hecate to whom she has Jason swear his oath of fidelity (94-5). Hecate's father was the Titan Perses.

**75** Note the chiastic word order which juxtaposes **umbrosum secretaque** and the sibilant alliteration suggestive of the rustling of leaves.

**76-7** The tenses are expertly handled and add to the immediacy and the pace of the story: Medea 'was being' (**erat** (imperfect)) strong (**fortis**), and her passion *had* died down (pluperfect (**resederat**)) when 'she sees' (**videt** (present tense)) and the flame 'has now rekindled' (**reluxit** (perfect tense)). Jason is named with the glorious patronymic **Aesoniden** again (see 9n.). For the image of sexual passion as a fire cf. 9, 21-2.

**78** **erubuere** is the shortened form of *erubuerunt* (third person plural, perfect tense of *erubesco*). The two verbs in this line indicate heat and light as Medea's face glows with desire.

**79-83** A wonderful simile to illustrate the rekindling of desire as analogous to the rekindling of a fire. A literal translation is: 'just as a tiny spark tends to draw nourishment (**alimenta**) from the winds, [a spark] which has lain hidden under a covering of ash [tends] to grow and, when stirred (**agitata**), to rise up again to its former strength'. The subject of the verb **solet** is **scintilla** in line 80 and the delay in revealing this word enacts the delay in the viewer seeing the hidden spark until it has been relit. The juxtaposition and verbal similarity of **scintilla favilla** bring out the spark lurking in the ash.

82 **lēnis** here means 'calm'. **iam** means 'by now': one might suppose that her former feelings would be inactive. **putares** (like **posses** in 85) is an indefinite second person singular verb addressed to the reader ('you might think').

83 The line is framed by the verbs. The subject of **inarsit** is **amor**.

84 **Aesone natus**: Jason is again named by reference to his parentage ('born of Aeson'). **solito** is ablative of comparison with **formosior** ('more attactive then usual'). Ovid amusingly ascribes Jason's sudden increase in beauty to chance (**casu**).

85 **illa luce** here means 'on that day'. **posses** is a potential subjunctive and **amanti** is the dative singular of the present participle here acting as the indirect object of **ignoscere**: 'you could forgive her loving him'.

86-8 Medea's protracted gaze is enacted in the phrasing which repeats the basic idea of 'look at' four times (**spectat ... viso ... lumina ... videre**).

86 **vultu veluti tum denique viso**: 'as if she had only then finally seen his face' (i.e. 'as if she had never seen him before'), with the repeated 'v' sounds suggesting open-mouthed admiration.

87-8 **demens** shows that the battle between *ratio* and *furor* (10) which she thought had been decided in favour of good sense and morality (71) has now ended with Medea losing her reason altogether. Her view of his face as being 'not that of a mortal' (i.e. divine) is not so strange in a poem where gods often come down disguised as humans.

**89–90** The subject of the verbs is only revealed in line 90 to be Jason. **hospes**: 'the stranger' recalls Medea's use of the same word to distance herself from him at line 21, but is also pointed: guests in ancient Greece were entitled to seek protection from their hosts and so the poet's use of this word justifies his begging for help (**auxilium**). It also enhances the shock value of this 'stranger' offering marriage one line later (91).

**91** **torum** is literally a 'bed' but here stands in synecdoche for 'marriage', like *thalamos* in 22.

**92** **faciam** is a present subjunctive in an indirect question ('I see what I am doing'). Her clear-sightedness extends also to her own future deception (**decipiet**) by love, recalling her struggle with her conscience at 20–1. **servabere** is the second person singular future passive of *servo* addressed to Jason ('you will be saved') and **munere** is an instrumental ablative ('by my assistance').

**93** **servatus** picks up **servabere**. **dato** is the archaic 'future' imperative with greater force than *da*.

**94–7** Jason swears by the 'rites of the triple goddess' (Hecate), by the Sun, and by his own future. Hecate is triple (**triformis**) as she embodied Diana and the Moon along with herself, being thus present in the underworld and the sky as well as on the earth. The Sun god is invoked as the ultimate witness since he 'sees everything' (**cernentem cuncta**) and so could call out misbehaviour as he did when he saw Venus and Mars in adulterous union in Homer's *Odyssey* (8.270–1); he is also related to Medea as she was his granddaughter, which makes him father of Jason's 'prospective father-in-law' (**soceri ... futuri**). To include any unknown gods Jason also swears by 'the divine power which was in that grove', although the grove was clearly linked to Hecate (74–5). **foret** is an alternative form of *esset* and is subjunctive in indirect speech. Finally he swears by the risks he is taking, in a cross-your-heart-and-hope-to-die form of oath. **eventus** – the 'outcomes' are (at this stage) unknown and **pericula** ('dangers') shows the uncertainty surrounding them: he is (it is suggested) risking his life if he commits perjury.

A Level

**98 creditus** is an abnormal passive participle from the intransitive verb *credo* ('having been believed') which in standard Latin would have to be an impersonal passive (*ei creditum est*).

## 100–21

The first task: Jason yokes the fire-breathing bulls and makes them plough the field.

**100** The pluperfect tense **depulerat** sets the scene as being (by now) daylight. Epic poetry likes to provide depictions of a personified Dawn to open a new episode (cf. IV.81, Virgil *Aeneid* IX. 459–60, Homer *Odyssey* 2.1) but here the epic motif may be pointed since 'casting out stars' prefigures the magic about to be set in motion.

**101** The **populi** are the Argonauts on the one hand and the native Colchians on the other, gathering appropriately in a plain dedicated to the god of war (*Mavors* is the archaic form of *Mars*).

**102–3** King Aeetes attends in person (**ipse**) in all his rich finery – hyper-expensive purple and ivory. **purpureus** - 'dressed in purple'. Take **medio . . . agmine** together ('in the middle of the platoon').

**104–5** **ecce** introduces the first combat in fine epic style. **aeripedes** is a compound adjective ('bronze footed'), the god Vulcan here stands in metonymy for 'fire' and the adjective **adamanteis** ('made of steel', explaining how the bulls can snort fire unharmed) is a resonant Greek word found here for the first time in Latin poetry. **naribus** is ablative with the verb **efflant** ('they breathe out of their nostrils').

**105–6** As if to prove that the act was not a stunt, grasses 'touched' (**tactae**) by their scorching breaths (**vaporibus**) 'do burn' (**ardent** emphasised in enjambement).

**106–10** A double simile from the blacksmith's furnace (**camini**) and the limekiln to illustrate the combination of fire and noise shown by the bulls. The similes, with their level of detail and real interest in the processes, are reminiscent of the analogies found in didactic poetry such as Lucretius (who explained thunder in similar terms at *De Rerum Natura* VI.148–9).

**107** The Romans invented the limekiln in the first century BC to produce cement and mortar by melting limestone (**silices** can denote a range of stones but here means 'limestone') in a clay oven (**terrena ... fornace**).

**108** Ovid points out that the sprinkling of water onto the kiln causes the stones to combust. **liquidarum** may seem otiose here – isn't water always liquid? – but the juxtaposition with **ignem** shows the sharp reaction of the two elements.

**109–10** The bulls' chest and throat act as a kind of bellows producing the roaring sound. Note how **sic intus clausas** is itself enclosed inside **pectora ... volventia**. **volventia** (literally 'rolling') well evokes the billowing flames inside the chest-cavity.

**110–11** After the lengthy description of their terrifying nature, Jason 'nonetheless' (**tamen**) goes to meet them and does so in a simple matter-of-fact way (**obvius it**) emphasised in enjambement. **illis** is dative with **obvius**.

**111–12** The poet emphasises the bulls' ferocity: they are 'savage creatures' (**truces**) and his face (**ora**) is met by their own 'terrifying faces' (**terribiles vultus**). **venientis** refers to Jason. Ovid adds the further frightening touch that their horns are tipped with iron.

**113–14** These lines are highly expressive. Note the alliteration and the rapid dactyls of **pulvereumque solum pede** to denote the beating of hooves, the sudden spondee as the pace slows with the sonorous **pulsāvēre** (the shortened verse form of *pulsaverunt*). Similar effects are produced in the four words which make up line 114: note the epic compound adjective **fumificis** (literally 'smoke-making'), the onomatopoeic **mugitibus** and then the highly unusual fifth-foot spondee and single word ending the line (**impleverunt**).

**115 deriguere** – from *derigesco* ('to become stiff') is an epic term commonly used of the effects of fear. **ille** refers to Jason and **subit** has the sense of 'undergo' as well as simply 'walk up to'.

**116–17** **tantum** is adverbial. The **medicamina** are the prophylactic drugs supplied by Medea (98–9). The subject of **mulcet** is Jason, who now humorously treats these fire-breathing monsters as domestic animals, stroking their 'hanging dewlaps' (**pendula** . . . **palearia**) to lull them into submission. Line 117 is a 'golden line', with a central verb framed by two adjectives before it and two nouns after in abVAB form: after the storm of the conflict Jason imposes poetic peace on the scene.

**118–19** Understand *tauros* with **suppositos iugo** which denotes the first stage ('he puts them under the yoke'): Jason then 'compels (**cogit**) them to shoulder the heavy burden of the plough'. **ferro** can go with the verb ('to tear open with the blade') and also with **insuetum** ('not accustomed to the blade').

**120–1** **Colchi, Minyae**: note the juxtaposition of the names: the stupefied Colchians over against the Argonauts (**Minyae**) who roar their support and so increase their hero's spirits (**animos**).

**121–2** The second phase is the sowing of the dragon's teeth which Aeetes had acquired from the goddess Athena. These teeth were left over from those which Cadmus had sown in the foundation of Thebes, as narrated earlier by Ovid (III.1–137), and the outcome would be the same in both cases. **galea** . . . **aena** is ablative of source ('from a bronze helmet').

**123** The seeds were 'steeped' (**praetincta**) in the venom from the dragon, but this poison had no damaging effects on their germination – quite the opposite, in fact – and the phrase may be concessive ('for all that they were steeped in poison . . .').

**124** The 'sown teeth' become 'new bodies' (**nova corpora**) but we do not see exactly what they look like for a few lines. The juxtaposition of **corpora dentes** emphasises the sudden shock of the transformation.

**125–7** As with the double simile at 106–10, Ovid here brings in an analogy from the natural world of childbirth. **ut** here means 'just as' and is picked up by **sic** ('in this way') in 128. The subject of the verb **sumit**

is revealed at the end of the next line (**infans**): **perque suos ... numeros** here means 'through its successive stages' and the lines beautifully depict the growing foetus being 'put together' (**componitur**) inside the mother's womb, taking on human appearance (**hominis speciem**) as it grows and emerging in the final word as the fully-formed infant (**infans**). **nec nisi maturus** 'and only when fully grown'.

**128-9** Ovid maintains the analogy with childbirth by using the metaphor of 'in the bowels of the pregnant earth'. Note also how **imago ... hominis** picks up **hominis speciem** in 125, and **feto ... in arvo** ('in the fruitful field') picks up **materna ... in alvo** ('in its mother's belly').

**130** The unexpected final stage of growth is now flagged up with 'what is more amazing is that ...'. **edita** could be read as nominative singular agreeing with **imago** ('as soon as it was born') but is more likely to be accusative plural agreeing with **arma** which were 'born' along with the men and which the newborn warrior at once 'clashes' (**concutit**).

**131-3** A complex sentence to indicate the mental confusion of the watching Greeks. 'When the Greeks saw these [men] preparing (**parantes**) to fire (**torquere**) their sharp-tipped spears at the head of the Aesonian young man'. **Pelasgi** here means 'Greeks' as at 49: *Aesonius* 'belonging to Aeson' is a variant of the patronymic form (see 9n.) to refer to Jason. **praeacutae** has to be scanned as three long syllables, swallowing the second syllable (*prae(a)cutae*) in what is called synizesis: this is a genitive of quality ('spears of sharpened tip').

**133** A good example of zeugma to emphasise the Greeks' instant loss of hope: they 'lowered their faces and their spirits'.

**134** **ipsa** is Medea, who has not been mentioned since line 99 and who is now shown to have been watching the events all along. Her doubts about her own powers to protect Jason remind us of her obsessive love for him.

**135** **ut** here means 'when' and **peti** is the present passive infinitive of *peto*: 'when she saw that the young man on his own (**unum**) was being attacked by so many enemies'. **unum** postponed to the end of the line brings out the disparity in the conflict (with **tot**) and the pathos of the lonely hero.

**136** Medea turns pale with fear, and **palluit** is here accented by its prominence at the start of the line. Note also the sibilant alliteration of the rest of the line which may suggest the shivering heroine, and the almost medical detail of her bloodless chill and sudden need to sit down. **subito** is adverbial ('suddenly').

**137–8** **neve parum valeant** – 'and in case the herbs she had given him might be insufficiently effective'. **ne** + subjunctive here is a negative final clause. The **gramina** were handed over at lines 98–9. Medea now adds singing to her sorcery, providing an incantation as back-up (**auxiliare**) and 'summoning her secret skills'. **auxiliare** is a word more commonly associated with military history, emphasised here in enjambement to bring out the novelty of the expression.

**139** **silicem**: in the legend, Jason threw a rock into the middle of the warriors who then blamed (and killed) each other for doing so. Ovid assumes that his readers will know the story.

**140** **Martem** (the god of War) here simply means 'conflict', which Jason 'diverts from himself' (**a se depulsum**).

**141–2** Ovid describes the mutual self-slaughter of the 'earth-born' (**terrigenae**) warriors in terms reminiscent of civil war, stressing that these are 'brothers' (**fratres**) perishing from mutual injuries and falling 'in civil strife', with the mutuality stressed by the assonance of **pereunt ... mutua vulnera** and their savagery suggested by the harsh 'c' alliteration of **civilique cadunt acie**.

**142–3** **Achivi** refers (like *Pelasgi* 133) to the Greeks, who now congratulate Jason in an orgy of celebration, 'clinging to him with greedy embraces'.

**144** In a nice segue, Medea sees the men embracing her beloved and would wish to be doing the embracing for herself, with the same word **victorem** repeated to bring this out: **velles** is an imperfect potential subjunctive ('you would want') addressed to Medea who is called **barbara** ('foreign woman') not in a spirit of xenophobic acerbity but simply to point out that Medea was not one of the Greek crew and so did not have access to their leader.

**145–6** The manuscript reading of these lines is suspect and the best modern edition marks them as probably spurious, added by a later hand and then mangled by scribes. They do (however) make better sense if reversed as printed here and the repetition of one idea in different words is not unparalleled in Ovid. Medea was held back from running into his arms by her **pudor** ('modesty') and then by 'respect for her reputation' (**reverentia famae**). **complexa fuisses** is a pluperfect subjunctive (equivalent to *complexa esses*) as part of the conditional sentence: 'you would have embraced him [if you had not been too embarrassed to do so]'. **ne faceres** – 'to prevent you doing so': the subjunctive is common after verbs of 'preventing'.

**147–8** **quod licet**: '[you are not allowed to embrace him] but – and this is allowed – you ...'. Medea conceals her passion in silence (**affectu tacito**). The **carminibus** are the incantations which she uttered both originally (98) and also as 'auxiliary' chanting (137–8): Medea gives thanks (**grates**) to them and to the gods who produced them. The sibilant alliteration here may evoke her whispered thanks to the gods.

## 149–58

Jason finally acquires the Golden Fleece and takes Medea home to Greece.

**149** **superest** – 'it remains to ...': this was the final hurdle in the path to getting the fleece. The line is framed by the dragon, whose unfailing vigilance is highlighted by its primary position (**pervigilem**). **sopire** recalls the term *insopitum* used of the dragon at 36.

**150–1** **crista, linguisque tribus** and **uncis dentibus** are all ablatives of specification going with **praesignis** ('conspicuous with its crest ...'). The tree itself was not golden but it housed the golden fleece. **aureae** is scanned as two syllables in synizesis (**aur(e)ae**) as with *praeacutae* in 131.

**152** The line is spondaic to indicate the soporific effect described. **Lethaei gramine suci**: 'the herb of Lethaean sap' is 'the Lethaean sap of the herb'. The river Lethe flows from the Cave of Sleep later in the poem (XI.603-4) and Plato had described (*Republic* 621a-b) souls falling asleep after drinking from it.

**153** As at lines 137-8, the words are as vital as the drugs and Jason recites them three times (**ter**).

**154** Witches traditionally have the power to move the moon and affect the weather: cf. Tibullus 1.2.45-6. The point here is that if Medea's magic can move the heavens, then it will be all the more capable of putting a dragon to sleep.

**155** Take **sibi** with **ignotos**: 'sleep came to eyes which were not known to it'.

**156 potitur** takes the ablative (**auro**). Jason is called the 'Aesonian hero' in suitably epic language to reflect his epic achievement. **spolio** is to be taken with **superbus** ('proud of his spoils').

**157** Medea, referred to as both the 'producer (**auctorem**) of service' and also as 'another set of spoils' (**spolia altera**) is suddenly promoted to being his wife (**coniuge**) in the next line.

**158** Where other epic writers devote hundreds of lines to the many adventures which beset the Argonauts on the way home (of which Medea was aware: cf. 62-5), Ovid here (as often in the *Metamorphoses*) simply tells us that they got there: his focus in this book is more on Medea than on Jason.

## 159-293

The story now turns to Medea's treatment of Jason's male relatives: the rejuvenation of his old father Aeson and then the murder of his uncle Pelias (297-349).

**A Level**

**159** **Haemoniae** – 'Thessalian'. **pro natis … receptis** is akin to the *ab urbe condita* construction and here means 'in thanks for their sons' return'.

**160** **grandaevi** is an epic term for 'advanced in age' and sets up the theme of 'old father' which we will see in the case of Aeson.

**160–2** When men sailed abroad it was common to make 'vows' which promised to show gratitude to the gods who brought the men safely home with animal sacrifice and other gifts to be dedicated in their temples. Here the gifts are lavish: 'heaped up' (**congesta**) incense is melted by fire to release the scent, and the victim has gold on its horns to enhance its value. The syntax of **inducta cornibus aurum** ('its horns smeared with gold') is complex: **inducta** is a passive participle from *induo* ('dressed') agreeing with the **victima** and **aurum** is a 'retained' accusative indicating what it has been dressed with (cf. 183), while **cornibus** simply means 'on its horns'. **vota** ('promised, vowed') is a perfect passive participle from *voveo* also agreeing with **victima**.

**162–3** **abest**: Jason's father is conspicuous by his absence. Note the heavy concentration of explanatory terms in 163 (**leto fessusque senilibus annis**).

**164** **Aesonides** ('son of Aeson' i.e. Jason) is not a mere formality: Jason is speaking here not as a hero but rather as a son concerned about his father.

**164–8** Jason speaks to Medea with a proposal to allow him to donate some of his own years to his father, making the old man younger and himself older in exchange. His short speech is skilfully persuasive, calling her his wife (**coniunx**) and praising her skills while also showing gratitude for what she has done for him so far.

**164–5** Translate: 'I admit that I owe my safety to you' (literally 'to whom (**cui**) I admit that I owe my safety').

**166** 'the sum total (**summa**) of your favours to me (**meritorum**) goes beyond what can be believed'. This is true when one recalls Medea's manipulation of fire-breathing bulls and unsleeping dragons.

A Level

**167 quid enim non carmina possunt?**: Jason flatters Medea with generalised confidence that her 'spells' (**carmina**) can do anything.

**168** The style brings out the transactional nature of the deed, with **deme** picked up by **demptos**. The polyptoton **deme** ... **demptos** is a rhetorical ploy to make the transaction sound natural. **parenti** here stands for *annis parentis*.

**169** Jason 'did not hold back his tears': whether this is real or feigned emotion is not clear, but Medea clearly bought it. **rogantis** is genitive singular of the present participle referring to Jason. *pietas* is dutiful integrity which makes epic heroes such as Aeneas sacrifice their pleasure for the benefit of others, especially their family, the state and the gods: here the word is effectively Medea's view of Jason's behaviour and is perhaps ironic to the reader who knows the full story.

**170** Medea recalls her own abandoned father: 'the deserted Aeetes came into her very different mind'. **dissimilem**: Medea defined herself as one who betrayed her father (38) and whose desire overcame the triple moral bonds of *Rectum Pietasque Pudorque* (72), whereas Jason is showing abundant *pietas* towards his own father.

**171** Medea does not admit to her own concern for her father Aeetes, but rounds on Jason with indignation. She is not annoyed that he wishes to rejuvenate his father but cannot bear for him to lose any of his own life. Her indignation is clear from the peremptory metaphorical language: 'what crime has fallen from your mouth?' meaning 'what criminal act are you talking about?'

**171-3** The intractability of the proposal is brought out in the complex style: 'do I seem to be able to transfer a section (**spatium**) of your life to somebody?' Her argument is of course more emotional than practical: she may well have been able to achieve this, but her love for him would not let her do so.

**174-5 Hecate**: Medea's patron goddess (74n.). **sinat** is a potential subjunctive ('would not allow'), while **petis** is an indicative ('you are asking for what is not right'). **isto** goes with implied *munere* from *munus* in 175 as an ablative of comparison ('a gift greater than that [gift]'). **experiar** is future indicative.

**176–7 temptabimus** – 'I will try' (not 'we'). The contrast is between **arte mea** and **annis... tuis** (both instrumental ablatives) as means to 'renew' (**renovare**) the long life of her father-in-law (**soceri**).

**177–8 modo** means 'if only' and takes the present subjunctives (**adiuvet... adnuat**) as it is a conditional in future time. The 'threefold goddess' is Hecate (see 94–97n.). The divine power is exercised with a nod of the head (**adnuat**) if the divinity consents to be 'present' and attentive (**praesens**). Medea admits that her enterprise (**ausis** from *ausum*) is a massive one (**ingentibus**).

**179–80** Medea's magic work begins, after waiting for the full moon. **ut... coirent** is a final clause meaning literally 'three nights were needed for the horns to come together complete and create an orb'.

**182–3** Religious ceremonies of all kinds are usually conducted with bare heads and feet and with no belts around the waist: cf. Tibullus 1.5.15–16n, Virgil *Aeneid* IV.511–18. Here the accusative **vestes** and **capillos** are (as at 161) 'retained' with the passive participle so that **vestes induta recinctas** effectively means 'having put on unbelted clothes' and **nudos umeris infusa capillos** means 'after letting her bare hair fall down on her shoulders'. **pedem** is an accusative of respect: 'naked as to her foot' and is singular for plural.

**184–5 gradus** is the object of **fert** and agrees with **vagos**, while **incomitata** ('unaccompanied') agrees with Medea who is the subject of the verb. **muta silentia** is pleonastic but emphasises the need for total silence in performing these rites – a good reason for doing so in the middle of the night.

**186–7** The twin themes of sleep and silence are elaborated in fine epic style as the scene is set: the inventory of 'men, birds and beasts' is followed by the pleasing image of the hedge (**saepes**) having no sound (**nullo cum murmure saepes**) with its assonance and sibilant alliteration aiding the meaning: and then the even smaller-scale details of the unmoving leaves and the moist air being silent complete the picture, with the repetition of the sibilant **silent . . . silet** adding to the soporific effect. For night as the favoured time for such rituals cf. Tibullus 1.2.63–4, 1.5.15–16.

**188** Ovid leaves the stars until last as these are the only things in any sense active (and they are 'shining' (**micant**)) and Medea can now raise her arms upwards towards them in prayer.

**189–91** Three is a magic number (cf. 153) and here Ovid aptly gives us a trio of threes (**ter . . . ter . . . ternis**). She rotates her body three times and then 'soaked her hair in waters drawn (**sumptis**) from the river'. **ululatibus** ('howlings') is onomatopoeic and the verb **solvit** well suggests the opening up of the mouth (**ora**) to utter these silence-breaking noises. **summisso poplite** is an ablative absolute.

## 192–219

Medea's prayer to a massive cast of divine forms.

**192 arcanis fidissima**: Medea begins by invoking Night as being 'most faithful to mystic rites': *arcanus* often has the sense of 'magical'.

**192–3** Medea now turns to the 'golden stars' (**aurea . . . astra**) which 'succeed (i.e. take the place of (**succeditis**)) the fires of day' along with the moon.

**194** Hecate is **triceps** (literally 'three-headed') as she is Diana and the Moon along with herself (see 94–7n.). *conscius* + dative has the sense of 'colluding with', and **coeptis** (from *coepi*) are 'undertakings'. This line is notable for its harsh alliteration.

**195 cantūs** and **artis** are objective genitives going with **adiutrix** ('helper of the spells and the skill'). **magorum** refers to Persian wizards (cf. Catullus 90, Horace *Odes* I.27.22) who (Medea assumes) are also working with Hecate.

**196 Tellus**: the earth is personified and addressed in the second person singular (**instruis**): she is the home both of the underworld and of the powerful plants (**pollentibus ... herbis**) which the *magus* and Medea need.

**197** A comprehensive list of natural features, linking Medea's magic with Nature in all its forms. The five nouns are all connected with polysyndeton.

**198** Medea turns to the divine spirits living in the groves (**nemorum**) and 'all gods of the night'. **omnes** is repeated to stress that she is addressing any and all the relevant divinities: in ancient polytheistic religion it was vital not to ignore any gods.

**199–206** Medea reminds these beings of her record as a magician: she admits that she used their help (**quorum ope**) at the start of the passage but from then on ascribes all the agency to her will (**cum volui**) and to her skill.

**199 ripis mirantibus** (ablative absolute) is a pathetic fallacy imagining the banks 'amazed' at the reverse-flowing river. Current reversal was a common trick of the witch: cf. Tibullus 1.2.46, Ovid *Amores* 1.8.6, Virgil *Aeneid* IV.489.

**200 rediēre** is the shortened verse form of *redierunt* (third person plural, perfect tense of *redeo*).

**200–1 concussaque sisto/ stantia concutio**: a brilliant piece of double polyptoton as in both cases the verb is used in both an indicative and a participle form, in chiastic (ABBA) order. The point is to show with verbal trickery the ease with which Medea can perform her trickery both ways. The object of both verbs is **freta**.

**201–2** The same ability to switch nature on and off is exhibited with regard to the clouds (**nubila**) and the winds (**ventos**): cf. Tibullus 1.2.51–2. Note how the three examples of this weather-magic (seas, cloud and winds) are described in phrases of diminishing length – what one might term a tricolon descrescendo.

A Level

**203 vipereas... fauces**: Virgil *Eclogues* 8.71 also lists the 'bursting' of snakes as a magic accomplishment. Note how the serpent's jaws physically enclose the line and are verbally broken up with the words inbetween.

**204 viva. ... saxa** – 'living rocks' are rocks emerging from the ground as if planted there, as opposed to loose rocks on the surface. Take **suā** with **terrā** ('from their soil') which verbally embeds the trees. **robora** are individual oak trees here seen as 'torn up' (**convulsa**, perfect participle passive from *convello*). Moving rocks and trees by the power of song was the skill ascribed to the legendary singer and magician Orpheus (cf. Ovid *Met*. XI.1–2).

**205 silvas**: Medea can also move whole forests, as well as making mountains shake. Note here how the line is framed by the objects and the key verbs are centrally juxtaposed.

**206 mugire**: literally 'lowing' like a bull: cf. Virgil *Aeneid* IV.490–1 where it is foretold 'you will see the earth bellow (*mugire*) under your feet and ash trees come down from the mountains' when the witch gets to work. **mānes** are the souls of the dead: Medea claims to be able to make them come out of their tombs (**sepulcris**: cf. Tibullus 1.2.47–8). The poet may be thinking of an earthquake in which the earth rumbles and stone tombs open up.

**207–8 Luna**: drawing down the moon/stars is a witches' trick familiar from Greek and Roman sources (e.g. Tibullus 1.2.45, Virgil *Eclogues* 8.69, Propertius 1.1.19). Medea addresses the moon directly in the second person singular. **Temesaea ... aera**: Temesa was a town in Italy famed for its bronze and it was believed that clashing bronze cymbals could prevent or at least lessen the danger of the moon being 'stolen' by an eclipse, a lunar eclipse being known in Latin as *lunae labores*. **quamvis** (+ subjunctive **minuant**) has the sense 'however much the Temneaean bronzes might diminish your struggles'.

**208–9 avi**: Medea claims to be the granddaughter of the Sun god who was father to Aeetes (see 94–7n.). **pallet** is repeated (with different metrical stresses) in anaphora to show how Medea can cause the fiery god to blanch. **venenis** is a surprise as (so far) her power has been verbal rather than medicinal and it may be that the personified goddess of the dawn goes pale with shock when she sees Medea's pharmacological arsenal.

**210–14   vos**: Medea addresses all her divine patrons at once in the plural, as she reminds them of what they have helped her to do in the recent past. This is standard prayer-formula – to remind the god(s) of what they have done in the past as prelude to a new request for help – and also allows the poet to recap the story for the reader.

**210–11   hebetastis** is the shortened form of *hebetavistis* (from *hebeto*) and is a metaphor as one cannot literally 'blunt' flames. **unco** goes with **aratro** (ablative). **impatiens oneris collum** go together ('a neck unable to tolerate the burden') and is concessive to mark up the force of **pressistis** – that neck had never tolerated a yoke before but 'you weighed it down' with one. Medea is inaccurate – it was the yoke which was laid on the necks and not the plough – but 'submitting to the yoke' was a standard phrase for subjugation in anient Rome. The story of Jason subduing the fire-breathing bulls into agricultural animals is told at 104–121.

**212   serpentigenis** is a compound term ('snake-born') found only here in Latin. Translate: 'you gave the snake-born men savage wars [to fight] against themselves (**in se**)'. The tale was told at 121–43.

**213–14**   The 'guard' (**custodem**) was the dragon keeping watch over the golden fleece. **rudem somni** reminds us that the dragon was 'inexperienced in sleep' and the golden fleece is simply called 'the gold' (**aurum**). **vindice decepto** is an ablative absolute ('after deceiving the defender') and refers to the dragon.

**215–16**   Medea gets to the point of her prayer: she needs 'juices' to rejuvenate Aeson. **opus est** means 'there is need of' with the thing needed going into the ablative (**sucis**). Medea uses three different terms for the rejuvenation, to ensure that there is no divine misunderstanding: **renovata senectus** ('old age renewed') is vague, but the metaphor of the flower of youth in **in florem redeat** is strong and **primosque recolligat**

A Level

**annos** ('reassemble his first years') reminds us of Jason's proposal to swap his own years with those of his father. The subjunctives (**redeat** and **recolligat**) are in a relative final clause after **per quos** ('through which his old age might ...' (i.e. so that his old age ...')).

**217-19**   **et dabitis**: a strong statement of confidence, almost imperative in tone. Medea's evidence is partly the dubious claim that 'the stars have not twinkled for nothing' (which proves nothing as stars twinkle anyway) and then the surprise announcement that her dragon-drawn chariot has turned up. **volucrum** here means 'winged' and is adjectival (from *volucer*) rather than the noun meaning 'birds' as at line 4, but the ambiguity would be present until corrected later in the line. The chariot (**currus**) is 'drawn (**tractus** from *traho*) by the neck of winged dragons'. Note the emphatic final present indicative **adest** ('is here'), at once repeated in the imperfect tense (**aderat**) with the explanatory phrase 'sent down from the heavens'. **currus** neatly frames the line.

**220**   **simul** here means 'as soon as' and **quo** picks up **currus**: 'as soon as she had climbed into it'.

**220-1**   Medea treats the dragons like horses, just as Jason treated the bovine monsters as tame farmyard animals at 117: she 'stroked' (**permulsit**) their necks which were 'bridled' (**frenata**) and took up the reins (**habenas**).

**222**   **rapitur** (from *rapio*) has the sense of 'races off' and the placing of **sublimis** ('on high') at the start of the line suggests the speed of her ascent. **Tempe** (neuter accusative plural) was a valley in Thessaly famous for its beauty.

**223**   **certis** here means 'specific': Medea knows exactly where to look. **applicat** is often used of 'landing' a ship into port: here the vessel is the 'serpents' (**angues**).

**224-6**   The main verb is delayed until 226: Medea 'surveys' (**perspicit**) the grasses (**herbas**) which (**quas**) ...'. We have to understand **tulit** with all the mountainous place-names mentioned. **Ossa** and **Pelion** are mountains, famous from the legend that the giants Otus and Ephialtes tried to mount one upon the other to scale the heights of Olympus where the gods lived. **Othrys** and **Pindus** are mountain ranges and Mt **Olympus** is the tallest mountain in Greece at almost 3000 metres. **Pindo** is ablative of comparison with **maior** ('higher than Pindus').

**226–7** **placitas** agrees with *herbas* (224): 'the ones which pleased her'. **partim … partim** means 'some … others …'. Notice Medea's botanical skill as she knows which ones have useful roots and which ones are only good for providing leaves. The plucking of the plants is conveyed in the alliteration of 'p' and 'r' in 226 and the snipping of leaves is enacted with the 'c' alliteration of 227. She clearly has with her a curved bronze sickle – the same tool used by Dido in her own magic moments (Virgil *Aeneid* 4.513). Note the epic periphrasis whereby 'the curve of a bronze sickle' means 'a curved bronze sickle'.

*The story continues: Medea uses her herbs and skills to rejuvenate old Aeson (228–93). She then uses similar techniques to opposite effect when she persuades the daughters of Jason's old enemy Pelias that he too could be rejuvenated. The girls eagerly follow her advice and end up killing their father instead of helping him (294–349). To escape the angry girls she flees to Corinth, where Jason has married a new wife: Medea murders both this bride and also her own children (350–97). She flees again to Athens and is received by king Aegeus who marries her in order to produce a son. When his real son Theseus appears, Medea tries to have him killed but Aegeus recognises Theseus just in time and Medea then leaves Athens and the* Metamorphoses *(398–424).*

*The book continues with the war waged by Minos king of Crete against the Athenians in revenge for their killing of his son Androgeos. Minos tries to secure help from Aegina but the Aeginetans refuse and agree to help Athens instead. Aeacus the Aeginetan entertains the Athenian ambassadors with an account of the plague at Aegina (which has decimated the population) and tells the tale of how he asked for help from Jupiter – at which a new race of men (the 'Myrmidons') was born from ants (490–660). One of the Athenians (Cephalus) then narrates the tale of* how the goddess Dawn, having failed to seduce him, had persuaded him that he needed to test the chastity of his new bride Procris: disguised as a stranger he seduces her and so proves her infidelity at which she leaves him to join a band of women devoted to Diana. Cephalus begs her to return to him and eventually she does so, but the book ends on a note of despair. Cephalus foolishly speaks to the cool breeze (aura) which fans his heated brow after he has finished hunting. He is overheard doing so by 'somebody or other' who reports that he is being unfaithful with a nymph called Aura: and Procris steals out to catch him in the act. Cephalus hears her rustling in the bushes and (thinking she is a wild animal) kills her with his javelin, leaving him inconsolable (661–5).

# Vocabulary

While there is no Defined Vocabulary List for A-level, words in the OCR Defined Vocabulary List for AS-level are marked with * so that students can quickly see the vocabulary with which they should be particularly familiar, although the meanings given in this book are not necessarily the same as the ones in the DVL as this vocabulary is tailored to this text.

This vocabulary lists every word in the text. Nouns are listed with their genitive singular, and verbs are listed with all their four principal parts. Adjectives are listed with the endings of the different genders (e.g. **Achīvus -a -um**) except where the three genders are the same in the nominative where the genitive is listed (e.g.: **dēmens, dēmentis**). Short vowels are unmarked but long vowels are marked with macra (e.g. **rapax, rapācis**). Where a word has different meanings in different lines this is indicated with line-references.

| | |
|---|---|
| *a, ab (*preposition + ablative*) | by, from |
| *absum, abesse, āfuī | be missing |
| abigō, abigere, abēgī, abactum | drive away |
| ablāta | *see:* **aufero** |
| *ac | and |
| accingōr, accingī, accinctus sum | gird oneself |
| *accipiō, accipere, accēpī, acceptum | receive, take hold of |
| Achīvī -ōrum *m.pl.* | The Greeks |
| Achīvus -a -um | Greek |
| aciēs, aciēī *f.* | strife, fighting |
| *ad (*preposition + accusative*) | to, towards |
| adamantēus -a -um | made of steel |
| *addō, addere, addidī, additum | add |
| adeō, adīre, adi(v)ī, aditum | approach |
| *adhuc | still |
| adiciō, ad(i)icere, adiēcī, adiectum | heighten, increase |

A Level

| | |
|---|---|
| adiūtrīx, adiūtrīcis *f.* | female helper |
| *adiuvō, adiuvāre, adiūvī, adiūtum | help, assist |
| adnuō, adnuere, adnuī, adnūtum (+ *dative*) | support |
| *adsum, adesse, adfuī | be present, be available |
| advena -ae *m.* | stranger |
| advocō, advocāre, advocāvī, advocātum | call upon, summon up |
| Aeēta -ae *m.* | Aeetes (king of Colchis and father of Medea) |
| Aeētias -adis *f.* | Daughter of Aeetes (i.e. Medea) |
| aēnus -a -um | made of bronze |
| *aequus -a -um | fair, right |
| āēr, āeris *m.* | air |
| aeripēs, aeripedis | having feet of bronze |
| aes, aeris *n.* | bronze |
| Aesōn, Aesonis *m.* | Aeson (father of Jason) |
| Aesonidēs, -ae *m.* | son of Aeson (i.e. Jason) |
| Aesonius -a -um | descended from Aeson |
| aetās, aetātis *f.* | youth |
| aethēr, aetheris *m.* | sky, heavens |
| aevum -ī *n.* | life-span, age |
| affectus -ūs *m.* | feeling, emotion |
| afflō, afflāre, afflāvī, afflātum | breathe on |
| *ager, agrī *m.* | field |
| *aggrediōr, aggredī, aggressus sum | embark upon |
| agitō, agitāre, agitāvī, agitātum | stir up (81), shake (reins 221) |
| *agmen, agminis *n.* | platoon |
| *agō, agere, ēgī, actum | *see* **grates** |
| ait | he/she said |
| aliēnus -a -um | belonging to another person |
| alimentum -ī *n.* | nourishment |
| *aliquis, aliquid | someone, something |
| *alius -a -um | another, other |
| aliud ... aliud ... | one thing ... another thing ... (19–20) |
| *alter, altera, alterum | other, further (157) |
| *alter, altera, alterum | somebody else (41) |
| *altus -a -um | deep (186), high (224) |
| alvus -ī *f.* | belly |
| amnis -is *m./f.* | river |

# Vocabulary 259

| | |
|---|---|
| *amō, amāre, amāvī, amātum | love |
| *amor, amōris *m*. | love |
| amplector, amplectī, amplexus sum | embrace |
| amplexus -ūs *m*. | embrace |
| *an | or |
| anguis, anguis *m*. | serpent |
| anhēlō, anhēlāre, anhēlāvī, anhēlātum | emit a blast of air |
| *animus -ī *m*. | mind (44, 170), fighting spirit (121, 133) |
| *annus -ī *m*. | year |
| *ante (*preposition + accusative*) | before (72) |
| ante (*adverbial*) | beforehand (46) |
| antīquus -a -um | ancient |
| applicō, applicāre, applicāvī, applicātum | bring to land |
| *aqua -ae *f*. | water |
| Aquilō -ōnis *m*. | The North Wind |
| *āra -ae *f*. | altar, |
| arātrum -ī *n*. | plough |
| *arbor, arboris f | tree |
| arcānus -a -um | mystic, secret |
| ardeō, ardēre, arsī, arsum | burn |
| ardor, ardōris *m*. | passion |
| *arma -ōrum *n*.pl | weapons, warfare |
| arō, arāre, arāvī, arātum | plough |
| *ars, artis *f*. | skill |
| arvum -ī *n*. | field |
| *ascendō, ascendere, ascendī, ascensum | climb on to |
| aspergō, asperginis *f*. | sprinkling |
| aspiciō, aspicere, aspexī, aspectum | look at |
| assūmō, assūmere, assūmpsī, assūmptum | draw, take up |
| astrum -ī *n*. | star |
| *at | but |
| atque | and |
| auctor -ōris *m*. | creator, producer |
| *audax, audācis | confident, daring |
| *auferō, auferre, abstulī, ablātum | carry off |
| *augeō, augēre, auxī, auctum | increase |
| aura -ae *f*. | breeze, air |
| aureus -a -um | golden |

A Level

# Ovid: Metamorphoses VII.1–227

| | |
|---|---|
| Aurōra -ae f. | Aurora (goddess of the Dawn) |
| aurum -ī n. | gold |
| ausum -ī n. | bold deed, venture |
| *aut | or |
| auxiliāris -e | assisting, helping |
| *auxilium -ī n. | help, support |
| avidus -a -um | greedy |
| avus -ī m. | grandfather |
| | |
| barbarus -a -um | foreign |
| *bellum -ī n. | war |
| bisulcus -a -um | cloven |
| brācchium -ī n. | arm |
| | |
| *cadō, cadere, cecidī, cāsum | fall |
| camīnus -ī m. | furnace |
| *campus -ī m. | field |
| *canis -is m./f. | dog |
| *canō, canere, cecinī, cantum | sing |
| cantō, cantāre, cantāvī, cantātum | charm by incantation |
| cantus -ūs m. | song, singing |
| capillus -ī m. | hair |
| *caput, capitis n. | head |
| carmen, carminis n. | sung spell |
| *cārus -a -um | dear, beloved |
| cāsus, -ūs m. | chance |
| *causa -ae f. | cause, explanation |
| celebrō, celebrāre, celebrāvī, celebrātum | hail, extol |
| *cernō, cernere, crēvī, crētum | see, observe |
| certē (adverb) | certainly |
| *certus -a -um | specific |
| cervix, cervīcis f. | neck |
| *cētera -ōrum n.pl. | all the rest, everything else |
| Charybdis -is f. | Charybdis (sea monster 63) |
| cinctus -a -um | girded, surrounded |
| cīvīlis -e | civil, internecine |
| *clāmor, clāmōris m. | shout |
| *clārus -a -um | famous, distinguished |
| claudō, claudere, clausī, clausum | enclose |

A Level

# Vocabulary 261

| | |
|---|---|
| *coepī, coepisse | begin, start |
| coeptum -ī *n.* | undertaking |
| coeō, coīre, coiī, coitum | come together |
| *cōgō, cōgere, coēgī, coactum | compel, force |
| Colchī, -ōrum *m.pl.* | the people of Colchis |
| collum -ī *n.* | neck |
| *committō, committere, commīsī, commissum | commit (wrongdoing) |
| commūnis -e | shared |
| complector, complectī, complexus sum | embrace |
| compōnō, compōnere, composuī, compositum | put together, build |
| concipiō, concipere, concēpī, conceptum | catch (fire: 9, 108), hold (17), hope for (22) |
| concitus -a -um | flowing rapidly |
| concurrō, concurrere, concurrī, concursum | clash against (30), clash together (62) |
| concutiō, concutere, concussī, concussum | brandish (130), stir up (200–1) |
| confiteor, confitērī, confessus sum | acknowledge (165), admit to (171) |
| congerō, congerere, congessī, congestum | heap up |
| coniugium -ī *n.* | marriage |
| *coniunx, coniugis *m./f.* | spouse |
| conscelerō, conscelerāre, conscelerāvī, conscelerātum | pollute |
| conscius -a -um (+ *dative*) | colluding with |
| *consistō, consistere, constitī | stand |
| consurgō, consurgere, consurrexī, consurrectum | rise up |
| contingō, contingere, contigī, contactum | arrive at, reach |
| convellō, convellere, convellī, convulsum | tear up, wrench |
| conveniō, convenīre, convēnī, conventum | gather together |
| convertō, convertere, convertī, conversum | turn |
| cor, cordis *n.* | heart |
| cornū -ūs *n.* | horn |
| *corpus, corporis *n.* | body |
| *crēdō, crēdere, crēdidī, crēditum (+ *dative*) | believe, trust |

A Level

| | |
|---|---|
| creō, creāre, creāvī, creātum | create, produce |
| crescō, crescere, crēvī, crētum | grow |
| *crīmen, crīminis *n.* | wrongdoing |
| crīnis -is *m.* | hair |
| crista -ae *f.* | crest |
| crūdēlis -e | heartless, cruel |
| *culpa -ae *f.* | sin, shameful behaviour |
| cultus -ūs *m.* | civilised culture |
| *cum (*preposition + ablative*) | with (59, 158, 186, 193) |
| *cum (*conjunction*) | when (77, 164, 199) |
| *cunctus -a -um | all |
| cupīdō, -inis *f./m.* | desire |
| Cupīdō, -inis *m.* | Cupid |
| *cur | why? |
| currus -ūs *m.* | chariot |
| curvāmen -inis *n.* | curve |
| cuspis, cuspidis *f.* | spear |
| *custōs, custōdis *m.* | guard, protector |
| | |
| *dē (*preposition + ablative*) | from (32) about (68) |
| *dea -ae *f.* | goddess |
| *dēbeō, dēbēre, dēbuī, dēbitum | owe |
| *dēcipiō, dēcipere, dēcēpī, dēceptum | mislead (92), cheat (214) |
| dēclīnō, dēclīnāre, dēclīnāvī, dēclīnātum | turn away from |
| dēmens, dēmentis | mad |
| dēmittō, dēmittere, dēmīsī, dēmissum | lower |
| dēmō, dēmere, dēmpsī, dēmptum | take away |
| *dēnique | just then, for the first time |
| dens, dentis *m.* | tooth |
| dēpellō, dēpellere, dēpulī, dēpulsum | scatter, put to flight |
| dērigescō, dērigescere, dēriguī | become stiff |
| despiciō, despicere, despexī, despectum | look down on |
| dēsum, dēesse, dēfuī | be lacking |
| dēterior, dēterius | worse |
| *deus -ī *m.* | god |
| *dextra -ae *f.* | right hand |
| di, deōrum *m.pl.* | gods (24, 37, 61, 148, 198) |
| *dīcō, dīcere, dīxī, dictum | speak, say |
| *dissimilis -e | unlike |

## Vocabulary

| | |
|---|---|
| *diu (*adverb*)* | for a long time |
| diurnus -a -um | belonging to daytime |
| dīva -ae *f.* | goddess |
| *dō, dare, dedī, datum | make (promises 94), give |
| *dōnum -ī *n.* | gift |
| dracō, dracōnis *m.* | dragon, snake |
| *dūcō, dūcere, duxī, ductum | pull (119) |
| *dum | while |
| *durus -a -um | tough, harsh (14–15), firm (191) |
| | |
| *ea | *see* is, ea, id |
| eburnus -a -um | made of ivory |
| ecce | look! |
| ēdiscō, ēdiscere, ēdidicī | learn about |
| ēdō, ēdere, ēdidī, ēditum | bring forth, give birth to |
| *efficiō, efficere, effēcī, effectum | produce, create |
| efflō, efflāre, efflāvī, efflātum | blow out |
| *effugiō, effugere, effūgī | run away from |
| *ego, mei | I, me |
| *ēgredior, ēgredī, ēgressus sum | walk out of |
| *enim | for |
| *ergō | therefore |
| ērubescō, ērubescere, ērubuī | redden, blush |
| *et | and |
| ēventus -ūs *m.* | outcome |
| excēdō, excēdere, excessī, excessum | exceed, go beyond |
| excidō, excidere, excidī | fall from |
| excutiō, excutere, excussī, excussum | knock out (i.e. extinguish: 17) |
| exeō, exīre, exi(v)ī, exitum | come out |
| exhortor, exhortārī, exhortātus sum | encourage, goad on |
| experior, experīrī, expertus sum | attempt |
| exstinguō, exstinguere, exstinxī, exstinctum | extinguish |
| extimescō, extimescere, extimuī | grow fearful |
| | |
| *faciō, facere, fēcī, factum | do, bring about (153), make (134) |
| falx, falcis *f.* | sickle |
| *fāma -ae *f.* | reputation |
| fateor, fatērī, fassus sum | admit to |

A Level

| | |
|---|---|
| faucēs, faucium *f.pl.* | jaws |
| favilla -ae *f.* | ash |
| fax, facis *f.* | wedding-torch |
| *fēlix, fēlicis | fortunate |
| fera -ae *f.* | wild animal |
| *ferō, ferre, tulī, lātum | bring (29, 160), bear (224) |
| feror (*passive of* fero) | be deemed, be said to be (61), travel (67) |
| gradus ferō | walk, stride (184–5) |
| *ferrum -ī *n.* | iron |
| ferus -a -um | savage |
| fessus -a -um | weary |
| fētus -a -um | fruitful |
| *fidēs, fideī *f.* | pledge of faith (46) credibility (166) |
| fīdus -a -um (*superlative* fīdissimus) | faithful, true to |
| *fīō, fierī, factus sum | become |
| fīxus -a -um | fixed, staring (87) |
| *flamma -ae *f.* | flame |
| flōs, flōris *m.* | flower |
| *flūmen, flūminis *n.* | river |
| *foedus, foederis *n.* | bond, contract |
| fons, fontis *m.* | source, origin |
| forem | = **essem** (*imperfect subjunctive of* **sum**) |
| forma -ae *f.* | beauty |
| formōsus -a -um | handsome, attractive |
| fornax, fornācis *f.* | furnace, oven |
| *fortis -e | strong |
| *frāter, frātris *m.* | brother |
| fraus, fraudis *f.* | deception |
| frēnātus -a -um | bridled |
| fretum -ī *n.* | sea |
| frīgidus -a -um | cold |
| frons, frondis *f.* | leaf |
| *frustrā (*adverb*) | in vain, to no purpose |
| fugō, fugāre, fugāvī, fugātum | put to flight, rout |
| fulgeō, fulgēre, fulsī | gleam, blaze |
| fūmificus -a -um | smoke-making |
| *furor, furōris *m.* | passion |
| futūrus -a -um | future, prospective |

A Level

| | |
|---|---|
| galea -ae f. | helmet |
| gena -ae f. | cheek |
| *genus, generis n. | noble birth |
| germāna -ae f. | sister |
| gestō, gestāre, gestāvī, gestātum | wear, bear |
| gradus -ūs m. | footstep |
| Graius -a -um | Greek |
| grāmen -inis n. | herb, grass |
| grandaevus -a -um | aged, elderly |
| grātēs, grātium f.pl. | thanks |
| grātes agō | give thanks to |
| grātia -ae f. | attractiveness, charm |
| grātor, grātārī, grātātus sum | congratulate, celebrate |
| gravidus -a -um | pregnant |
| *gravis -e | heavy |
| gremium -iī n. | lap, bosom |
| guttur, gutturis n. | throat |
| | |
| habēna -ae f. | rein |
| Haemonius -a -um | Thessalian |
| haereō, haerēre, haesī, haesum | cling to |
| *hasta -ae f. | spear |
| hebetō, hebetāre, hebetāvī, hebetātum | blunt, deaden the force of |
| Hecatē -ēs f. | Hecate |
| herba -ae f. | herb, grass |
| hērōs, hērōōs m. | hero |
| *hic, haec, hoc | this |
| *hīc (adverb) | here |
| *homō, hominis m. | human being |
| horrendus -a -um | dreadful (8), terrifying (151) |
| *hospes, hospitis m. | guest, stranger |
| *hostis -is m. | enemy |
| *humus -ī f. | earth |
| | |
| iaculor, iaculārī, iaculātus sum | throw |
| *iam | by now |
| Iāsōn, Iāsonis m. | Jason |
| *ignis -is m. | fire |
| ignorantia -ae f. | ignorance |

# 266 Ovid: Metamorphoses VII.1–227

| | |
|---|---|
| ignōscō, ignōscere, ignōvī, ignōtum | pardon |
| ignōtus -a -um | unfamiliar, unknown |
| *ille, illa, illud | that |
| imāgō, imāginis *f.* | appearance (128), shape (181) |
| immōtus -a -um | motionless |
| impatiēns, impatientis | intolerant of (+ *genitive*) |
| impleō, implēre, implēvī, implētum | fill up |
| impōnō, impōnere, imposuī, impositum | apply, bestow |
| *in (*preposition* + *ablative*) | in the case of (21, 43), in the hands of (24), in (33, 62, 66, 95, 125, 129) on (86, 191) |
| *in (*preposition* + *accusative*) | against (35, 132, 139, 140, 212) to (46, 216), into (81, 99, 101, 127, 155, 200, 214) onto (122) |
| inardēscō, inardēscere, inarsī | catch fire |
| inceptum -ī *n.* | undertaking |
| incomitātus -a -um | unaccompanied |
| indūcō, indūcere, induxī, inductum | cover with (80, 161), summon (202) |
| induō, induere, induī, indūtum | dress |
| īnfāns, īnfantis | infant |
| īnfēlix, īnfēlicis | unhappy |
| īnfundō, īnfundere, īnfūdī, īnfūsum | let fall down |
| *ingēns, ingentis | massive, huge |
| ingrātus -a -um | ungrateful |
| *inimīcus -a -um | hostile |
| inops, inopis | helpless |
| inquit | he/she said |
| *īnsignis -e | conspicuous |
| īnsōpītus -a -um | unsleeping |
| *īnstruō, īnstruere, īnstrūxī, īnstructum | equip, furnish |
| īnsuētus -a -um | unaccustomed |
| *intereā | meanwhile |
| *intrā (*preposition* + *accusative*) | inside |
| intus (*adverb*) | inside, within |
| invītus -a -um | unwilling |
| Iōlciacus -a -um | of Iolcus |
| *ipse, ipsa, ipsum | oneself |
| irrōrō, irrōrāre, irrōrāvī, irrōrātum | sprinkle |
| *is, ea, id | he, she, it, that (43–4) |
| *iste, ista, istud | that |

## Vocabulary 267

| | |
|---|---|
| *iubeō, iubēre, iussī, iussum | command |
| iugum -ī *n.* | ridge, slope (102) yoke (118) |
| *iungō, iungere, iunxī, iunctum | join together |
| iūrō, iūrāre, iūrāvī, iūrātum | swear an oath |
| iussum -ī *n.* | order |
| *iuvenis -is *m.* | young man |
| | |
| *labor -ōris *m.* | toil, suffering |
| lacrima -ae *f.* | tear |
| lacus -ūs *m.* | lake, pool |
| laetor, laetārī, laetātus sum | be delighted |
| *laetus -a -um | joyful |
| langueō, languēre | droop, be feeble |
| lateō, latēre, latuī | lie hidden |
| latrō, latrāre, latrāvī, latrātum | bark |
| lēnis -e | calm |
| Lēthaeus -a -um | of Lethe |
| lētum -ī *n.* | death |
| *levis -e | light |
| *lex, lēgis *f.* | law |
| *licet (*impersonal*) | it is allowed, one may |
| līmōsus -a -um | muddy |
| lingua -ae *f.* | tongue |
| linteum -ī *n.* | sail |
| liquefaciō, liquefacere, liquefēcī, liquefactum | melt, dissolve |
| liquidus -a -um | flowing, running |
| *locus -ī *n.* | place |
| *longus -a -um | expansive (67) long (176) |
| *loquor, loquī, locūtus sum | speak |
| lūcus -ī *m.* | grove |
| luctor, luctārī, luctātus sum | struggle, wrestle |
| lūmen, lūminis *n.* | eye (87) |
| lūna -ae *f.* | moon |
| *lux, lūcis *f.* | day |
| | |
| magis (*adverb*) | more |
| *magnus -a -um | great |
| magus -ī *m.* | magician, sorcerer |

A Level

| | |
|---|---|
| *maior, maius (*comparative of* magnus) | greater |
| mānēs, mānium *m.pl.* | spirits of the dead |
| *manus -ūs *f.* | hand |
| *mare, maris *n.* | sea |
| Mars, Martis *m.* | Mars (god of war) |
| *māter, mātris *f.* | mother |
| māternus -a -um | maternal |
| mātūrus -a -um | fully grown |
| Māvors, Māvortis *m.* | Mars (god of war) |
| maximus -a -um (*superlative of* magnus) | greatest |
| mēcum | on my side |
| Mēdēa -ae *f.* | Medea |
| *medius -a -um | central, in the middle of |
| medicāmen -inis *n.* | drug, medical treatment |
| meliŏr, melius (*comparative of* bonus) | better |
| *mens, mentis *f.* | mind |
| meritum -ī *n.* | service |
| metuō, metuere, metuī, metūtum | fear |
| *metus -ūs *m.* | fear |
| *meus -a -um | my |
| micō, micāre, micuī | twinkle, gleam |
| minuō, minuere, minuī, minūtum | reduce, lessen |
| Minyae -ārum *m.pl.* | Argonauts |
| *mīrōr, mīrārī, mīrātus sum | be amazed |
| mīrus -a -um | amazing |
| *miser, misera, miserum | wretched |
| *mittō, mittere, mīsī, missum | send |
| *modo | recently (15), if only (177) |
| molliō, mollīre, molli(v)ī, mollītum | soften |
| *mons, montis *m.* | mountain |
| mora -ae *f.* | delay |
| mortālis -e | human |
| *moveō, movēre, mōvī, mōtum | stir (28, 169), move (205) |
| mūgiō, mūgīre, mūgiī, mūgītum | bellow |
| mūgītus -ūs *m.* | bellowing |
| mulceō, mulcēre, mulsī | stroke, caress |
| *multus -a -um | much, many |
| *mūnus, mūneris *n.* | assistance (93), service (157), gift (175) |
| murmur, murmuris *n.* | sound |

## Vocabulary

| | |
|---|---|
| mūtus -a -um | dumb |
| *mūtō, mūtāre, mūtāvī, mūtātum | exchange |
| mūtuus -a -um | reciprocal, mutual |
| *nam | for |
| nāris -is *f.* | nose |
| nātālis -e | native |
| *nascor, nascī, nātus sum | be born |
| nātus -ī *m.* | son |
|   Aesone nātus | son of Aeson (i.e. Jason) |
| *nē | in case (16), so that ... not (155) |
| *nec | and not, nor |
|   *nec ... nec | neither ... nor (174) |
| nefās | wicked act |
| nempe | without doubt (53), in fact (66) |
| nemus, nemoris *n.* | grove, forest |
| *neque | nor |
| nescioquis, nescioquid | some ... or other |
| nēve | and so that ... not |
| *nihil | nothing |
| nimis (*adverb*) | excessively |
| nimium (*adverb*) | excessively |
| *nisi | if not, unless |
| nōbilitās -ātis *f.* | distinction, excellence |
| *nōmen, nōminis *n.* | name |
| *nōn | not |
| *nōs, nostrum | we, us |
| *noster, nostra, nostrum | our, my |
| nōtitia -ae *f.* | knowledge |
| *novus -a -um | new |
| *nox, noctis *f.* | night |
| nūbilum -ī *n.* | cloud |
| nūdus -a -um | bare, uncovered |
| *nullus -a -um | no, not any |
| nūmen, nūminis *n.* | divinity |
| *numerus -ī *m.* | stage, category |
|   per suōs numerōs | through successive stages (126) |
| *nunc | now |

A Level

| | |
|---|---|
| ō (*exclamation*) | oh (addressing another person: 164) |
| oblīvium -iī *n.* | forgetfulness |
| obstō, obstāre, obstitī, obstātum | stand in the way, obstruct |
| obvius -a -um | in the way |
|   obvius eō | I go to meet (111) |
| occidō, occidere, occidī, occāsum | die |
| *oculus -ī *m.* | eye |
| Olympus -ī *m.* | Olympus (mountain) |
| *omnis -e | all, every |
| *onus, oneris *n.* | burden |
| *oppidum -ī *n.* | town |
| *ops, opis *f.* | power (39, 199) help (29) |
| *opus est (+ *ablative*) | there is need of (215) |
| orbis -is *m.* | world (22, 59) orb, circle (180) |
| *ōs, ōris *n.* | face (4, 78, 111), mouth (29, 172, 190) |
| Ossa -ae *f.* | Ossa (mountain) |
| Othrys, Othryos *m.* | Othrys (mountain range) |
| | |
| Pagasaeus -a -um | of Pagasa (town in Thessaly) |
| palear, paleāris *n.* | dewlap |
| palleō, pallēre, palluī | be pale (136), grow dim (209) |
| *parens, parentis *m.* | father |
| *parō, parāre, parāvī, parātum | prepare (to do something: 132) |
| partim ... partim ... | some ... others ... |
| parum (*adverb*) | too little, not enough |
| *parvus -a -um | small |
| *pater, patris *m.* | father |
| *patior, patī, passus sum | allow |
| pectus, pectoris *n.* | heart (17, 28), chest (109) |
| Pelasgī -ōrum *m.pl.* | the Greeks |
| Pelasgus -a -um | Greek |
| Pēlion -iī *n.* | Pelion (mountain) |
| *pellō, pellere, pepulī, pulsum | banish (48, 76), drive away (201) |
| pendulus -a -um | hanging |
| *per (*preposition* + *accusative*) | thanks to (40), across, through (67, 184) by (in oaths: 94), by means of (141, 215) |
| *pereō, perīre, periī, peritum | perish, die |
| *perīculum -ī *n.* | danger |
| permulceō, permulcēre, permulsī, permulsum | stroke, caress |

# Vocabulary 271

| | |
|---|---|
| perpetior, perpetī, perpessum sum | suffer |
| perpetuus -a -um | unending |
| Persēis, Persēidos *f.* | daughter of Perses (Hecate 74) |
| perspiciō, perspicere, perspexī, perspectum | survey |
| pervigil, pervigilis | unsleeping |
| *pēs, pedis *m.* | foot |
| *petō, petere, peti(v)ī, petītum | target (135), ask for (174–5) |
| Phāsis, Phāsidos *m.* | Phasis (river in Colchis) |
| Phīneus -eī *m.* | Phineus |
| Phrixēus -a -um | of Phrixus |
| pietas -ātis *f.* | dutiful behaviour |
| Pindus -ī *m.* | Pindus (mountain) |
| placeō, placēre, placuī, placitum | please |
| placidus -a -um | peaceful |
| *plēnus -a -um | full |
| *poena -ae *f.* | penalty, punishment |
| pollens, pollentis | potent |
| pondus, ponderis *n.* | weight |
| poples, poplitis *m.* | knee |
| *populus -ī *m.* | people |
| *portō, portāre, portāvī, portātum | convey |
| *portus -ūs *m.* | port, harbour |
| *poscō, poscere, poposcī | ask for |
| possideō, possidēre, possēdī, possessum | possess |
| *possum, posse, potuī | be able |
| posterus -a -um | next, following |
| *postquam (*conjunction*) | after |
| *potior, potīrī, potītus sum (+ *ablative*) | take possession of |
| praeacūtus -a -um | sharp |
| *praeda -ae *f.* | prey |
| praefīgō, praefīgere, praefīxī, praefīxum | coat the tip with |
| praepōnō, praepōnere, praeposuī, praepositum | prefer |
| praesens, praesentis | in person (83) present (178) |
| praesignis -e | distinctive |
| praetingō, praetingere, praetinxī, praetinctum | steep |
| *precor, precārī, precātus sum | pray for |

A Level

| | |
|---|---|
| prehendō, prehendere, prehendī, prehensum | grasp |
| premō, premere, pressī, pressum | squeeze, press |
| *prīmus -a -um | first |
| *prō (*preposition* + *ablative*) | (in gratitude) for |
| probō, probāre, probāvī, probātum | approve |
| *prōdō, prōdere, prōdidī, prōditum | betray |
| profundō, profundere, profūdī, profūsum | shed, pour out |
| profundum -ī *n.* | deep water, sea |
| *prōmittō, prōmittere, prōmīsī, prōmissum | promise |
| *propior, propius | closer, nearer |
| proscindō, proscindere, proscindī, proscissum | plough |
| prōtinus (*adverb*) | at once |
| pūbēs -is *f.* | youth, young people |
| pudor -ōris *m.* | modesty, shame |
| pulsō, pulsāre, pulsāvī, pulsātum | beat, strike |
| pulsus | *see* pello |
| pulvereus -a -um | dusty |
| puppis -is *f.* | ship |
| purpureus -a -um | (dressed in) purple |
| *putō, putāre, putāvī, putātum | think |

| | |
|---|---|
| *quamquam | although |
| quamvis | although |
| *quantus -a -um | how great |
| *-que | and |
| *quī, quae, quod | who, what |
| quī, quae, quod? | what, which? |
| quid? | why (21, 47) |
|    quid quod | what of the fact that ... |
| *quiēs, quiētis *f.* | rest, peace |
| quīn | in fact, furthermore |
| *quoque | also |

| | |
|---|---|
| rādix, rādīcis *f.* | root |
| rapax, rapācis | grasping, greedy |
| rapidus -a -um | fast-flowing |

## Vocabulary 273

| | |
|---|---|
| *rapiō, rapere, rapuī, raptum | catch up (*passive:* race off) |
| *ratiō -ōnis *f.* | reason, intelligence |
| ratis -is *f.* | ship |
| recandēscō, recandēscere, recanduī | glow again |
| recēdō, recēdere, recessī, recessum | go back into |
| recingō, recingere, recinxī, recinctum | unfasten |
| *recipiō, recipere, recēpī, receptum | recover, get back |
| recolligō, recolligere, recollēgī, recollectum | reassemble, regain |
| *rectus -a -um | correct, right |
| *reddō, reddere, reddidī, redditum | return, pay back |
| *redeō, redīre, rediī, reditum | go back to |
| regiō, -ōnis *f.* | area |
| rēgius -a -um | royal |
| *regnum -ī *n.* | kingdom |
| *relinquō, relinquere, relīquī, relictum | leave behind (52, 55, 170) abandon (41) |
| relūceō, relūcēre, reluxī | shine out |
| renovō, renovāre, renovāvī, renovātum | renew |
| repugnō, repugnāre, repugnāvī, repugnātum | fight back |
| *rēs, reī *f.* | thing, possession |
| resīdō, resīdere, resēdī | subside (76) sit down (102) |
| resonō, resonāre, resonāvī, resonātum | resound |
| resurgō, resurgere, resurrexī, resurrectum | rise up again |
| revellō, revellere, revellī, revulsum | pluck up |
| reverentia -ae *f.* | respect |
| *rex, rēgis *m.* | king |
| *rīpa -ae *f.* | riverbank |
| rōbur, rōboris *n.* | oak tree |
| rogō, rogāre, rogāvī, rogātum | ask |
| rudis -e (+ *genitive*) | lacking experience of |
| *rumpō, rumpere, rūpī, ruptum | burst open |
| | |
| sacer, sacra, sacrum | sacred |
| sacrum -ī *n.* | religious rite |
| saepēs -is *f.* | hedge |
| *saevus -a -um | cruel (53), savage (64) |
| *salūs, salūtis *f.* | safety |
| *sanguis, sanguinis *m.* | blood |

A Level

| | |
|---|---|
| sānus -a -um | sane |
| sati | see **sero** |
| saxum -ī *n.* | rock |
| *scelus, sceleris *n.* | crime |
| sceptrum -ī *n.* | sceptre |
| scintilla -ae *f.* | spark |
| scopulus -ī *m.* | rock |
| Scylla -ae *f.* | Scylla (sea monster) |
| *sē, suī | himself, herself, itself, themselves |
| secō, secāre, secuī, sectum | cut through |
| sēcrētus -a -um | remote (75), secret, mystic (138) |
| *sēcum | with himself |
| *sed | but |
| sedeō, sedēre, sēdī, sessum | sit down |
| seges, segetis *f.* | crop |
| sēmen, sēminis *n.* | seed |
| *semper | constantly |
| senecta -ae *f.* | old age |
| senectus -ūtis *f.* | old age |
| *senex, senis *m.* | old man |
| senīlis -e | of an old man |
| *sentiō, sentīre, sensī, sensum | feel |
| sepulcrum -ī *n.* | tomb |
| *sequor, sequī, secūtus sum | follow after |
| serō, serere, sēvī, satum | sow (seeds etc.) |
| serpentigena -ae *m.* | one born from a serpent |
| servātrix -icis *f.* | saviour |
| *servō, servāre, servāvī, servātum | save |
| *sī | if |
| sīc | in this way |
| Siculus -a -um | Sicilian |
| sīdus, sīderis *n.* | star |
| *silentium -iī *n.* | silence |
| sileō, silēre, siluī | be silent |
| silex, silicis *m.* | rock, stone |
| *silva -ae *f.* | forest |
| *similis -e | similar to |
| *simul | along with (130), as soon as (220) |
| *sinō, sinere, sīvī, situm | permit |

A Level

## Vocabulary 275

| | |
|---|---|
| *sine (*preposition + ablative*) | without |
| sistō, sistere, stetī, statum | halt, make to stand still |
| socer, socerī *m.* | father-in-law |
| *soleō, solēre, solitus sum | be in the habit of |
| solidus -a -um | unbroken, complete |
| solitum -ī *n.* | what is usual |
| sollemnis -e | solemn |
| solum -ī *n.* | land, ground |
| *sōlus -a -um | alone |
| *solvō, solvere, solvī, solūtum | melt (107), relax (186), open up (191) |
| *somnus -ī *m.* | sleep |
| sonō, sonāre, sonuī, sonitum | make a sound |
| sōpiō, sōpīre, sōpīvī, sōpītum | put to sleep |
| sorbeō, sorbēre, sorbuī, sorbitum | suck up |
| *soror, sorōris *f.* | sister |
| sospes, sospitis | safe |
| spargō, spargere, sparsī, sparsum | scatter (122), sprinkle (152) |
| *spatium -iī *n.* | section |
| speciēs, -ēī *f.* | appearance |
| speciōsus -a -um | fine-sounding |
| *spectō, spectāre, spectāvī, spectātum | watch, look at |
| *spolium -iī *n.* | spoils, prize |
| *stō, stāre, stetī, statum | stand |
| stella -ae *f.* | star |
| suādeō, suādēre, suāsī, suāsum | urge |
| *sub (*preposition + accusative*) | subject to (2), under the command of (4), under (80) |
| subeō, subīre, subiī, subitum | walk up to (115), come into (170) |
| subiectus -a -um | lying underneath |
| *subitō | suddenly |
| sublīmis -e | on high |
| submissus -a -um | soft, low (90), lowered (191) |
| succēdō, succēdere, successī, successum | succeed (take the place of) |
| succīdō, succīdere, succīdī, succīsum | cut from below |
| sūcus -ī *m.* | juice, sap |
| *sum, esse, fuī | be |
| summa -ae *f.* | total |
| *sūmō, sūmere, sūmpsī, sūmptum | take (121, 189), take on (125) |
| superbus -a -um | proud |

A Level

| | |
|---|---|
| *supersum, superesse, superfuī | remain, be left |
| suppōnō, suppōnere, supposuī, suppositum | put under |
| *suus -a -um | one's own, their own |
| *tacitus -a -um | silent |
| *tālis -e | of such a kind |
| *tamen | however |
| *tandem | at last, finally |
| *tangō, tangere, tetigī, tactum | touch |
| *tantum (*adverb*) | so much (116) |
| *tantus -a -um | so great |
| taurus -ī *m*. | bull |
| *tēctum -ī *n*. | house |
| *tegō, tegere, texī, tectum | cover over, shroud |
| tellus, tellūris *f*. | earth |
| Temesaeus -a -um | of Temesa |
| Tempē *n.pl.* | Tempe (valley in Thessaly) |
| temptō, temptāre, temptāvī, temptātum | try |
| tendō, tendere, tetendī, tentum | stretch out |
| *teneō, tenēre, tenuī | hold (66, 87, 143), restrain (145, 169), |
| ter | three times |
| *tergum -ī *n*. | back |
| tergum dō | retreat |
| ternī -ae -a | three |
| *terra -ae *f*. | land, earth |
| terrēnus -a -um | made of clay |
| terribilis -e | terrifying |
| terrigena -ae *m*. | earth-born creature |
| testis -is *m*. | witness |
| *tetigit | *see* **tango** |
| thalamus -ī *m*. | marriage-bedroom |
| Thessalus -a -um | Thessalian |
| tigris, tigridis *f*. | tigress |
| *timeō, timēre, timuī | be afraid of |
| *timor, timōris *m*. | fear |
| titulus -ī *m*. | distinction |
| torqueō, torquēre, torsī, tortum | shoot, fire |
| torus -ī *m*. | marriage-bed |

## Vocabulary

| | |
|---|---|
| *tot | so many |
| *tōtus -a -um | all of, whole |
| *trahō, trahere, traxī, tractum | drag out (2), pull (19, 218), draw down (207) |
| transcrībō, transcrībere, transcripsī, transcriptum | transfer |
| tremescō, tremescere | shake |
| *trēs, tria | three |
| triceps, tricipitis | three-headed |
| triformis -e | having three shapes, triple |
| trux, trucis | savage, brutal |
| *tu, tuī | you (*singular*) |
| *tulit | *see* **fero** |
| *tum | then |
| *turba -ae *f.* | crowd |
| turbō, turbāre, turbāvī, turbātum | stir up, disturb |
| tūs, tūris *n.* | incense |
| *tūtus -a -um | safe |
| *tuus, tua, tuum | your |

| | |
|---|---|
| *ubi | when |
| ululātus -ūs *m.* | howl |
| umbrōsus -a -um | shady |
| umerus -ī *m.* | shoulder |
| ūmidus -a -um | moist |
| uncus -a -um | curved |
| *unda -ae *f.* | wave |
| *ūnus -a -um | one |
| *urbs, urbis *f.* | city |
| ūrō, ūrere, ussī, ustum | burn |
| *ūsus -ūs *m.* | use |
| *ut (+ *subjunctive*) | even though (27), so that (40, 45, 179) |
| *ut (+ *indicative*) | as, when (83, 89) |

| | |
|---|---|
| vagus -a -um | wandering |
| *valeō, valēre, valuī | have power, be effective |
| *validus -a -um | powerful, strong |
| vapor -ōris *m.* | scorching breath |
| *vel | even |
| vellus, velleris *n.* | fleece |
| *velutī | as if |

A Level

| | |
|---|---|
| venēnum -ī *n.* | drug |
| *veniō, venīre, vēnī, ventum | come (155, 195), approach (111) |
| *ventus -ī *m.* | wind |
| *verbum -ī *n.* | word |
| vereor, verērī, veritus sum | fear |
| *vērō (*adverb*) | however |
| vertex, verticis *m.* | head |
| *vertō, vertere, vertī, versum | turn |
| *vērus -a -um | true |
| *vestis -is *f.* | clothing |
| *vetus, veteris | old |
| victima -ae *f.* | victim |
| *victor -ōris *m.* | victor |
| *videō, vidēre, vīdī, vīsum | see, look on |
| *videor, vidērī, vīsus sum | seem (14, 173) |
| vigeō, vigēre, viguī | be powerful |
| *vincō, vincere, vīcī, victum | overcome |
| vindex, vindicis *m.* | defender |
| vīpereus -a -um | belonging to a snake |
| *vir, virī *m.* | husband (41) |
| *vīrēs, vīrium *f.pl.* | strength |
| virgineus -a -um | virgin |
| virgō, virginis *f.* | virgin |
| *virtūs -ūtis *f.* | courage |
| *vīs, vis *f.* | power, force |
| viscus, visceris *n.* | bowel |
| *vīta -ae *f.* | life |
| *vīvō, vīvere, vīxī, vīctum | live |
| *vīvus -a -um | living |
| *vocō, vocāre, vocāvī, vocātum | call (13), summon (202) |
| *volō, velle, voluī | want |
| volucer, volucris, volucre | flying |
| volvō, volvere, volvī, volūtum | roll |
| *vōs, vestrum | you (*plural*) |
| vōtum -ī *n.* | prayer, vow |
| *vox, vōcis *f.* | voice |
| Vulcānus -ī *m.* | Vulcan (god of fire) |
| *vulnus -eris *n.* | wound |
| *vultus -ūs *m.* | face |